IL VAGABONDO: AN URBAN OPERA

Guernica World Editions 33

Canada Council   Conseil des Arts
for the Arts   du Canada

ONTARIO ARTS COUNCIL
CONSEIL DES ARTS DE L'ONTARIO
an Ontario government agency
un organisme du gouvernement de l'Ontario

Guernica Editions Inc. acknowledges the support of the Canada
Council for the Arts and the Ontario Arts Council.
The Ontario Arts Council is an agency of the Government of Ontario.
We acknowledge the financial support of the Government of Canada

IL VAGABONDO:
AN URBAN OPERA

Libretto
by
Glenn Carley

GUERNICA
World
EDITIONS
TORONTO • CHICAGO • BUFFALO • LANCASTER (U.K.)
2021

Michael Mirolla, editor
David Moratto, cover and interior design
Guernica Editions Inc.
287 Templemead Drive, Hamilton, ON L8W 2W4
2250 Military Road, Tonawanda, N.Y. 14150-6000 U.S.A.
www.guernicaeditions.com

Distributors:
Independent Publishers Group (IPG)
600 North Pulaski Road, Chicago IL 60624
University of Toronto Press Distribution
5201 Dufferin Street, Toronto (ON), Canada M3H 5T8
Gazelle Book Services, White Cross Mills
High Town, Lancaster LA1 4XS U.K.

First edition.

Printed in Canada.

Legal Deposit—First Quarter
Library of Congress Catalog Card Number: 2020947873
Library and Archives Canada Cataloguing in Publication
Title: Il vagabondo : an urban opera / Glenn Carley.
Names: Carley, Glenn, author.
Series: Guernica world editions ; 33.
Description: Series statement: Guernica world editions ; 33
Identifiers: Canadiana (print) 20200359614 | Canadiana (ebook)
20200359657 | ISBN 9781771836364 (softcover) |
ISBN 9781771836371 (EPUB) | ISBN 9781771836388 (Kindle)
Classification: LCC PS8605.A7547 V34 2021 | DDC C812/.6—dc23

Il Vagabondo is dedicated
to the Molinaros, the Mascitellis, the Strohs,
the Carleys, the Swedenborgians and the *Castropignani*
... and for Adriana, my daughter,
who was constantly present during the 'Installation'

A Tale of Gusto and Enchantment, Adaptation, Loss, Preserving the Old Ways of Making a Life in Canada.

To the Enchanted Ensembles of
The Urban Opera:
How to Perform This Book.

Gather with me, all Patrons of the Living Opera and we will sing together in the dialect of the love. Is not all opera about the life? Cannot the life be simple in its truth? Yes, life is not always about the fun, but there is fun in the life, when we can see it. Il Vagabondo wishes to see it with you and if you see it, you will become enchanted and when you are enchanted you will see the humanity.

Yes, this is a book, but what is a tale but a libretto in disguise? If you are tired or on the airplane, you may wish to read the thing to yourself. It is okay. It is better if you read him out loud, though, and become the performer. You are in the total freedom to do so.

An Urban Opera is an Installation Art and you are meant to be participant-readers on the stage of your own design. In this way, you complete the experience and open your imagination into the sweet melodies that lie deep within your cuore—your heart. I tell you this! You are part of the Installation Art and the work is truly complete if you preform her. Comprendi?

Like Il Vagabondo you do not have to be the good singer. All you have to do is recite either alone or together with your friends in "sing-speak (singspiel)." This is the basic unit of communication in all of the normal and the modern operas. When you have the time, perhaps you will go see them and know what I mean. They are so beautiful, yes, but you can do it on your own! In the hilltown, in the fields, tending sheep, gathering the wheat, to work is to sing … and then rest and pass time.

I will give you the example.

Gather your friends together in your home, in your classrooms, in your book club, outside when you are camping, anywhere you wish. You are performers in Opera Della Casa, the Opera of the Home, or Opera Della vita, the Opera of the Life, or Opera Della scuola, the Opera of the School. Do not sit.

To sing-speak is to read with a little music in your voice, like the chant. Perform the words, but do it with a little melody in it. Yes, it will seem silly at first. Yes, you have not trained for years and you are not the professional. Imagine you are in the shower or the car. This is all you need. Someone can read the address like the Puck in Shakespeare, or like the ancient messenger in the piazza of the hometown to gather you all around. Someone else can sing-speak the Stage Sequence. Then you can imagine where you are and why. Divide each part among you, double up if there is only one of you! Imagine the stage design in your mind because I am not the good drawer.

Il Vagabondo likes to warm up like a buffone.

Ripete (repeat after me) in the call and the response. This is Installation Art, remember? This is not the normal book. This is kinetic performance, and it is meant to be done, like you are in the ancient hill towns of your ancestors, no matter where they are or who they are. You do not have to be Italian. Il Vagabondo is not the Italian, but he loves his Italianioni. Especially, the mother—and the father-in-law in the story, and O yes, his sposa, his wife.

> **Like I say, ripete after me.**
> **Il Vagabondo:** La la la lay-O!
> **You:** La la la lee-O
> **Il Vagabondo:** La la la lay-O!
> **You:** La la la lee-O
> **Il Vagabondo:** La la la lay
> **You:** La la la lee
> **Il Vagabondo:** La la la lay
> **You:** La la la lee
> **Together:** *(sing with me, Bud!!)* La la la la lahhh/ la la la la la leeee/ la la la la la laayyy/ la la la leee! (repeat till someone throws the shoe at you)

There, you see? You are how do we call it? You are "warmed up." That is all you need to do. It is so easy. Bravo! Do not fight the enchantment. Encore!

Table of Performance

Signore e Signori, The Ladies and The Gentlemen
(an address to the audience of the Urban Opera)

Come with me to *Garibaldi's* Court and I will tell you
tales of gusto and enchantment.
We will sing, dance, laugh, cry and eat polenta at
midnight, al fresco.
I promise you homemade red wine and frittata.
Have some more! For me!
We will work hard, and then we will rest.
Always there will be the *lezione*: something to learn
and then something to eat.
Together we will sing in the living opera and, like
Il Vagabondo You will make a life too.

ACT I

ACT I: Scene 1

A Sauce-Making Tableau. Canto in red
(The English-speaking guy (Il Vagabondo) *spends the day making sauce with the Italian-speaking guy* (Garibaldi) *and his landlady. Powerful memories of the mother-in-law are invoked. Ancient lessons are shared in the doing—The Instruction and not the Education. Cultural dissonance, so apparent, is bent like a sapling.)*

Players:

Il Vagabondo—The English-speaking guy
Angelo/Garibaldi—The Father-in-law
Pasqua—The Mother-in-law (in spirit-form, a memory)
Santuzza—The Landlady
Maria (Vagabondo's wife)—offstage

[*The scene opens in the present time.* Il Vagabondo *is invited to "La Scuola di Salsa" (sauce school), to make the tomato sauce by* Angelo, *The father-in-law and his landlady,* Santuzza. *He must drop everything and attend or forever be doomed to be an ill-fated cultural tourist. He is excited by the chance, but remembers the drama of his past, 'red as fire' and the memory of his departed mother-in-law, Pasqua, is invoked.*]

Vagabondo: *(on the telephone)*
The tomatoes are ready? No!
I don't believe it!
(Exuberantly, to the audience)
It is not possible!
For months I send reminders
To this father-in-law and his landlady
I am captivated,
I am enchanted!
The state of gus-to/ Is the gate to paradiso
I must make la bella salsa with them.
I must make everything
for I ... am the student ...
of Salsa ... la scuola!

Angelo and **Santuzza:**
Could it be
that he is really interested
in the old ways?
He is young
and always in a hurry!

[*Memory invites the time change and it is the past now.* Pasqua, *the mother-in-law and matriarch of the family, is alive and healthy.* Il Vagabondo *is summoned to 'help make the sauce' after playfully cajoling and blackmailing the elders with their grandchildren but he arrives late in the morning after a meeting at work. The in-laws are already cleaning up and hosing down the driveway.* Vagabondo *snarls in defeat.* Pasqua *takes pity and later sends a small colander, some tomatoes home with him and* Maria, *to crush. The death of* Pasqua *is foretold.*]

Vagabondo: *(to the audience) (shrug shoulders, here)*
I will tell you:
I am ill-fated.
I am doomed.
Once, I made Maria tell her mother
Our Pasqua/ her Love
To invite me/ to make the sauce
Dio No! No Non!
Not to help/ but to make,
comprendi?
Do you not see?
Work through me/ to teach/ the children

Our halfbeeds must learn/ This spirit/ of their being.
Eh? Do you want them/ to lose/ the old ways?
(It is my dialect act/ of love's sheer blackmail)
Ha ha! / Bravo, / I break them,
Pasqua, you comprendi!
Grazie!

Pasqua: *(in spirit form, as memory)*
We make it on giovedi
You must come early

Vagabondo:
Dio! I am not retired
I must go to work!

Pasqua:
Eh? What am I to tell you?
When they are ready
you have to go.

Vagabondo: *(to the audience)*
O my geezis!
I came as fast as I could!
Broke the land-speed record
Four-wheel skid/ into the curb
of North York.
Only to find
the hose is out:
The Old Guy squeegeeing,
the clean wet concrete
in front of the garage
The plastic colanders and steel pots
all on their sides.
Dammit I hate my life!
I came as fast as I could!
Still/ they think/ I am/
an Inglese tourist
After all these years!

Pasqua:
You have to do the sauce
when the tomatoes are ready.
Do not weep

I see it/ in your eyes
I understand/
Your need to learn
Your need to love
But we/ are not teachers
We are/ how do you say it?
We are doers
You must be here/ to learn.

Vagabondo: *(to the audience, intimately)*
Canto: (Lament in blue light) "Season's Pass"
Later in the month
In the gentle ways of women
Pasqua quells my spirit
Brings my yearning in
Through deep pools of her eyes
She sent Maria home
With the colanders, the pots, the hand grinder
Two twenty litre pails,
purple, like grapes/ Vin bon!
And the lit-tle ba-by bush-el
of the Pom-o-doro, so-red-as-fire.
But this is not the real way
Geezis/ I am sentenced/ to the hobby-way,
Tour-i-si-mo ... class.
Dio!
Time passes.
Death, she comes and goes
I convince myself to give up
To always be the tourist
If you are lucky enough to be around
or better? To live there?
You may partake.
Otherwise, you can forget it. *(shrug shoulders here)*

[*The scene jumps back to the present time. The 'Inglese', the
Canadian, gets a second chance and arrives early at the
garage. He is immediately put to work by* Santuzza. Angelo
names him as Il Vagabondo *for the first time, and Garibaldi's
Court is named.*]

Vagabondo: *(on the phone)*
When do you want me there?

Santuzza:
You come in the morning,
the nella mattina.
Do not get up early
you have such/ a long way/ to travel!

Vagabondo:
Seriously!
Signora. What time do you start?

Santuzza:
You should be here
by the 7:30/
before/ it is too hot.

Vagabondo:
Perfetto! I will be there by 7
Before the sun has time
for the aqua sporca!

[Vagabondo *arrives curb-side at the house in North York. The garage is a hive of activity. There are big tubs of tomatoes bobbing, newspaper and tomatoes spread everywhere, drying and ready.*]

Santuzza:
Ahh! You are here!
You are early. Good!

Angelo: *(the father-in-law)*
Oh-oh, Il Vagabondo is here!

Vagabondo: *(with a flourish)*
It is I.

Angelo:
You are on time.

Vagabondo: *(with mock indignity and in pidgin Italian)*
Dio, Signore
Do you think/ that I am/ the tourist?
I must inform you
I have come to work/ not—how do you say it?—? To Talk!
I am no Inglese parrot

I am no buffone
I am not a jester
Yes, I dropped out of Italian night school, once
But I am here/ in the Redemption!
I will show you/ how we work!

[*Quickly, for it is their way,* Vagabondo *is put to work by* Santuzza. *Like "KP" duty he begins washing the tomatoes, drying, cutting out bad parts to prepare them for grinding.*]

Vagabondo:
How do you know?
Which tomatoes are good to buy?

Santuzza:
Ahh. A tomato is a tomato.
They are all good.
You just know

Vagabondo:
Signora! This is my first lesson:
La Prima Lez-i-o-ne!
They come in the morning
They come in the evening
They come in the middle of the day!
I must watch for them
O tell me when they are coming
So, I can tell my Inglese friends
"A tomato/ is a tomato/ You just/ know!"

[*Vagabondo begins to lift the bushels of tomatoes to carry to the back.*]

Santuzza:
No, Dio No!
You do not carry them/ to the back!
Put them on/ our little scooter
Mio sposo built it
To improve on the process
The how do I say it? The macchina
Never do for yourself/
What the machine/ Can do/ for you.

[*The action shifts to the back yard.*]

Vagabondo:
Canto: (in blue light): "That is the way she makes it"
Ma-key-na ... Ma-key-na. *(to the audience of the living opera)*
I must show you
how to prepare the tomatoes
for the macchina.
Observe. The beautiful lezione
Everyone does it their own way/
it depends what you like/
The Landlady, she cuts the fat ones/ in fours
But Pasqua? She cuts them/ long and thin/
Divide the cores/ the pieces are smaller/
they won't break the sieve.
O my friends/ Can you not understand?
the simple ways of love?
Weep with me
I will make it Pasqua's way/ Forever!

I am so happy
In the sauce school
in the pre-sence/ of an-cient ways
With two elders.
Enjoying one day
and all that fills it
While bees sip clear drippings
of cut tomato nectar
and sun has chased us
to the back yard.
You can tell/ It is going/ to get hot/ soon
But for now, we are cool
I pop/ a piece of tomato/ into my mouth
and pretend I feel the spirit of it.
Whisks me back in time/
Like a wanderer, a lucky tramp
I am witness to a thousand stories/
of Old days, and Old Ways,
History up close/ and personal
I listen to tales, the lezioni/
and learn to speak them.
I taste them/
upon the roof/ of my mouth
They cling to me/ like the scented sting/
of the basilica, from sprigs/ hooked in shadows.

I am in the shade
A breeze/ takes me fully/ into each moment
Consider my lilies—There is no Rush!
For I know exactly/ what is happening to me/ and Why.
It is the enchantment
of the Court/ of Garibaldi.
It is—How do you say it?—
It is ... Everything!

[*In his concentration,* Angelo *drops a tomato on the ground.*]

Vagabondo:
My father-in-law.
Why do you do this?
Are you wasting it/ or teaching me a lezione?
Santuzza! I must start throwing/ the to-ma-toes/ on the
    ground
So I can/ how do you say it?/ get the technique right!
It is the difference between
The Instruction/ and the Educazione!

Santuzza:
Write that down in your recipe book
You are such a joker!

[Vagabondo *is enchanted. He marvels at the 'sistemi', the systems everywhere, so efficient: the compost, the garden, the cadence of hard work. Preparation done; they begin to make the sauce. The crushing is complete and they pause for wine.*]

Vagabondo:
O I am a mah-kee-na
All the nasty malvagio we set aside/
She goes into the compost.
What a work of art!
Nothing is wasted!
Greatest of the lessons
But better still? The giardino!
Embrace of engineering and ingenuity
With little aisles the "old guy"
plays bocci in!
My fagiolini, so tall
form their high narrow arch

amidst steel rebar/ fused with wire
Gawd! It is not an Italian garden
unless you have rebar/ holding up the world
How do you get it?
Listen! I will tell you.
It is magic!
You get it/
from someone you know!
I am sure/ my "old guy" sleeps/
hidden in the beans
atop shady recesses/ of grass/ holding the moisture.
The basil/ laid out so nicely!
How does he get/ his tomatoes so tall?
I should water mine every day
I never make the time to do it.
While zucchini/ play hide and seek
Behind starr-y/ yellow-turgid leaves
Home free!
Everything plays together
The harmony/ The order/ The organization!

Vagabondo: *(by the macchina, using a plunger to push the tomatoes through)*
So ...
Can you see, Old Man?
That I/ have the most/ importante job
The one you must go/ to the school for
The Education/ and not/ The Instruction

Angelo: *(ignoring him, intent on his work)*
If you push too hard
You will break the sieve
Like I did, last year

Vagabondo:
I see the lesson!
You must experiment with the thing/
to see how it is done
and once you see how it is done
you work to do it right! *(He makes a note in his little sauce procedural book)*
I know you kept notes
In the hometown too!

Angelo:
Watch out for the bees!
They have come/
to greet you.

Vagabondo:
Geezis Dio! Why is it/
that every time/
I make/ something with you/
Wasps show up/
and I get stung?

Angelo:
It is be-cause/
you are not/ Italian!

Vagabondo:
Mamma mia!

Santuzza:
Because you have worked/
You can drink the wine.
First, we work/
and then we eat.

Vagabondo: *(turning to address the audience of the Living Opera)*
(Brindisi Canto: "The Instruction not the Education")
O can it be true?
To drink the vino
like Inglese acqua sporca
at 10:30 in the morning?
My reward/ for working hard!
It is paradiso
So full/ So warm/ so primitive
I cannot/ go to the LCBO any-more
I feel so masculine!
All women so feminine
My life is the enchantment/
the passion play/ How can I/
ex-plain it ... to you?
The rhythm of the garden:
the rows

the systems
the tendings to
the division of tasks
from soil/ to table and back again!
The cycle of seasons/
The efficient current of life
The immensity/ and choreography of Souls!
Perceptions/ so slightly/ out of view/
You have to be/ The Vag-a-bondo/ to see them!
The Education/ is not/ The Instruction
This sacred moment/ by a burning bush
O take off your sandals!
Be bathed in light!
Do nothing/ but listen/ watch/ be humble!
Time. Patience. Solitude. Listening. Presence
To Listen/ to let things be/
To not try/ to explain it all.
You just know.
It is like faith/ and tomatoes!

[*Garibaldi is named.*]

Angelo: (*clinks glasses*)
I am a rich man
Not in terms of the mon-ey
but in terms of my life/ mia famiglia!

Vagabondo:
You are My Italian/ My Garibaldi.
And I am/ an apprentice
in the dialect/ of your Court.

[Vagabondo *and* Garibaldi *return to work. They dismantle the macchina, the machine. There are references to* Garibaldi *grieving the death of his wife,* Pasqua. *He refers to her in the third person.* Vagabondo *professes his undying love for* Pasqua. *They fill the jars with sauce and start the water boiling on the burner.*]

Vagabondo: (*to the audience*)
No one announces/
the return to work
There is no bell/
The resting time/

passes naturally.
Observe as I observe:
Santuzza rinses tools/
by the yard barn.
Monkey see? Monkey do
My Observation/ is the great dialect of love,
the great communicator.
What beauty!
What ingenuity!
Condensation sweating from her furnace
runs along a tube
from inside to outside
to 50-gallon drum/
a perfect/ out-door-sink!

Santuzza: *(proudly)*
No matter what—how do I say it?—
No matter what tragedy happens,
We are self-sufficient.

Garibaldi:
Why are you rinsing
directly in the barrel?
That is not/
the way to do it.

Vagabondo:
I do it the way/
I am instructed!

Garibaldi:
Then you have/
been instructed wrong!

Vagabondo: *(ignoring him) (speaking intimately, to his
    audience)*
The water
cools my hands and arms
After his grief
When he moved
He gave away so many/
50-gallon drums.
There is a mystique
to their beauty

I remember six of them
Standing at parade-rest
at the old, dead house.
Some carried lard/
some carried the vegetable oil.
I ask him where he gets them
He says/ you just get them/
from people you know.
It is like rebar/ so useful!
I took one home/ but it/
does nothing:
Overturned, avoiding mosquito larva
and the West Nile virus
Home to spiders, maple keys
and leaf debris/
Empty/ devoid of life
disconnected from its system/
like the modern ways
But when drums live?
When they are alive?
I tell you this.
Filled to brim?
The muscato, the carignane, the alicante/
covered in thick poly-ethy-line/ the plastic
To hear/
the warm sizzle/
of wine fermenting/
This hiss of afternoon/
Hear it?
It is like the bees/ whispering!

Santuzza:
It is time/ to pour la salsa
Observe.
The lids
the jars
the salt
the basilico.
First you put in/
each teaspoon of salt.
Then the sprig/
of the basilico.
Take this pot/
It holds exactly/ a litre
Pore it into the jar/

Be careful not to drip!
Use the funnel/
the way I showed you.

Garibaldi:
My wife/
She used to put
the salt all at once
in the big pail.
But Santuzza?
she likes to do it/
this way.

Santuzza:
However, you like to do it.

Garibaldi:
Everyone does it their own way.

Vagabondo: *(loyally)*
I will do it/
the way Pasqua has done it.
With a dash of/
Canadese/ on the side.

Santuzza:
Why do you bring/
such big jars?

Vagabondo:
Signora/ do you not see?
Maria and I
Like to give it a-way/
to our Inglese friends.
They love me for it/
It gives them the big stomachs/
like me!

Santuzza:
So, I see.

Garibaldi:
It is time
to boil the jars.
Observe

Vagabondo:
The Instruction
and not/
The Education?

Garibaldi:
Si!

Santuzza:
Angelo
That is not the way to do it!
Do not be such/
a testa dura!
The water?
Will never boil/ that way.

Garibaldi: *(bending down to light the burner)*
Eh, Eh, Eh, Eh!

[*WHOOOOSH!!!!*]

Vagabondo:
Holy Mackerel!

Santuzza:
An-ge-lo!
you will kill yourself
That is not the way?
to light a burner!

Vagabondo: *(bending down beside the old guy)*
She is right you know.
I know you know.

[*WHOOOOSH!!!!*]

Garibaldi and **Vagabondo:**
Holy Mackerel!

Garibaldi: *(trimming the flame)*
There. You see?
That is how you do it!

[Garibaldi, Santuzza *and* Il Vagabondo *have lunch.*]

Santuzza:
It is time/
to eat now.
Go and wash up/
in the barrel.
Then sit with us/
where it is cool.

Garibaldi, Santuzza, Vagabondo:
Signore benedice/
questo cibo/
che stiamo/
per prendere,
Cosi sia.

Santuzza:
Mangia!

Vagabondo: *(addressing the audience)*
Look!
It is the zucchini lasagna
So crusty
Panini, so crisp/ still warm
The sausages, all raggedy at the end
The green beans, the insalata
with oil and vinegar and e sale.
Where is the Inglese dressing *(facetiously teasing)*
The garlic, the oregano
It is everything!

Santuzza:
You like to be/
with the old people
I cannot believe/
what a passion you have/
to learn!

Vagabondo: *(grandly)*
That is because/
I am—how does he say it?—
I am ... a rich man!

Garibaldi: *(looks up, as if to see him for the first time)*
Have some wine.

[*The jars of sauce continue to boil in a big pot of water on a propane burner. Garibaldi decants the hot water to start a second pot.*]

Garibaldi:
I will show you/
what we do.
You take the piece of hose/
and you go like this.
See how you transfer/
the hot water?
while it is/ still hot?
This saves time!

Vagabondo:
You are a buffone/
if you ever throw out/
a piece of the hose
There a thousand uses/
and it is importante!
To save the time!

Garibaldi: (*playfully*)
Especially in the cantina, eh?

Vagabondo:
Signore.
Why do you accuse me?
I only decant
the vino/
for you and la signora
Geezis! I do not
drink it for myself
I am not / the brigande.

[*The work completed, Vagabondo is walked to his car by the ancients. He feels complete. Molto contenti, you could say.*]

Vagabondo:
Grazie signora e signore
per lezione/
salsa la scuola.
I lead a charmed life!
io sono molto contenti!

Santuzza:
You have done everything.
You can go home.
Now you know/
how to make it/ next year.
Remember/ to put the jars/
upside down/
on a newspaper.
That way you can tell/
which ones
are not sealed.
Ciao, Vagabondo!

Vagabondo:
Ciao!
You never know/
when you will/
see me next!

ACT I: Scene 2

Variations on Red Peppers. "The Dance of the Mudcat"
(Magnifico! Garibaldi invites Il Vagabondo to return to his
Court to make the Peppers. Lessons and sistemi abound!
The seeds of making a life are sown. The cycle, cadence and
trance of hard work are revealed.)

Players:

Maria
Adriana—Vagabondo & Maria's daughter (offstage)

(Stage note: Choreography: This scene could be punctuated
by an imaginary dance, or ballet by red clad spirits in slow,
languid gyrations of motion, like fire flickering in the back-
ground, on stage, on a shimmering curtain and up the aisles
of imagination. [i.e. The Dance of the Red Peppers] [This is
a counterpoint to the sorrow-besotted and troubled blue
demons, who appear at intervals, and to show that love finds
its way in making a life as does grief.])

[*The scene opens with a telephone call. Il Vagabondo is*
invited 'to make the peppers' in North York with Garibaldi
and The Landlady. *He knows as an outsider; he must have*
made an impression and the invitation to return is a gift of
acceptance and understanding. The ancients know he is
interested in being instructed.]

(The phone rings and one of the children answers it.)

Adriana:
O! Hi Nonno!
Do you want/
to speak to Mamma?
Daddy? It's Nonno/
He wants to speak to Vagabondo!

Vagabondo:
Canto: "If you can make the time, you come" *(andante,
with excitement, expressive)*
O Heavens to Betsy!
Before I can breathe
I am asked
If you can make the time/ you come
Am I interested, tomorrow?
In coming to Santuzza's
to make the Peppers?
Incredibile!
Magnifico!
it is a—How do I say it?—
A Miracolo!
For the first time/
I am invited
without having to ask/
to Pepper La Scuola!
Come prima,
piu di prima,
I'm in love.
What time/
Do you want me there?
Is it only/
going to be hard work? /
because I only like/
to work hard.
I don't believe it!/
It is not possible
They must have had/
a lovely time.
They actually comprendi
They know I am In-ter-ested
in learning to be taught.
It is the Instruction/

and not the Education.
To decline the invitation?
Would violate my Father's
Rule G!
And no-body knows/
what-ever-that means.
It must mean loyalty
and it must mean love.
A knowledge/
that certain things/
must be done.
Otherwise?
Do you not see the thing?
You violate Rule G.
I must make haste!
Tidy up!
Get a shave
Play some jazz/
in the car to celebrate.
Mamma mia!
I must leave time/
for the drive thru acqua sporca!
They want me for 8
but I will make the time
to be there at the 7!

[*After all the fuss of the importance of arriving early and on time,* Vagabondo *sleeps in and arrives late. Nonetheless, Inglese patterns intact, he still makes the time for morning coffee at the drive-through; the aqua sporca (dirty water). He plays the free jazz of John Coltrane triumphantly as he drives south.*]

Offstage: *(Decidedly non-Italian, imaginary jazz music plays. There is a pause and an iconic voice is heard)*

Drive Through:
May I take your order?

Vagabondo:
Large double double please
and make it snappy/
I'm late!

[Vagabondo *arrives and enters into a playful dialogue with* The Landlady. Garibaldi *is busy in the morning shade of the backyard preparing the barbecues for roasting peppers. There is a large, functional BBQ for the ancient Italians and a "baby" BBQ for the Inglese.* The Landlady *gives a practical lesson on getting the coals right and imparts ancient knowledge to* Vagabondo.]

Vagabondo and **Santuzza:** *(duet w/ Garibaldi at intervals)*
Canto: "The Instruction -not the Education!"

Vagabondo:
I am late!

Santuzza:
Oh, you are here!

Vagabondo:
It is unbelievable
I cannot/
believe it myself!
You will not believe me/
but I slept in!

Santuzza:
You are so funny!

Vagabondo:
As you can see/
I have come for the hard work/
Grazie, for inviting me/
to Pepe La Scuola.
I will not drop out today!

Santuzza and **Garibaldi:**
Ehh,
We shall see!

Santuzza:
No, no An-g-e-lo/
you don't do it like that! /
you don't put the wood/
in with the charcoal.

Now it will burn unevenly/
Now we have to wait! /
You are such a testa dura!

Vagabondo:
Dio Angelo! /
What are you doing?
You have been/
taught wrong!

Garibaldi:
Eh, eh, eh ...
It will be o-kay/
Do not be/
so nervous!

Vagabondo:
Holy Mackerel!
Geezis! Santuzza
Now I will look/
for an old style/
Bar-be-cue/
at the yard sale

Santuzza:
Write that down!
That is one thing I would like/
to go to/ The garage sales
but I don't need anything/
and there is never/
enough time to go!

Vagabondo:
If you go/
look for Mio glasses/
For me!
I am so worried/
when the last one breaks
I can no longer drink/
any more vino!
It is a—come si dice—a tragedy!

Hey! (Eh?) Why does the Old Guy/?
have the large Bar-be-cue
and this baby/
picolito one, is for me?

Santuzza:
It is because/
you are learning.
Now observe!
You take the peppers/
and prepare them
like this!
The key is not to/
burn them too much!
Then when you cook
the pepper/
It will not taste too good.
Angelo!
This is too black.
What are you doing?
Mamma Mia!

Angelo:
O-kay, O-kay
Why do you peck me?

Vagabondo:
The embers
are like the foundation
of the house.
If you don't/
build the bottom right
everything on top/
will have the problem.

Santuzza:
Exactly!
See? You understand.
Good!
I will leave you now. *(she disappears inside the house)*

[The Landlady *goes inside and the men begin their work, fanning the fire and roasting the peppers. Later she will return with a banana and teach the next step in the process.*

Il Vagabondo *takes the time to ask about* Pasqua *and* Garibaldi *grows quiet and far off. He is not in the Instruction mode. Frustrated,* Vagabondo *sings an arietta to the audience of the living opera lamenting a cultural dissonance that nobody—how do you say it?—Yaks!*]

Vagabondo: *(an arietta) (He addresses the audience)*
Canto: "Why does nobody talk?"
We stand beside each other
So busy together in our work
Did you make the peppers
with Pasqua? I ask.
No, we never made them ...
He says, just like that!
No elaboration.
No Conversation.
A simple call and response,
Then ... silence.
O why does nobody talk?
I come from a family
of yakkers.
I love to yak!
My mother loved to yak
I yakked with my brother
and everything had to be said!
I ask my wife, Maria
Why does no one like to yak?
Garibaldi won't yak
Pasqua never yakked,
Your Brother is so quiet
We could spend
forever in an afternoon
and no one/
would need to say a thing!
You don't have to talk/
to be together
is her logical defense.
Yes, we kiss,
Yes, I love her/
but sometimes/ it takes me years
to understand the thing
Sometimes?
I tell you this!
I still don't.

[*Nonetheless,* Il Vagabondo *grows enchanted by the cadence of hard work, of learning, the ancient order of life. He falls into the thoughtless trance of repetitive work and begins to understand the universal language where there is absolutely no need to say anything. He yearns to show it all to his children! Competently,* Garibaldi *is fanning his large BBQ while* Vagabondo *is comically fanning his. He is again taught the importante lesson: "Nothing is wasted."*]

Vagabondo and **Garibaldi:**
Canto: "The Ancient Order of life" (You have to be crazy, to be the Inglese)
We pick/
blackened pepper/
off grill/ with tongs/
Pile flaccid shapes
on large trays.
Steam escapes/
from cracks.
Blackpartsofskin/
flakeoffinhand.
Strong and nauseous smell
peeled open/ the seeds/ the steamy juice
and fibrous inside.
I am shown/ to stand them on end
Hook stems/ through grill
They stand like/
Old, bent red men
in the piazza.
O nothing. Nothing is wasted.
In the bella giornata
Shade hides under umbrella/
Old Barbecue and its baby/
in the sun.
Eyes so teary from shifting smoke
We are intent/
Upon our task.
Enchanted,
to know exactly/
where we are now
in the cadence of our being/
in the unity of our hard work
Everything within our gaze?
exactly how it should be

Feel the Order!
The backyard sistemi quietly/
knows exactly/
what they/ are made to do.
In air so
masculine and feminine/
we can tell/
which of the beans/
are boys and/
which of the tomatoes
are girls!

Vagabondo: *(alone, with emphasis)*
You have to be crazy/
to be an Inglese/
Alone. In Garibadi's Court.
Yes, you have to be crazy/
to be an Inglese/
Alone. In Garibaldi's Court
But I have my lessons now
I know/ what contenti means!
In the presence of silence/
In the cadence of hard work?
Yes you have to be crazy
to be an Inglese ...
This dialect of love/
is a gift.

[The Landlady *returns with two bananas and declares it is time to eat. She announces the last lesson in the process of skinning peppers, will leave the men and later return with a beautiful pizza and wine in a Mio glass. It is the time for telling stories.* The Landlady *shares the early days of her arrival to Canada.*]

Santuzza:
I will teach you/
the next step now.
But first you/
will have/ something to eat.
Are you still/
Enjoying yourself?
Observe!
Take a pepper like this

Pull it open/
scrape off the skin
The fire must be right/
Otherwise, you waste time.
Do not leave the skin on/
if you want the peppers/
to taste good.
Now pick it up like this/
and tear it like this/
It depends/ how you like to do it
Put them in baggies and freeze
When the company comes/
add oil, the parsley and the garlic
You always have something/
That is good you can eat!

Vagabondo:
About ten peppers in/
the tedium, she takes o-ver
and I en-ter/ the thoughtless trance/
of hard-work.
The Universal Language/
(no need to say nothin'!)
Within a day so warm/
A neighbour's dog is barking/
a jet flies over/ airport bound
Like the seagull/
gliding by in our sky/
a wish dives/
across thoughts
and I wish the Children/
could be here/ to learn
to know what I now know/
to feel what I now feel.
And reach automatically
again, and again/
for brittle black skin/
pulled off with our hands/
the scraping, and scraping/
inspect/ pluck seeds/ stand up
stretch the stretch-supreme
over to the compost/
sweet system, Repeat!

Santuzza:
Time to stop working!
We are going/ to eat now.
You must/ wash up/ in the barrel

Vagabondo: *(to the audience)*
Old Garibaldi/
is not back
from his journey through dreams.
The water so cool/ drips from cupped hands/
And I wash face and neck
Exactly like him!
I cannot read/
if he is hap-py or sad.
I know if I ask him/
O tell me your thoughts?
He will shrug me off
as Pasqua retreats/
from his spirit.

La bella tavola!
(my Italian complete)
Santuzza!
It is come si dice—it is Everything!
So dolce—so sweet!

Santuzza:
It is nothing

Vagabondo:
Poco, poco vino Signora?

Garibaldi:
Chin Chin!

Santuzza: *(after praying)*
Buon appetito!
You are so hungry
Have some pizza
I see/ you have found/
the vino!

Vagabondo:
Grazie per la lezione/ Pepe la scuola

Io sono/ in paradiso
O Geezis:
Homemade Pizza/
lightly crusted/ smothered
in the onions
the cheese
zucchini
With flick and flop/
still within
our glorious peppers!
The Caravaggio/ the Angelico/ The Botticelli
bathed in oil/ the herbs ...
More pizza!
More sausages!
More bread!
More salad!
More vino
O my Dio!
More ... More!

Santuzza:
You have/
such a passion to eat!

Vagabondo:
I am learning to!

Santuzza: *(an arietta)*
In Italy, our life was hard/
but it was not
easy here, either.
The first job?
Eh! We put tomatoes in trays/
dressed tightly in cellophane
The girls in the factory/
the mean ones
called us names
A British war bride/
was nicer than the rest.
They asked us to work weekends/
The other girls said no/
but we were glad to do it/
The overtime paid better
It was a struggle/

But I tell you this!
We made do/ with what we had/
and that is why
we are/ The way we are now!
O, this story/ makes me so tired
I rise to collect the plates
Now you go and get
more wine!

[*The wine bottle is empty.* Vagabondo goes *inside to the cantina and its magical "ali baba" contents are explained in precise enchanted detail. Enter the* "Piccolo Coro" (Small Chorus) *who sing* the "Cantina Song" *to extol the virtue of simple, ordinary things. It is the enchantment of making a life, creating systems and making do, with all the exquisite micro-joy in-between.* **Stage note:** *The Reader(s) will note that the* Vagabondo *part is demanding. To add variety to the Urban Opera, a small chorus may be invited into the read to sing enchanted interludes and to punctuate the 'hyper-details' of the Italian culture. These will later be referred to as "observation songs" where additional voices add texture to the experiences resonating in any particular scene. (To preserve* Vagabondo's *vocal cords, the small chorus sings to the 'meta-view' of the operatic narrative.)*]

The Piccolo Coro (Small Chorus): "Cantina Song"
The cantina
is my root cellar
Deep red gallons perched/
on two-by-fours, under shelving
made from solid ends/
of wine cases, reborn.
Sapore Dolce
DutchBoy Carignane
Ballentine
E Dolce
L Bar L and
Ma-Ma-Mia!
With the picture of signorina/
and her dress is so ...
in need/ of the supervision!
O musty smell!
How do I explain/

this space to you?
Cold not freezing/
Chilly enough to keep/
everything so nice.
Benches and shelves/
run entire length/ of foundation
Jugs of wine,
The Brio, the Mio, fifty-gallons drums
and demijohns.
Clear plastic tubing/ for siphoning
Cases of sauce/ cases of paste
canned chick peas/
Onions and the garlic/
drooping on nails/
There are things/ I cannot name
... I have yet to discover.
Sour wine vinegar/ so pungent!
Put my finger inside/
to taste.
I am enchanted
each time/
I set foot in there.
Remove plastic tube
Take the long, hard pull/
slowly, agelessly to brim
Quickly pull tube
above gravity line/
to arrest the flow
Happy task complete?
I release myself and return
warmly/
To the enchantment
of Garibaldi's Court.

[Il Vagabondo *returns to the table and talks of his love for music. He teases* Garibaldi *about wasting money on luxuries in the Hometown. An opera buffa moment of playful banter in the libretto.* Santuzza *gets the portable stereo and* Vagabondo *puts on Italian hill songs (the Alan Lomax recording of The Abruzzo) and then some ersatz opera and then some Coltrane jazz.* Garibaldi *tells a story about the Hometown while they go back to work, to finish.*

Santuzza:
You have done/
everything now!
You know—how do I say it?—
you know/ the process.
You help so much/
If you want to go downtown/
to buy la musica/ you can go.

Vagabondo:
Signora! I do not/
wish to go.
Do you think?
That I am rich?
Do I have the money/?
like the old guys
to squander/
Like it is nothing?
Music is everywhere!
Dio/ It is here already!
Can you hear it?
Play the Abruzzo one!
We still have/
the peppers to skin!

[*Santuzza fetches her portable stereo and puts in a CD.*]

Garibaldi:
Ha!
You think/
we had the money
for that?

Vagabondo:
Garibaldi!
We must have/
la musica.
Surely you had the stereo going
in the fields/
when you worked?
Surely you had la musica/
feeding Rosie/ the donkey/ and your peegs?
Remember?

I bought this/ for you!
Alan Lomax
He is so autentico!
His treasury of Italian songs
are like the vino/
rough ... prim-i-tive ... full bodied/
filled with presence
Listen with me!
Al fresco
A symphony of the shade
Songs of love/ of death/
of shepherds/ of lost sheep found.
Gawd, don't you comprendi?
Observe.
It is possible to work
It is possible to listen.
Now pass me/ a pepper.

Garibaldi: *(arietta)*
It was not possible/
for the boys and the girls
to meet.
The only way
Was to go into town/
to the piazza
and mill about.
Someone had
an Old Victrola/
with a small bell speaker
and only one record.
A boy
would wind up
the stereo.
Errrrrr, errrrrrr, errrrrrrr
Suddenly la musica!
Clapping/ dancing
all coming to life
under the stars.
This was how
we passed time.
We had/
to make
our own ... fun!

Vagabondo:
Bravo Garibaldi!
There is nothing finer
You sing the libretto/
for this day, alone.

(to the audience of the living opera)

I sing the gaiety
I sometimes see
in the Old Men
being silly
So out of stoic character
So funny to watch
It is a bit embarrassing:
He reminds me
of a Young Me!
But I will tell you this!
My Inglese segreto
During the holiday season/
when you are stuck
For the idea?
Buy them Hill songs
Buy them opera
For the man
who has everything,
for the man
who needs nothing!
O it is hot-time
We are so tired
We call it stanco
Old Man
I tell you
I will be seeing
the peppers
in my dreams
But hark!
Is that the sliding door?
On time
In time
like the traverse of sun
across this North York sky
Like a system
Do I smell espresso?

Is that the biscotti
on your tray?

[Santuzza *returns to announce proudly (and prematurely)
that the work is done.* Vagabondo *knows there are still
peppers to skin. He will no longer allow himself to be 'tourist
class'*]

Santuzza: *(duet)*
It is time/
to stop now.
You have helped
so much!
Last year/
Angelo only had
finished one box.
He still had half to do!
If you want to go now
You can go.

Vagabondo:
Signora
I can-not go
until the work
is done.
You know
that this/
is the true lezione!
and I?
I am not a tourist

Santuzza:
The young/
they do not/
usually show/
this much interest.

Vagabondo:
I am older than I look!
Grazie for this/
my third espresso
There is a hole
in the pot/
It is empty!

Santuzza:
I could make more?

Vagabondo:
No, I am
Content. Thank you.

(to the audience)

A slight breeze/
As afternoon
begins to dance/
with the earliest part
of our evening.
The end is in sight!
We know we will finish
in an hour, or so.

Santuzza! Don't go!
Look how much
I have done
compared to this
Old Italian.
He is ruthless
He is a testa dura
He sleeps when you are gone
He makes me/
do all the scraping
all of the cleaning
He claims all hard work
for Himself!

[*As a sign of respect* Vagabondo *lets* Garibaldi *scrape the last pepper. Maria and the children arrive and they dine al fresco. Vagabondo, enchanted, sings to his daughter to impress upon her the importance of ancient ways in the living opera. They exit. (Red peppers continue their slow, flickering imaginary ballet.)*]

Vagabondo:
Garibaldi?
I will teach you
My lezione
You see?

When you love someone/
you do not always
take the black peppers.
Sometimes you take
the not-so-black peppers/
so the other guy
is not always scraping away.
I am worried
you are always taking
the black peppers.
What do you think?

Garibaldi:
You are right.

Vagabondo: *(to his audience, affectionately)*
For some reason
It is important to me
that Garibaldi
has the last pepper/
to finish.
Like everything else
A system of respect
Must be tilled/
and planted in little rows,
watered, tended
and above all?
Harvested.
Deep down I know this.
(turning and arching his back to stretch)
Old Man?
I cannot believe
we have finished.
Eh? Someone is here
Bravo. It is Maria and the children.

The Children:
Hi Nonno!

Maria:
I did not know
if you would be done or not
but I decided I would come
anyway. Hi Santuzza!

[*In twilight, they all sit al fresco.* Santuzza *brings trays of food, there is silent bustle at the table, merriment without sound. The music is warm and melodic. A short recitative between Vagabondo and daughter ends the day.*]

Adriana:
Did you have/
a good day, Dad?

Vagabondo:
My daughter?
Did you know/
there is a song/
In every day?

Adriana:
Yes, Dad

Vagabondo:
You can compose, live
and sing with each minute
If you want to.
It is ...
It is like going to the cantina
You will always find
Something!

Adriana:
Were you in a song/ today Daddy?

Vagabondo:
Exactly!

ACT I: Scene 3

Dinner al Fresco
*(A week has passed. The Light has changed. It is evening.
A tablemass. The death of Pasqua is foretold and the arrangement of the companions of the life and not of the bed,
explained. Cracks in the culture are lamented. "If you move
the compost it will stink." Garibaldi and The Landlady are
leaving for his hometown of Castropignano in the morning.)*

The Players
(as in Scene 2)

*(Stage note: The action takes place in the backyard, al fresco.
The light changes and the music should be wistful and
romantic.)*

[*La famiglia arrives for dinner and* Vagabondo *is virtually
ignored by the (exaggerated) joy of seeing the nipoti.
(**Imaginary music note:** a robust fanfare could be played
at the opening of this scene to punctuate the sacredness of
the nipoti, the grandchildren, to their grandfather.)*]

Vagabondo:
Buona sera to all
La famiglia
Vagabondo
is here!

Santuzza:
Angelo!
Maria is here!

Garibaldi:
Hel-lo!

The Children:
Hi Nonno!

Maria:
Hi Daddy!

Vagabondo:
So.
I have returned
I was so worried/
I left the peppers
All of the sauce
And now?
I fear?
It is gone!

Garibaldi:
You are right
There is no food here
You can go
back home!

Vagabondo:
Buona sierra, signora
You see?
I had such a good time
you cannot/
get rid of me.

Santuzza:
That is true!

[Garibaldi *and* Santuzza *are going on a trip to Europe and to his Hometown. Maria and her father consult an overly large Michelin map of Italy. It is the first time that* Garibaldi *has returned to his Hometown and the second time he has travelled since the matriarch, his wife,* Pasqua *died.*]

Vagabondo: *(to the audience of the living opera)*
In a few days
they will depart/
On the senior's tour
To the Europe and to the Italy
Be religious
Tour Rome
Take a bus to Boiano
retrieved by sister and love eternal
My friends from last year!
to be whisked
up back roads impossible
to the burning bush!
Cas-tro-pig-na-no!
Let it roll/
off your tongue
like meat off the rib.
See me speak
The Italiano?
Castro-Castro-pig-ni-ano
Sing it with Il Vagabondo! *(gestures to the audience)*

All:
Castropignano!

Vagabondo:
Bravo!
Do you not see
The Instruction/ not the Education
Geezis ...
You are—how do we say it?—
Bilingual
And there?
In the piazza
you will drink the benezine/
and play the skopa.

[Il Vagabondo *explains the emotional role of* Santuzza *and* Maria *and he reflects on this notion of "a companion of the life and not of the bed." It is hard for them but they recall the matriarch's famous lesson: 'you will not die from this.'*]

Vagabondo:
Canto: "Companions of the Life (and not of the bed)"
I tell you this
It is his first return
to the Hometown
The second time
travelling without his wife.
She died/
three years ago.
He lives now
as a tenant
the last year
and a half
in this home.
He pays the rent/
She makes the food
He fixes things/
she does the cleaning
They grow the garden
Do things together
to make a life
Return it to order
the way it all should go/
like systems
like planting
like a sun
coming up and going down.
This alternately Modern/
yet ancient
—how do you say?—
Arrangement.
Companions of the life
Not of the bed
Dio! I know/
there is a huge lesson here
It does not come all at once
Most of my generation
choose not to learn it ·

Can you pass time
with a Landlady?
What are you going to do? *(Shrug shoulders here)*
He is happy/
So I am happy
It is foolish to argue
with the weather
If it rains?
You watch it.
If it is sunny?
You find the shade.
You will not/
die from this
Pasqua, she used to say.
She is right
Maria and I
We are not dying
But do you not see?
It is hard/
for my wife.
So, what
if it is hard
She weeps in my arms
It is not/
going to
change a thing.
I tell her
Garibaldi—He is like the corn plant
in the field/
the year after the harvest
No matter what crop
No matter what field
No matter how fallow
there are always
one or two plants
left over from the season/
growing tall
despite the odds
Go and see for yourself
I tell you
I am smarter than I look
for I, Il Vagabondo
have married
my corn plant.

It is/
My good fortuna.

Vagabondo:
Santuzza!
I am so happy
Watch out!
Or I will travel with you.
Bring me an atlas!
So I can see
Where you come from
and where you
are going.
Dio Signora!
Do not bring me the globe
Pasqua used to do that too
You are not
leaving the planet
Are you?

Santuzza:
No/
It is too
expensive.

[*A most beautiful, iconic, Italian dinner occurs. All are filled with gusto and enchantment.*]

Vagabondo and **Maria:** *(recitative)*
In time
the map is folded
To the airport
we will take them, tomorrow
But for now?
The sun leaves
the patio area
Her heat gives way
to soft coolness.
A tablecloth replaces
Thick plastic covers of work
Maria will go
help with the meal
I will take the bottle
to the cantina and fill

the rosy brim
Vino racing to the top
Pinched off in the nick of time
I tell you
this siphoning:
It is an art
But like everything?
It takes the practice.
We return
to dishes stacked
and food arriving.
She says it is nothing really
Grilled chicken breast
Boiled pork shoulder
(I think)
Food so strange and wonderful
Green beans glistening
Look! Our fire-red peppers
Burn Caravaggio's light
The bread
the insalata
a dance of oregano, salt and the oil
kissed by red wine vinegar.
Ti amo amore
Wine for the grownups
Orange pop for the kids
And after the melon
and after the chocolate
Bambini are excused to play.
Dusk comes
to usher cool evening
Under umbrella
We sip espresso and talk
about important things.

[Il Vagabondo *begins a song describing* Garibaldi *and* Pasqua *as his role models of love. The cancer narrative is explained briefly from alpha to omega and this segues to some marital advice from* Garibaldi *to* Vagabondo. *He is befriending his son-in-law and sharing a 'hard tale' of his marriage to* Pasqua *and how to resolve it.* (**Canto: "A decade is a long time"**)]

Garibaldi:
If you are having
any trouble
I want you to
come to me.

Vagabondo:
Did you go through
rough times?
I once asked him
In the early days/
when we smoked
Export A's
with abandon.

Garibaldi:
Canto: "A decade is a long time"
Si
I will tell you this
A decade is a long time
I was mad
at my wife and at my family
for ten years, once.
I would come home
and go out
I did not talk to them
She could not listen
I was always so nervous
But one day
I woke up
I kept saying to myself
You are wrong
to be so mad
all of the time.
They cannot help
who they are.
They are not
doing anything wrong.
From then on
It was better
And my life is happy now.
We still fight
She is so stubborn
But it does not last

We are always laughing.
The neighbours
they tell me now
We are like the newlyweds
But I tell you this
A decade
is a long time.

[*Memory-love is in the air and* The Landlady *shares the tale
of her husband, how he lived and how he died.*]

Santuzza: *(arietta)*
It grows softly dark
around the table now
And the light from the TV
beats its languid strobe
inside the house.
I think about my widowhood
the crushing pain
of living alone
when your sposo dies.
He was a "bookman"—
An engineer who
played the piano
who loved the music.
He was younger
than I—
I used to tease him
Ha! You think you know
More than I know?
I tell you, you are wrong.
He told me
I should not worry
After he died
(of the cancer/
it was horrible)
I must look after myself
and never fear.
For he will be
Happy in heaven
find a foreign girl
and she will
massage his feet.
What can I tell you?

That was our life
You have to make do.

[**The first imaginary 'blue demon' appears.** *It is a harbinger of the unhappiness of life between and amongst family and friends; some of the harsh realities of Italian culture observed, the grudges, the family arguments that last forever. A cautionary tale of a mother (a Strega or witch) who would not accept an Italian/Canadian match and how the couple had to elope, forever in exile.* (**Canto: Se sposti il compost puzza. ("if you move the compost, it will stink.")** *Imaginary Choreography: gossamer clad blue demons slowly dance in blue light in the background.]*

Vagabondo:
Canto: "Se aposti il compost puzza"
Like you/
We talk of family
of unhappy grudges
between mothers and daughters
between sons and fathers,
between sisters and brothers,
the sons and the mothers-in-law
We grow tired
Yet the urgency in the night
this urgency to be known
sets down/ the eternal
burden of despair
So that we/ may rest.

In the dark
if only for a moment
My blue demons appear
My enchantment fades
ridden away
on blue wisps of grief
across the fields of my scorn.

(to the audience of the living opera)

Family is everything?
I doubt it
I snarl to myself.
All they ever say?

We only see one another
at the weddings or the funerals
You are like everyone else
You get angry
Like my friend/ at work
He married the Inglese
She is so sweet
but his Mamma
treats her like a Strega—
the Witch!
Old Nonna cannot be invited
to grandson's wedding
a generation/
after the fact.
She is so nervous
Time passes/
the intermediaries sought
Yet still my friend/
his Strega and the Children
are dead to her
Jesus Christ
(Help us all!)

O Santuzza
I push back
blue demons
Gently in this soft night
My enchantment returns
With tenderness
I do see/
you so love
your sposo/
will miss him forever.
I understand
io comprendi
Garibaldi and Pasqua
They are my
—how do you say it?—
My role models
My heroes of the love.
I hope Maria and I
can be that way
when we are old.

Santuzza:
That is why/
you go so well together.
You are ...
a good match.

Vagabondo:
Such a waste it is
to stay mad/
to never be able
to forgive and forget
O I am growing weary
from the weight
Life is too short!
O Garibaldi
Help me push back
these blue demons.
In an urgency of youth
and the useless ways of spirits,
Before they flutter off,
I am back in my mind
sitting at downstairs kitchen table/
It is late.
I am angry.
Even in Garibaldi's Court
There is a problem
with the family
O patriarch!
Solve it now
Lay down the law
with your people.
Just say something!
I say like a hothead
Smacking the table
for emphasis.
You should not be so nervous/
He says so tenderly
covering my hands.
When we were back home/
before we came here
We used to say:
"If you move the compost/
It will stink."

He looks straight through me
Through my eyes/
into my Soul
so, he knows/
I get it.
One of the few times
I see him pound table
with palm of hand/
to drive off my blue demons
Perhaps he is saying
That I Am the one
who stinks?

[*The light changes and it is time to go home. The children
are full and content to be led like sheep. The scene closes
beautifully with the intimate repartee between* Maria *and*
Vagabondo. *This punctuates the notion that problems do
not need to be held and kept but rather peeled and discarded.
It is a small loop of completion and ties the three scenes
together.*]

Maria:
Santuzza e Garibaldi
they are stirring now.
I am so tired
I sigh the way
my Mother sighs.
We gather the espresso spoons
stack cup upon saucer
to signal the end
of this nativity of friendship
Our field-mass al fresco
and we all know
without staring at watches
that it is time to go home.
Something has grown
between us
the way the Zucchini
suddenly look grande
in the moonlight
Do you not see the lesson?
There is a time to talk
and a time to stop talking

It is different/
than your distracted silence
of repetitive work
in the sun
Let us stand and stretch
Gather up our Children wordlessly
A chorus of kisses
a bevy of hugs ushers/
our sweet walk
to the car.

Vagabondo:
Ciao Santuzza!
Ciao Garibaldi
We will see you domani/
We will take you/
to the aeroporto!
Arrivadello!
Arrivaderlla
Santuzza do you know/
this is how I am taught
to say goodbye
at the night school?

Santuzza:
Then they have taught you
to be the buffone!
You are/
so funny.

Vagabondo:
Garibaldi!
Make sure/
that you pack your cane.
There is no rush!
Let the vacation/
come to you
Don't run after it/
and everything
will be fine.

Garibaldi:
Eh! I know, I know

Vagabondo:
We glide North
on the Highway 400
Our children
sprawled in the back, dreamy
Led like sheep to bed
the way children do
when they are tired
and know that their parents
are contenti.

Maria?
Translate your Papa's saying
This amazing thing:
If you move the compost/
it will stink

Maria:
"Se sposti /
il compost puzza"

Vagabondo:
I see it now
Tonight was like
scraping the skin
off peppers!
It flakes right off
burnt to nothing/
and then you throw it
all into/ the compost.

Maria:
Yes my love/
but keep your feet/
out of the mess.
Now kiss me!

ACT II

ACT II: Scene 1

*Aria. Il Vagabondo and Maria take the
children to the Hometown*

*(Il Vagabondo and his family settle in, in the Old World. The
Court of Garibaldi supersedes time and space. Loved by
relatives they behold the importance of the past within the
past. An enchanted passegiata leads them through memories
of ancient tales, once told. Il Vagabondo claims Castropignano
for his own. As the light changes, they make their way to
Domenico's for dinner. A loyalty of love courses through their
awakened heart.)*

Additional Players:

Il Vagabondo and Maria
Their Children
Emmanuelle—a driver
Biagio and Nina (uncle and aunt)
Domenico (an uncle)
Nicola (a cousin)
Assunta (Cousin Johnny's sister)

[*There is a shift in time. The scene opens with* Vagabondo
and Garibaldi *sitting together in the downstairs kitchen.
This is his area in the Landlady's House. It is a "veglia"—a
sitting at the table to reminisce.* Vagabondo *has returned
from taking his family to Garibaldi's Hometown. He realizes
the treasure he has gained from taking the grandchildren to
see their roots. This occurs three years after* Pasqua *died and*
Vagabondo *speculates that the act of his going, freed up the
old man to eventually go and return to his ancient roots for
himself.* Vagabondo *complains about constantly walking
"up" in a hill town and announces with a flourish, that he
has lost twenty pounds.*]

Vagabondo:
You know/
you will not believe me
but I think you left/
for Castropignano/
because of me.

Garibaldi:
Eh! Maybe
You cannot be certain.

Vagabondo:
Maria and I
would be poor
if we had not taken
the nipoti
to see where you lived.
It is a treasure
they have now.
I cannot believe it
You will not believe me
In your Hometown?
I always seemed
to be walking ... Up!
Even when you walk down?
you are walking up!
Look at my belly!
Even though/
you will think/
that I am lying
You will not/
be able to tell
It will not show, Yes!
But I lost the twenty pounds!

Santuzza:
Well
If you are hungry/
You must eat!

Vagabondo:
Signora?
I am hungry/
Now.

Garibaldi:
There is/
no food.

[*The action shifts to landing in Rome. The family is retrieved by Emmanuelle, a family friend, who drives them to Castropignano, removes their red, Canadian luggage (bag upon bag) from the trunk of his car, has a word with Maria's Uncle (Zio) Biagio and then leaves.*]

Vagabondo:
Canto: "The Americanos have Arrived!"
(He addresses the audience of the living opera)
The lines of North York
They shrink so quickly
They grow
smaller and smaller
fading
until the sudden burst
of white cloud
turns our gaze
to Rome.
We are retrieved
by Emmanuelle
Such a handsome driver
arranged thru
Cousin Bar-bar-a
O! the enchanted sound
of the names
of the Italian women!
Bar-bar-a
Bharrr-bharrr-ahhhhh
Bar-bar-ah
I am so Happy!
Like efficient sheep
We are taken east
three hours.
From the base
of the valley
Look up!
See proud ruins
of the Castello
Set like a jewel
in a clean blue sky!
Up and up again

around hairpin turns
Voila!
it is the magic
My first Piazza!
Steps cascade to meet
The house of Biagio e Nina.
Canadian flag-red luggage
stands politely
like the peppers
waiting to be shed!
Before I can say a word
Emmanuelle is gone
Bar-bara has made
the excellent arrangements
We are left with
vague feelings of importance
The Americanos/ from Toronto/ have arrived!
These are/ the Big Leagues
The Hometown
La famiglia Garibaldi
Maria was born here
The scared soil
The burning bush
Take off your sandals
The Americanos/ from Toronto/ have arrived!

[Biagio *takes them next door to the "apartmento" where they will stay.* Maria *surveys the space with fascination, like she is trying on a set of clothes for the first time.* Maria *sings an* **arietta**.]

Maria:
My beautiful town
so emptied by the sun
I feel on the back of my neck.
My uncle shows us
our refurbished casa
and gives me the key
Like I somehow, never left
It opens to brown tile
and lemon Mediterranean colour
An outcrop of rock
pushes through the wall!
Kitchen, gas stove, dining table, some chairs.
Our own bathroom, two bedrooms

And a door opens to the roof.
It feels so smartly dress casual
I try it on for the first time
So new and stiff and clean
I know already, it will be my favourite
The piazza seems to fit
I cannot wait
to try on the Castello!
Gingerly, we close the door
Lock our lock
Climb steep stone stairs
Part beaded curtain and
adjust our eyes
to the dark of the kitchen
It is time to meet
my family.
We go to dinner
At Garibaldi's father's
house in town.

[*They go next door to la casa di Biagio e Nina, Maria's uncle
and aunt and their family and grandchildren. Over dinner,
Il Vagabondo is enchanted but begins to realize how
impoverished his Italian really is.*]

Vagabondo:
We sit at the table
of Biagio the Great
His family all bustling
In the happy motion
of their routines.
Quietly I say all names
ph-o-ne-tic-ca-lly
to ensure I will remember/
Everyone forever.
O my lovely names!
There is Sal-va-tor-e/ e Mar-i-ca
Their No-e-mi/ Ga-bri-ele/ e E-ster
Sweet En-rica/ e En-zo
Bambini Val-en-ti-na/ e Kris-ti-na
Bar-ba-ra and handsome Gra-zi-ano
a lawyer from the Roma.
Giovanina, lovely matriarch
of the stove.
O when your Italian

Is impoverished
Get the names right
and the rest
will come later!
For now we rely
so bold and independent
on my Berlitz "Self-Teacher"
Dio "if you can speak English
you can speak Italian"
Do you not see?
All other times
I will stick like glue
to my wife,
who reverts so easily
back to her mother-tongue
O I feel so fluent
speaking the dialect of love
Lina is Pasqualina
Lucy is Lu-chee-ah
My Mary is My Mah-ree-ah
Hold your arms out
so wide and in love
It is—how should I say it?—
Ro-man-ti-ca!

Giovanina (Nina):
He does not/
speak Italian then?

Maria:
No.
But he is—Trying!

[*Vagabondo's recitative*: **"Io sono la scuola serale italiana, come si dice, drop-out."** *(The Italian night-school Drop-out)*]

Vagabondo:
I am the
Italian night school
Drop out.
You see
early in our marriage
I signed up for
the lessons—the lezioni
Every Wednesday night.

On the second night
I am asked
to describe
my Italian meal
in Heaven.
That is easy, I say.
La tasse, carne,
polo, pane/
Insalata!
Vino/ e/ espresso
Cosa è la tasse?
asks the Instructor
With a grin
that looks like
the shit.
O my Geezis
You would not like it.
Boil the water
for the pasta
Before it is ready
spoon some out
into the bowl
Add One-two penne rigate
bathed in steam
Add the homemade vino
Bring the bowl
Up to breathe
Presto.
And if you have a cold
Tomorrow
it is gone!
I never heard of it
The instructor laughs.
An entire class
giggles at me crudely
They stand, point the fingers
Place hands over the mouth
He is an idiot
I hear someone ... whisper.
The next thing I know
I am fighting
with my fists.
There is no point
in being here.

How can you
.teach me anything?
When you do not know
What la tasse is.
O my Geezis
it must be
the Education
and not
the Instruction!
So I dropped out
in triumph!
But! Listen to me.
I tell you this!
I went to another school
Maria did not make me
And now
I am so happy to tell you
I have the certificate, picolito
Italian conversazione uno
Tourist class!
Bravo!
It is a gift.

[*Dinner concludes and the children go outside with their cousins to play with lizards and scorpions.*]

Maria:
By now/
our first feast
is ending.
Our children decline thirds/
And go willingly out
into the tiny courtyard
to catch lizards!
Later, there are screeches
We all step out/
to see the scorpion!
So blackish red/
sharp and oily
My Vagabondo
wants to crush it.
We are surprised
by how small it is
and rather than crush it

The children move it around/
with sticks and screaming.

[*The party shifts to the piazza and the men play skopa with*
Cousin Nicola *and* Uncle Dominic, *Garibaldi's first cousin
and brother. It is ferragosto, the feast of the Assumption and
Vagabondo's son is "pressed into service" to play soccer. He
departs.* Vagabondo *is introduced to "benzina", the gas,
birra ... the beer.*]

Vagabondo:
Later in the week
I will behold a three-act play
starring a large slug,
a toothpick crucifix
and some tomato sauce
Take note!
There is a lack of
shiny bicycles
The pogo sticks
skateboards
and tiny plastic cars/
to sit in.
I see no Star Wars spaceships
or Jurassic Park raptors
Only Ferragosto/
The holiday time/
when all leave the city/
to come to town to relax.
Soon our son/ is swept away
to the soccer tournament
He will be given the medal
Triangolare Di Calcio/ Castropignano
Nonno will be/ so proud.
While I am with the men
in the piazza
in the cool shade
playing the skopa
and sipping the benzina
the birra—the how do I say it?—
the gas!
Like a cat swiping the mouse
la bella seta
the beautiful seven

is thrown down/ with a flourish
Cousin Nicola
has taken the trick!
The game is over/
I sit back in my chair
Sip the benzina
Watch men smoking
laughing in clusters
while children scoot away
up stone steps/
to parts unknown/ games unseen
It is all al fresco
The sun stomped away
in a huff!
Now shadow softly mixes
the sweet air and
The enchantment sets in ...

[*Segue to Garibaldi reminiscing about his childhood. (imaginary lighting top corner, stage left, elevated)*]

Garibaldi:
At that time
there was no money
for the toys
(you fold the stocking
and roll it like this,
wind it tight,
make it round)
We used to make
our own fun.
We used to
go into town
and just go around.
Here!
That was our
soccer ball!

[Zia Nina *arrives to take* Maria *and* Il Vagabondo *('The Americanos') on a magical tour of the Hometown. Acute observations about the museum and the Castello are made. On the way they happen upon a villager who recognizes* Maria *and who made the wedding cake for her parents.* Vagabondo *is enchanted by his witness of the roots of his*

*wife and her family, before his very eyes. He breaks out
into a song of reverie* **("Io sono un uomo ricco"** [I am a
rich man]). *From the Castello, he observes the fields being
burned of stubble on a hillside across the way. He beholds
the moment!*]

Maria and **Vagabondo:** *(recitative, duet)*
We walk now
with Nina.
Up narrow lanes
past the postale building,
and a store/
where you can buy the meat.
Wooden doors
Have round holes
in the bottom
to let in/ the cats.
Houses newly renovated
Not yet lived in/
Derelict abandoned houses
of bones, socketless windows/
rubble and beams
crashed to the floor/
like the ghosts
of ancient neighbours.
Through those beads/
a variety store
our Nina retrieves the key.
While old Madonna
sneaks a peak
at the Americanos!
In a moment
we are in a museum/
two/ three rooms
packed with artifact and memory
It is not unlike/
having dreams filled in
as if, a work-in-progress.
Over here is canvas
over there thin pencils sketches
suggest possibility
Our subject takes shape/
in glorious Technicolor.
We see a wall of porcelain plates/

wooden bowls and spoons
the wooden pitchforks
an old wine press.
Shocking cans of
poison mosquito spray,
a wall of keys!
A huge stone/
pulled by the horses
to flatten Garibaldi's grain.
We have it all/
to ourselves and
Nina takes the time
to explain.

Vagabondo:
We leave now/
and return the key
to Old Madonna next door.
"Grazie signora,"
I say feeling brave.
"Io sono Canadese/
Mia moglie e/
Italiana da Castro-pignano/
figlia di Angelo Molinaro!"
Si she nods
with the worried look
that strangers give.
It is the same look/
Pasqua gave to me
when I started
to come around.

Maria and **Vagabondo:**
We walk up again/
squeeze through laneways
crest a hill so narrow/
Steps within our dream
There is no sense/
of time or space here.
The town could hold
11 spirits or 11,000
but you would never
know it!
We happen upon

a woman in her fifties.
Recognizes Nina
In happy singsong greeting/
speaking urgently, together.
There are kisses/
first for you and then for me.

Vagabondo:
You are held/
arms stroked with affection
By an old woman/
making sure her dream
is real.
So long ago/
This angel's mother
prepared the wedding cake
for the feast/
when Garibaldi and Pasqua/
promised themselves
to one another.
My Maria/ rubs her eyes
Our Nina/ looks delighted
And I
feel strangely tall/
with a loyalty so elemental
so primitive and instinctual.
I awaken to my Inglese heritage
Feel I would do anything
to make this woman's
life happier!
anything, anyhow, anytime—
like she is family.
Suddenly/
I am embarrassed
by my passion
within ...

Vagabondo:
Canto: "Io sono un uomo ricco"
Stone upon stone/
cut from stone
Pristine/ clean
splashes of colour/
from textile to flower/

perched on ledges
over valley below
Maria/ I tell you this!
We will come back here
to live!
I seal my oath/ with a kiss.
In your enchantment/
you take my kiss
and ignore me completely!
Walk arm-in-arm/
deep in conversation
with your aunt.
I behold this nativity/
this rebirth
and I see the lesson
completely.
I, Il Vagabondo
am witness to your roots/
to the heritage of
our half-Italian children.
This birthplace
of Garibaldi's stories
The treasury of lezioni/
the motherlode.
Everything is in the day
and the day is in everything!
The Alpha and the Omega of it!
I see the libretto/
I am the rich man.
Io sono un uomo ricco!

Vagabondo: *(to the audience of the living opera)*
We are on our way
to the Castello now.
We must walk faster
to catch up!
Dog bark startles/
chickens milling about.
They poke their stupid heads
right up to the street.
There are buckets and shovels/
hay and seed strewn about
the House-scapes and terrain
of Castropignano

The funny thing is?
is that it all makes sense.

Nina:
The Castello
has a respectful/
weathered look.
This sign/
warns us in Italian
to stay out!
There is no room
to walk around/
because the outside/
is the edge/
of our mountain.

Vagabondo: *(in reverie, enchanted)*
The tower is somehow
smaller up close.
Its fine lines/
have tumbled into slackness
in some places.
It has a history
I will never really know.
Like the old guys/
who play cards
at the club.
There are stories there/
and lessons to find
If you want to look for them.

Once a little girl/
was playing up here
I tell Nina.
She tumbled over the edge/
and went down the side.
The women were crying/
the bells were ringing.
Some men went/
to get the rope!
Scaled down the side/
to find her.
At that time/
there were no cars

like there are today.
Some people/ went down the road
right to the bottom
of the hill.
It took a long time.
When they found
the little girl/
She was playing
and picking the flowers!

Nina:
You know this?

Vagabondo:
Si!

Maria:
He talks a lot/
with Daddy.

Vagabondo: *(to the audience of the living opera)*
Maria pats my cheek and sighs
Together they walk gracefully
over to the castle/
arm in arm,
completely present
in feminine/
conversation.
I sit solitary on bench
overlooking the valley/
The light is changing.
I am riveted!
I sit up
Look!
Far across the valley/
hills rise up.
Bold angles suggest vertigo.
The fields are patches/
Hedgerows border squares
Stone fences sculpt space.
I see only
texture and contour
colour and form/
moving shadows/

shimmering atmosphere.
Frothy orange flames
peel the mountainside
Smoke curls black/
in that tiny corner of sky.
Farmers burn off the stubble
berm soil ridges herd flames/
now this way, now that
I see/
the black patterned wake/
thick, white smoke boiling.
From the bench/
beside the Castle
in the midst of family
I am permitted/
to see/ The Divine Sistemi
The Grand Garden unfolding/
before my eyes.

Vagabondo, Maria, Nina: *(together)*
This landscape lives!
Glimpse the lesson/
Watch!
It moves faster than flames/
flickers out
before you fully understand it.
But you can understand it
In Garibaldi's Court.
It is as if to see/
the Soul of something
but you cannot tell/
for no one/
will believe you.
This eternal tableaux/
of the way life was
and the way
life is going to be.
Revealed/
in one animate landscape.
Be quick!
The lesson is a shooting star!
You might miss it.
Perhaps you will see it/

out of the corner
of your eye
Or perhaps/
you will be crestfallen
to miss it completely.
One day? Perhaps?
You will see it/
head on.

[*Nina's enchanted passegiata takes them to Camillo Caperchione's ... a home of an ancient relative. They pass through
beaded doors which stick to them like tentacles. The iconic
meeting of the great elder.* Camillo *leans in close to recognize*
Maria. Vagabondo *is accepted and offered his wine.*]

Maria:
Camillo Caperchione's
is around the corner
from the war monument.
If you get lost/
all you have to do?
Climb to the Castello/
Look around
and find your bearings!
To get to the ancient house/
You must pass
the open door
where younger girls
sell the handwork
of their mothers.
Past the Morte posters
announcing, boldly,
blackly/
Who has died and when.
The street hairpins/
to overlook the prison.
Dio, there are no prisoners
there now
unless you count the children/
who once left their school building
rendered unsafe/
by the earthquake.

Vagabondo:
Nina, did you know
In your Hometown
The school was/
the prison?
La scuola
was on the second floor
They kept the prisoners over there
When I was young/
you could only go
to the Grade 5.
If you had the money/
you could send your kids/
to Campobasso.
But the rest of us/
had to go to the work.

Maria:
He is smarter/
than he looks!

Nina:
Ah, si!

Vagabondo:
We climb steep steps/
to Camillo's home.
Father to my friend/
The Johnny from Woodibridgi.
Maria! Translate per favore
Johnny played saxophone/
so did his Dad.
Back then/
there was a little Orchestra/
Garibaldi tried to organize it.
One musician in the town
knew how to teach.
Angelo got the young people together/
He never played himself
Johnny kept playing
and now, Nina/
you should hear him play!
Come prima!
For me!

Only for me!
Can you believe?
They call him the Johnny Sax/
back home.

You take your chances
climbing cement steps/
in Castropignano.
No rails and angles
calibrated for pitons/
and mountain axe.
Four or five cats
inevitably/
Sun themselves on landings.
Split off into laneways?
which lead to other houses.
Vaguely, my knees are reminded/
of Navajo cliff dwellings.
Drop offs abound!
You take your chances
climbing cement steps/
in Castropignano!
Suddenly?
Of course!
Inglese Baby fences and socket guards
make no sense/
to my nonnas and nonnos
in Garibaldi's Court!
You take your chances
climbing cement steps/
in Castropignano!

Garibaldi: *(elevated, light, stage left, a voice, sonorous)*
No!
You don't see
the safety devices/
in my country.

Maria:
We pass through
the beaded tentacles
of all doorways/
into darkened rooms
while My Nina calls out

Hello! We are here!
Sticky tentacles/
cling to neck and arm
then fall free
to keep the air in
and the flies out.
We meet Assunta/
who cocks her head
in avian inspection
Listens intently/
Suddenly explodes in understanding!
"Ah Si, Si Si"
The Yes, Yes Yes.
This is her cousin/
and Americano Husband
in tow.
Camillo sits to my right/
So old/ so very old.
His mind/ leaves gracefully
for an interior world
where involuntary movements/
of arm and leg/
his beautiful sway of head
no longer matter.
To me/ he is simply beautiful
My eyes well up!

Vagabondo:
There are kisses
there are touches/
Intense ... Listening ... gazes
We are met by Filomena/
another of Johnny's sisters.
Camillo looks so happy
but I can tell/
he is not quite sure
who Maria is.
Assunta explains
So close to his face/
A flare of the recognition!
Suddenly/ I am asked
if I would like a glass of the wine/
and I accept.

Assunta:
He is not/ Italian then?

Vagabondo: *(to the audience)*
I am used
to the question.

Maria:
Non. Non parlo Italiano
He is/ my wonderful Cake

Vagabondo: *(mockingly)*
"Ah, Si Si!"
And at this point
get ready for it!
The natural love
in the room/
the joy of it
and the laughter
Be prepared/
(I warn you)
You will be completely, Ignored!

[Vagabondo *addresses the audience and sings to them about
the dissonances of culture and his pleasure in exact moments.*
(arietta)]

Vagabondo:
I tell you this!
Lesser men/
will grow bored/ fidget/
complain grumpily
to their wives.
If you want?
you can be happy
"You will not die from this"
C'mon
You still have your sight
You still have your sound
Your heart
Your thoughts
Your power of the observation.
Your smile
Your laugh,

You possess your love.
You are Il Vagabondo!
The Tramp
Thrown into an ancient story/
with all your wits!
The Mosto in the Mundane
A bit player/ stage left
of the Living Opera!
A Canadese shot down/
befriended by an entire hill town/
Hidden from the Germans/
You are just past the light
in the Caravaggio
Curled in the dark/
so slightly out of view
with the pure freedom/
of Alberich's invisibility!
The heightened sense of wonder/
that dreams create!
It is an Enchantment/
induced beyond
and without the thickness/
of homemade wine.
Happily I toast Old Camillo/
and then? The entire room!
Tell them all/
that Johnny is my amico!
and I am honoured
to be here.
Like a fool/
Like an Inglese out of water.
My Maria, half-heartedly translates:
(She is so present
in this room)
You must remember/
and will be told
that the privilege
of invisibility, is a toll/
on the double duty
of your translator!

[*The recitative is interrupted by a phone call. It is* Johnny
*calling from Woodbridge, back home. The son of the patriarch
and cousin to* Garibaldi *(who plays a tenor saxophone*

almost as big as himself). In a flurry of bottled-up English,
Vagabondo *speaks to him urgently of his joy ... finally able
to speak like water flowing.*]

Vagabondo:
The telephone, it rings.
Assunta retrieves it ...
Animated conversation/
the disbelief!
Johnny is on the phone/
calling from The Wood-a-bridgi!
He does not even know/
That Maria and I
are here!
Everyone speaks to him/
Excitement raises its notch
Maria speaks to him in Italian
Then he asks/
to speak to Me!
My English pours out/
like water from
the fifty gallon drum!
Johnny!/ We are Here!/
In Your Father's House!
It is so beautiful!/
Yes, he is fine./
He looks good.
Johnny, I am drinking/
your father's wine
in the house/ you grew up in!
it could not be better/
Are you playing
a wedding tonight?

[*The light begins to change; the shadows in the room grow
longer (across the whole imaginary stage). The cedars begin
their silhouettes.* Nina *and the Americanos leave and on the
way, pass* Valentina, *a granddaughter with* Vagabondo *and*
Maria's *children in tow. We are walking to Zio Domenico's
for dinner and Nina calls out to them to meet us there in the
early evening. Il Vagabondo is content ("io sono contenti") The
disorientation has passed; he begins to recognize landmarks.
He can now claim Castropignano for his own.*]

Maria:
I can see/
by the shadows
in the room/
The sun/ is now/ on the move.
There are kisses and touch/
as one by one/
we part/ the beaded curtain/
step over the cats
to sidestep our way down cliffs.
Everyone is out
on the landing
to say goodbye.
Perhaps forever.
The cedars stand out first/
then warm yellow fields
vivid green of woods beyond
stretching in the shade.
We leave
go up and around
Children selling lace/
have all gone home.
At the large piazza/
People collect, mill about
A Barbecue is smoking.
We climb up
to main street/
past old School Prison
the shop to buy meat
past the small piazza
where we all play cards.
A restaurant yawns open/
Gelato and benzina
invite the happiness
of dusk.
O Our Children pass
O is this not love?
Headed the other way/
In a gaggle of fun ...
Of cousins and laughter.
They stand out
Like Americanos/
but look to be content.

Nina:
Kristina/ Valen-tina
We are going
to Zio Domenico's
Bring them/
We will meet you there!

Vagabondo:
I am not sure/
which angle we ascend.
I think it is in
the direction of
the church.
A stairway takes us
down to a road
We amble along
get over close/
when the cars pass by.
A break in the stone
reveals the road ascending/
to the house of Domenico.
In the corner of my eye
I recognize the prison/
Cross checked
with a sighting of the Castello.
Eureka! All disorientation has passed!
I know how
to get to the home.
Suddenly?
It feels like home!
I am home.
We have broken in/
our new set of the clothes.
They are no longer stiff!
We are none the worse for wear
I find myself/
flopping on the bed
Leave my toothbrush on the sink
My laundry on the floor/
Castropignano
has claimed me
for its own!

ACT II: Scene 2

Serenade. An evening at Domenico's
(The Inglese gets to know the Old Guy's brother. A series of
dinners begins. Enchanted memories are invoked. A farewell
under stars. Il Vagabondo is that much more in love.)

Additional Players:

Biagio and Nina
Domenico and Maria
Their Children and Grandchildren (many)
Maria and Vagabondo
Their Children

[*The action takes place at Domenico's, Garibaldi's brother*
(who stayed in Italy and chose not to emigrate.) A dinner is
being prepared at Garibaldi's ancestral home. There is lots of
bustling around the BBQ and the table, adults going in and
out of 'beaded tentacle' doorways. Il Vagaondo sees his
children look tired; they all are and he and his daughter play
a hand clapping game called "Hi Lo Chick-a-Lo". Soon all
the children are doing it.]

Vagabondo: *(recitative)*
Everyone/
is now at Domenico's
Biagio e Enzo intent
around the barbecue
Gabriele is crying/
Tired Noemi squabbles
Enrica looks intense
Marica serene
Zia Maria e Nina/
move to and fro
to ready our table.
Salvatore rigs a karaoke/
Older children/ sing lyrics
A thin-looking dog/
a couple of new cats
Join the throng
Our children look tired/
a little disconnected.
I hug Adriana/
whisper a game:
O-pen and closed hand/
O-pen and closed hand/
Hi-Lo-Chikolo/
clap, clap, clap.
O-pen and closed hand/
O-pen and closed hand
O-pen and closed hand/
clap, clap, clap.
Gabriele stops crying/
Noemi is no longer shy
Soon/ they are all having a go
with the Americano!
This happy trance/
of play.
Maria gravitates to kitchen/
I go stand with the men
To bask in our manliness
I am told/
Domenico has killed
one of his chickens/
It smells too good!
Domenico is younger/
then our Garibaldi

His white hair/
makes him older
We met once before/
20 years ago/
Came from Italy
to Welland, then Toronto
making the rounds/
of family and love.

[Il Vagabondo *naturally gravitates to* Domenico. *He wants to know Garibaldi's brother. Domenico speaks no English, looks with amusement and the libretto is awkward at first.*]

Vagabondo:
When he talks
in the Italian
He speaks even less/
than his brother.
Gestures with hands
A "Choo sound"
changing thoughts.
Crinkled face/
around the eyes
the slow-moving look
of a man ...
Who works hard
speaks little
sees all
knows much
Eyes that twinkle/
When he is amused
He observes me/
and already forms
the opinion!

Pidgin English/ blended nouns/
Italian gestures of hand
You look/
like your brother/
I work hard/
at how/ to engage/ him.
La terra e molto bene/
La casa e Bellissima/
tumbles out like/

the stutter steps.
And my spirit, it translates/
through my eyes/
Do you not see it?
Your house/ your land
so beautiful/ I am so honoured
to be here.
It is all/
wonderful!
Did you know?
Your Brother I love?
And did you know?
I will get to know you/
whether you like me
or not.
Your wife, Maria/
has eyes that laugh
like our Pasqua's!

There is a pause/
all emotion suppressed/
Forced into mock drama
Do-men-i-co, I ask/
Do-you-play/ the-scopa?
Do-men-i-co, I mime
Do-you-make/ the-wine?

He says something/
I don't understand
Gestures to follow/
past apple trees and wall
Over thin cat wincing/
Old Moosh-Moosh
scoots indignant.
I am made to see/
my sight so fluid
my spirit walks through
oily contours/ earthen smells
of living art.
Breathing reddish sun
lifting off fields leading/
to the cool pulse
of the cemetery.
Bordered by cedars/

patiently standing vigil.
Beyond that/
the green roll
of the woods/
swells indefinitely!

[*The action shifts to Garibaldi's kitchen back home. Il Vagabondo is talking with him there.* **The Piccolo Coro** *sings an*
Observation Song *of the downstairs kitchen and the Living
Equinox of the place setting.* Garibaldi, *remembering* Pasqua
begins a beautiful **aria** *called* **"We Had Nothing (but we
were happier than we are today)"**, *about being so poor but
making a life. The libretto is peppered with a tender vignette
of Vagabondo telling Garibaldi's stories back to him, as a
sign of pure respect that is not lost on the Old Man. In the
dialect of love, it is called speaking stories together.*]

Garibaldi: *(with Vagabondo, elevated, stage left, lit)*
Back then/
if you wanted to
get someplace/
there were no cars
or even roads/
like there are, now.

Piccolo Coro (small chorus):
Garibaldi built this kitchen
with his own hands/
and with his own, son.
The drywall
the plumbing/
gas line, the wiring.
A paesano came in/
to do the ceramic
Twenty years later/
it still looks
like the grouting
was just done.
I tell him/
It is the "ceramica bella"
that makes the kitchen/
look good!
I tease him
while he takes the bait/

I shake my head
at the way guys/
do the work now.
Cutting corners/ fudging it
Once the paint dries/
and they are all gone
You see more of
what they didn't do
and what they did do/
looks like the shit!
There is very little pride now/
It is all/ about the money
I tell him.
Surprisingly?
He concedes/ the point.

Garibaldi is always/
at the end
at the head of the table/
in front of the hutch.
It holds wine glasses/
espresso cups and percolator
ground coffee e Barzula/
beside a box of paper filters.
Alcohol is behind
the sliding wooden doors:
the rye
the Sambucca
the vermouth
always full/ rarely used/
except to toast the Holidays.
Over left shoulder/
next to crucifix
He will erect/
a jerry-built shrine
to his departed wife/
who left him ...
Pictures of family/
descending in proximity
to his heart.
He will move his spot/
to sit/ always/ where she sat
where he alone/
can see her shrine.

And in that living equinox/
I realize I have moved
to face him.
A little gas stove
a steaming pot of water/
the gurgling spattering
pot of the sauce.
Garish magnets/ of hens pecking roosters
Jesu and a guardian angel
airily watching children/
cross a bridge
Over my head/
a plate we brought back
from our Honeymoon.
Inevitably the dishes
so efficiently done
by our woman/
who leave us/
to go outside and pass time.
While children watch TV
after the meal/
when the work is done.
I have already gone/
to the cantina
to fill the bottle
And it is the time/
when old men
talk to young men/
if they will listen.

Garibaldi:
We had nothing!

Vagabondo:
He continues in a tone/
that makes me
sit up and listen.
Holds my gaze now/
looks me straight
in the eye.
I can tell/
he wants me
to listen.

Garibaldi:
We had nothing/
but we were happier then
than we are today!
We would get up/
in the dark
Make a little piece of bread/
if we were lucky
Then we would
walk for miles
Go to work/ in the fields
Whatever there was to do
Pick the corn/
gather the wheat
dig the field.
We did not have the tractors/
like they do today.

Vagabondo: *(to the audience of the living opera)*
Sometimes I will tell/
his stories back to him.
It is my way
of showing respect/
of connecting with the signore
For while I may be/
the Italian Night school dropout
I show up for his stories/
and in the dialect of love
learn to speak them/
fluently.
Yes/ and do you remember?
That time Pasqua/
walked out to bring you food?
Late in the morning
when the women arrived/
It was time/ for the break.
One time your sister in law
walked past the ridges/
and fell down.
The container of pasta
jumped off her head/
and into the dirt.
They were so afraid/

You know what they did?
They gathered it up
they brushed it off
they brought it out
to the men as if/
nothing was wrong!
You all started to eat/
made faces
and spit out the dirt.

Garibaldi:
Yes, I remember

Vagabondo:
Sometimes/
when I feel like teasing him
I will completely take/ his story over.
I don't know if you did this/
I say in my Instructive tone
We did not use the water/
back then
to clean the dishes.
No. We grabbed the plates like this/
rubbed dirt around them like this
and made them clean, like this!
The women gathered them up/
went back home
and came out later/
with more food.
And that ... is the way ...
It used to be/
I tell him with a flourish!

Garibaldi:
You are right!

Vagabondo:
That was our life!
I say and shrug my shoulders
to make his point.
You will not remember this!
We used to bring/
the ears of corn
all the way back.

Dump them on in huge piles
On your father's front yard
People from other farms
would come over
Everyone would sit/
around in a circle
and husk the corn.
There was singing
There was dancing
There was good food
It was—how do I say it
in your language?—It was/
your recreazione
Do you want
some more wine?

Garibaldi:
The wine was better/
back in Italy.
It was—ahhh—I can't think
of the word now.
It was ... more natural
We did not use/
the chemicals like they use today
to keep the grapes/
from ripening.
Everything was natural.

[*The scene shifts from the reverie with* Garibaldi *back to the ancestral home in Italy.* Il Vagabondo *sing/ speaks a Garden recitative. The libretto is rife with observations of the vegetable gardens of Italy, the gardens back home and their parallels to immigration.*]

Domenico:
Choo!

Vagabondo:
My eyes/ walk in/ from the hills
and the tree line
I see now/ the giardino autentico
The authentic garden/
in a free-spirited backyard
that could run to the cemetery/

and back.
There is a new lesson here
Subtle/ slightly out of view
Garibaldi's garden/ back home/
Is a work of art.
Every square inch/
connected to its purpose
Zia Enedina's garden/
has a woman's beauty
logic
thoughtfulness
grafted/
to its system.
Zio Giovanni's garden
has a different personality
His tomatoes are from
the lost planet/
over six feet tall
he plants peppers/ around trees
in the front.
Sank his own makeshift well
into the ground/
to keep his water cool.
Yet with Domenico/
in Castropignano
I see/ that the gardens back home
While beautiful/
are little restrained replicas
Like a spirit in a box
Like a horse in a stall
Like a housecat/
devoid of Serengeti roots.
Maybe ... even like an immigrant/
Magnificent/ despite restrictions
on a little piece of land/
that cannot really sing
old songs/
No matter how hard/
you till it.
You lose things forever/
when you immigrate
But your spirit/
will still produce/
You will still/

make a life
You will come from nothing
and make a garden/
that still puts every Inglese garden
in need of that much more water.
It is different back home/
I can see it now.
Domenico's garden is wild!
There are no fences
Soil reddish brown and crusty
It crumbles like the cake/
with interior moistness.
The rows are longer/ wider
There are more of them.
The tomatoes/ you see first
Zucchini/ the eggplant/
all the usual stuff.
And then you see the vines/
elevated on tripods/
hooked up to poles/
connected to every row!
This so-called "Grade 5" Engineering design/
Will bring water
from the house
to anywhere in the garden.
Your Brother/ has got to see/ This!
I tell him/ and I think/ he gets it.
We laugh/
we are starting/
to comprendi!

[Domenico *and* Il Vagabondo *are getting to know one another.
The Elder is showing him things the way* Garibaldi *does.*]

Vagabondo:
He takes me now/
to his cantina.
Talks to me/
the way Garibaldi
talks to me.
Not with the words/
but by walking
pointing
showing

tasting
gesturing
watching
demonstrating/
passing me the things
to touch.
This expansive expression/
but you will/
miss it completely
if you do not
sing the libretto/
of Garibaldi's court.
You could grow impatient
You could excuse yourself
Look to be rescued/
from deafening silence
by your wife.
Later you could/
get angry with her
know you are wrong
but argue anyway.
It is impossible/
to get through
to old Italian guys.
You complain to your
Canadian friends later/
at the pub.
They will nod/ shake their heads
There are a thousand ways/
to avoid getting to know
the strange/ the unique
and the different.

[*There is an opera buffa scene where, during a pause in Domenico's internal tour of the cantina, Il Vagabondo regales the women about cooking for Maria during their courtship and serving her Spaghetti-in-a-can.*]

Vagabondo:
Later at night/
with Maria's help
We will stand/
with Zia's Maria and Nina
In open air kitchen/

converted from stall
Where pigs, sheep/
and Rosie the mule were kept
I will tell them/
my story of Gusto.
It can only be told/
under the stars
When you are taking the break/
from frittata la scuola
nibbling cheese/
and sipping wine al fresco
When my wife and me
were first going out/
she came to see me
for the dinner.
I would feed her/
Heinz spaghetti sauce
opened expertly
from the can.
She would refuse it/
get mad at me/
threaten me
throw my pots
all over the room!
How will we fall in love?
What am I going to do?
We will starve to the death.
Then she took me to Pasqua/
the first time
for the pasta
My first red boiling smells/
My first finocchio—the fennel
I did not know/
that olives were black.
I did not know/
they came out of the can.
Warm, shivery sips/
of la tasse
Spare ribs/ sliding off the bone/
hard pieces of the sausage
shredded veal clinging
to steamy ridges of
the penne rigate
Chewy bread to soak it

Oil and vinegar insalata/
with glorious, glorious salt
stinging the inside of my mouth
Glorious thick/ red wine
to gulp down and refill
O my geezis/
biscotti, the frutta/
the espresso for later
Maria, Nina, Dio!
How do I say it?
It was Everything—
it was The Enchantment.
And that is how/
I got so fat
I say to you, so sadly
But I am in love/
and I know what Gusto means
I say to them triumphantly!
Like Il Duce,
and get the mouth corners just right!
Bravo! Vagabondo they cry!
I bend my neck/
I shrug my shoulders/
What can I tell you?
Choo!

[*Domenico and Vagabondo are now in the 'inner sanctum'
of the cantina. He is offered a birra, the gas. The observations, rich and beautiful, segue to an ancient cantina story
of Garibaldi's about a boy stealing sausages from the bottom
of a clay urn. Domenico shows Vagabondo: "il torchio di
nonno," the great wine press of his father's father. It is akin to
a sacred object.*]

Vagabondo:
I tell you this.
The cantina/
is not necessarily
a guy-place/
but I feel comfortable here.
This one is wild/
seems to span the underside/
of half of Domenico's house.
Ledges and recesses

dark anterooms
I know Ali Baba
and his forty thieves
would be at home here.
Sausages hang/
a prosciutto, I think.
The air/
smells musty and damp.
I want to eat again
in this sacred ark-
sample two of every jar.
With Domenico/
as my guide
My tour guida
I am offered the benzene/
the birra, the gas
Always
there is a bottle opener
in the cantina.
You are a fool/
If there is not!
Systems-within-systems
trial and error
Experiences that make/
the life efficient/
simpler/ running smoothly.
Using all nouns
I can muster/
all gestures and hand signs
Just growing comfortable/
talking plain, clumsy English
I take a good run/
At the cantina story
About the boy/
who stole/ the sausages.

Garibaldi: *(an image of him, singing softly to Domenico, stage right) (an arietta)*
When we were little kids
We were hungry.
We could never/
get anything to eat.
We kept our sausages/
in the clay pot/

like an urn.
Fill it up
with grease/
from the pig.
That is how
we kept them
From growing bad.
There was one guy/
that tipped over the pot
and he made a little hole/
in the bottom.
He used to sneak in/
all of the time
take a little piece/
and stand the pot, back up.
One day, the father/
went to the cantina
to get some sausages.
He pushed down/
broke through the top/
and found the pot
was empty.
Boy did that boy/
get some trouble!

[*A friendship is forged; Domenico smiles and brings Vagabondo to the table. (There is dinner and later, more food, laughter, squawks, whines and singing. A cigarette is lit and the smoke hangs in the air, then catches a breeze and slips into the night. When it is somehow time, they hug, there are kisses, ciao's and promises to see each other tomorrow.) Maria and Vagabondo holding hands, with the children in tow, ambling like sheep, pick their way in the night back to their lodging.*]

Vagabondo: (arietta)
It is hard to know
if Domenico understands
Somehow/
It does not matter.
He carries/ a large bottle
of wine now
out of the dark cantina
We step into the light.

My eyes adjust
I trail behind him/
along the back
of his house.
He shows me
the outdoor kitchen
the gas stove
Beside that
near the end of the house/
where patio table awaits
I see a wooden door
He opens it/
We enter the stone chamber
Standing majestically/
the wine press/
of Garibaldi's grandfather.
Il torchio di nonno.
I am made to understand/
it still works.
I touch it
feel it to be
a living thing/
Diol! Magnifico!
is all I can say.
He smiles and nods
We step outside/
and walk to the table.
There is dinner
later more food/
from polenta la scuola.
Laughter, squawks, singing/
Enzo lights a cigarette
The smoke hangs in the air/
catches a breeze
slips into
the night.
When it is somehow time
We hug/
there are kisses
and ciaos
Promises to see
each other, Domani.
Maria and I
our children in tow/

pick our way
up worn steps
around the bend
to Biagio's and home.
We are home/
I am a rich man
and that much more/
in love.

ACT II: Scene 3

The Cemetery and Fig Pastoral
(The hometown passegiata concludes at the cemetery. Pasqua's spirit is returned to her parents and grandparents. Birthplace of Pasqua visited. The honey-gold sun of family gives way to the next dinner. A goodbye party at a train station in Boiano. The beginning of the lamentations of Garibaldi.)

Additional Players:

Nina (Garibaldi's sister and guide)
Nicola (Garibaldi's cousin)
Old Zia Maria (Pasqua's Sister, Maria's maternal aunt)
Her Children and Grandchildren
Old Zia Ermelinda (Pasqua's other sister)

(Stage note: The action takes place at the Village Cemetery, the Matriarchal Home (Abandoned) and Dinnermass with Pasqua's "side" of the family)

[*The evening passes and the next day is hot and bright.* Vagabondo *takes the towels out and hangs them to dry.* Zia Nina *calls out something in Italian and he panics.*]

Vagabondo:
Bravo!
The next day is here
I take out/ our laundry
Hang it on the line.
Bright white/ from stone/
makes me squint.
I look to solid blue of sky/
to clear my vision.
Somehow?
Our day is already arranged
The sheep/ will be led.
It is a wonderful feeling.
There is Nina!
On the next step!
Ciao Nina, I say
Buongiorno, I say
La bella giornata!
She sings something back/
and something else
Maria later translates/
Did I sleep well?
O my geezis!
What is it with me?
Dormi, dormi, dormi/
I repeat/
over and over and over
to bake it permanently/
in the oven/
of my mind.
It blows a fuse
each time I have to
converse with someone.
Si, grazie/
I say so cleverly
Tu sei—come si dice?
Stupido!

[*La famiglia Vagabondo leave the 'apartmento' and stroll over to meet Cousin Nicola, his wife, Maria and Old Maria, Pasqua's ancient sister. The Old Matriarch is described.*]

Vagabondo:
We leave the tiny courtyard
fiddle with the lock/
and get it right.
Up a little laneway
above the piazza/
We part new/ beaded curtains
Maria calls out
to her Zia.
The kitchen is always/
the first space/
to greet us.
There are hugs
sound and kisses.
There is Cousin Nicola!
In his sixties/
walks with a swagger
It suits his/
Clarke-Gable style moustache.
I like him immediately
We meet his wife, Maria
and then/
we are presented to
Old Zia Maria.

Maria: *(bella canto)*
O she is stooped/
and beyond beautiful.
My eyes well up/
her eyes well up
We hold one another/
grasp both arms
slightly apart/
the way women do
to look deeply/
into one another's spirit.
We stroke arms/
nod, beam and say things.
We sit together
on the couch
holding one another/
not really talking.
O my husband/

Do you not see?
We are simply/
being present.
Talk if you want/
or do not talk
Look at each other/
and smile.
Let silence/
remember and evoke
Quietly live!
Our Children understand/
this lovely sphere.
See! They don't complain/
They are content
to be led
where ever we go.
Like Papa says:
the unspoken lesson:
We are shepherds/
on the stage
of the Divine System.
They know/
that this is Mamma's time.
That Father is happy.
In less than a minute/
they sweetly sip/ the orange pop
accept strange-looking cookies/
from far-away lands.

[*Nicola takes the family on a passegiata and they drink "benzina" along the way, at the pizzeria, La Palma, the huge hotel on a hill, and near there, a hut in Nicola's remote garden, outside of the village.*]

Vagabondo: (*recitative*)
Slowly/
when it is time—
there is no rush
We learn that Nicola
will show us around
Take us willingly/
on the passegiata.
The expedition/

takes us up
around the piazza
past the monument
to a new part of town.
A pizzeria/
our first glorious
pizza margherita!
Children repeat, ripete:
The green is the basil
The white is the cheese
The red is the sauce!
Bravo! Now you know!
O Italian flag
of my stomach/
you are the best pizza
I will ever eat!
We stand at the bar/
Sip the Blue Ribbon
Nicola! You must let me pay!
He smiles/ brushes off
poorly spoken nouns/
sign language and gesture/
accepting only/
our newly minted friendship.
It is time to go/
we are outside
on the move
Winding our way/
slowly up!
To La Palma.
Pretender to the throne/
modern resort/ dance hall
all in glorious one.
It stands pinkly/
on the edge of town
so moderno.
Beckons us all
up from the monument
up from the piazza
up from the soccer pitch
and other, old fashioned places
that need/
no preservative. *(to the audience of the living opera)*

Arietta: ("It is like that, here")
It is like that here
All in one place/
flames burn up
the side of the hills.
On one side of town/
Ancient castle crumbles
a prison/ the cemetery/ a school
Farmed land
a modern house
beside a yard
full of chickens/
poking their stupid heads
under the fence.
A bar with roll-up awning/
astride cobbled stones
perched up on the hill
within walking distance/
from everywhere!
La Palma the pink giant
And in the evening/
when you are ready
pizza margherita/
to stay or to go

It is like that here
Everything blends together
You make do/
with what you have.
No wonder/
first and second wave
adapted to the tales
of Toronto.
Come to think of it?
No wonder/
an English guy
can make the life
in Garibaldi's Court.
You will not believe me/
but I tell you this.
Everything blends together
You make do/
with what you have.

Be exactly who you are/
It is like that here.

Maria:
Nicola takes us/
to his piece of land
Forever walking up/
to his garden and his hut.
The soil has that same/
wild crumbly look
with its moisture
kept secret on the inside.
His Maria already there/
with the bread
and the cheese
a thin dog
and a little shed
planted between
fruit trees and vines
rows of tomato and zucchini
fagioli and cabbage.
Little lizards scurry about
Vagabondo has benzina.
The land/ the couple/ the Americanos
the dog/ the sky/ the air ...
Everything/ is content.

[*They go now, as a processional to the Cemetery. It is on the far side of the village. The names on the tombstones read like the wedding list at our marriage reception.*]

Maria:
The road/
leading to the cemetery
is over by Domenico's house
It ends/ straight as a plank
a half-mile past/ the prison.
Nicola leads us/
up stony side-path
to black, wrought iron gate.
Pushes the latch/
and walks in
with the deliberate steps
of a man/

who has been here, before.
He takes us directly/
to my mother's grandparents.

Vagabondo:
We gaze at names/
on ground and on walls
They read like the names/
from our wedding invitation list:
Sergneses, and Tullos and Meffes
Mascitelli and Molinaros
Our Iocca and Venditti
And my mind
is swept back/
to our moment of love.
The dark cognac/
is for the men
The light cognac/
is for the women
Swan bonbonniere/
flocked at the end
Hard white candy/
symbolizing fertility
and broken teeth
carefully collected
in netting.
I see a procession/
of small, beautiful spirits
making their way towards us.
The men in their dark suits/
The women in new dresses
of green and blue
lilac and pink.
The glint of gold jewellery
so warm in the light.
From the sideline/
I see each of them
steal a glance
at Garibaldi and Pasqua/
to see if he is happy.
Word is out!
His daughter wed the Inglese/
a non Italiano, and non Catolica, to boot!
They see The Father is happy

And when they see
he is happy
My face is pulled down/
to gaze again and again
deeply into beautiful faces
wrinkled and smiling
so eager to kiss me
on each of both cheeks.
Grazie Signore e Signora/
My Prego is breathless.
Later at the bar
with my brother
amidst music/
the merriment and dancing?
He comments/
on the same enchantment
He is loved too!
Like I say ...
It is the way/
things are with them.

[*Maria tapes her mother's picture on the gravesite of her parents. Pasqua had come to Castropignano to rest with her parents on sacred ground. Il Vagabondo in the recitative is reminded of the mausoleum where Pasqua rests back home. Nicola waits patiently.*]

Maria:
A gentle breeze
brings me back to
the gravesite.
Vagabondo holds me
I push things/
around in my purse.
Carefully I find/
my roll of tape
my palm frond
and a picture/
of my mother.
It adorns the granite
of Pasqua's apartment
in the Holy Supper mausoleum
back home.
We secure our gifts gently

Say the Italian prayer/
stand back
and sigh.
Our pilgrimage is complete
Pasqua has come back/
to Castropignano
to her parents
I return her/
to Holy ground.

Vagabondo:
Nicola waits patiently.
When he thinks
that we are ready/
He walks us
to Maria's paternal nonni
We move down
cobbled pathway
suddenly shocked to see
a picture we recognize.
Rita died too young
She is daughter/
to my friends
Johnny e Marianina.
Her smile is so lovely
Somebody has taped
her spirit
to her nonna's grave.
We pray for her/
for her parents
for her brother
for her husband
for her children.
They are Garibaldi's people
Because I am in his Court
they become my family/
My Italians
Each of them/ all of them.
I look over my shoulder
to ensure the children/
see everything.
The prima lezione.
Pleased to have them/
stand witness to it.

La famiglia is everything
Nicola nods.
At Maria's paternal nonni's
we touch the stone
uneasily take its picture
to bring to Garibaldi.
I notice the children/
now stand reflexively
in the shade.
To learn
you have to
experience the thing!
The old guy/
he always says so.

[*Nicola takes them deeper in memory into a foul-smelling crypt which holds the ancient bodies of the great-grandparents. The family surfaces and remembers to stand in the shade as Nicola locks the cemetery gate.*]

Vagabondo:
Canto: "Underground passegiata"
With half a heart
We follow Nicola
through narrow maze
walkways descending
sidestep cobwebs
fight to exhale
damp urinous smells.
Maria whispers to me
"These are the great-great nonni"
I turn to tell the children
The words echo-
call eerily above us
around and below.
It is remarkably cool
under ground
with our dead
We are glad
to pick our way
back up to life
the sun and fresh air.
It is time to go
Nicola leads us out

He lifts the latch/
The gate's sharp clang
ends the moment
as everyone exits.
We are back
along the road
that leads past
the prison.
Walking slowly/
vaguely shaking off
wisps of memory
that cling to us
and beckon us
to stay.

[*They return to Nicola's home in the village. Old Maria comes out to walk with her Maria, her niece. They go to see Nicola's vineyard, in the middle of the village, on a small piece of land. It is one single, fertile vine* (**"una vite!"**). *Vagabondo is desperate for a translation but Maria has given up and is locked in touch and conversations with her ancient aunt. "Pidgin Italian and hand signs" make up the dialogue. Il Vagabondo sings an* **arietta** *(or the libretto reflects a recitative) about the early days in Garibaldi's Court and being "invisible" to the culture.*]

Maria:
Soon we appear
along stone steps
across the little street
from Nicola's house.
Zia Maria is out
to meet us
She wears a head scarf
like a towel
draped across her hair/
Her dress is black
She carefully picks her way
across cobbles with cane.
Moist translucent shade
of Nicola's garden in town
a breeze gently flutters/
Sunlight through grape leaves.

Vagabondo:
E Magnifico!
I turn to Nicola
Bending down to enter
his beautiful space
My eyes focus/
on tightly packed
clusters of grapes
weighted sensually/
Throughout the green canopy.
These are kiki
I say out loud
I touch them tenderly
and Nicola nods.
I know a little bit
about the vines
I know a little bit
about the grapes
For I have attended
Garibaldi's Wine School/
so many times.
The kiki are tightly packed/
clusters of grapes
bunched together
no spaces.
It is a sign/
It is a good year/
for the grapes.
Remember!
tight together/ evenly sized
You buy them this way
at the Jane and the Sheppard
Back home/
in the Court of Garibaldi!
"Maria! Tell me how you say
Oasis in Italian?"
O tell me how to say it.
But Maria ignores me!
Tired of translating/
she finds Zia Maria's arm
Together they sit/
on stone bench
Holding hands/ talking quietly
touching.

I tell you this!
A lesser man/
would be offended
by such rebuttal
But Vagabondo/
has learned his lesson.

(Arietta)
In the early days
of courting and love
It is not unusual
to sit downstairs
In the kitchen
with any number of Italians/
who laugh and talk
all at once/
punctuate their joy
with bangs on the table!
It is so loud/
and so happy.
At some point/
you ask for translation
It is not unusual for them/
to look up at you,
surprised that you are even there
in the first place!
Skip a beat/
and then they go on
laughing or talking or arguing.
As if the entire conversation
bunches up arm-in-arm
walks away from you
barely looking over its shoulder.
Yes some men/ would complain
but others know
and have learned/
it is the way it is with them
and frankly/ like I say
You won't/
die from This!
Ahhh, abbi pazienza
I say to Maria
with a scowl/
I make the up and down

chopping gesture
in her direction/
with my hand:
You are not
the boss of me
for I/
can speak the Life!
Nicola!
It is like a—come si dice?—
oh-ay-sis in here!

Nicola:
Una vite!
Una vite! he repeats proudly
Index finger
Punctuates my claim
Do you not see it?
Una vite!

Vagabondo:
E incredibile
I say in reply
One extraordinary plant/
singing its bright green song
between white and grey
stone buildings.
I feel so proud/
just looking at it!
With the children/
we inspect
the strong pale undersides
of leaves/
touch clusters of grapes.
There is motion
I see it is time to go inside
for some panini and cheese
banana and melon
wine and orange pop!
It is a bella giornata/
We are beyond content?
We are so alive/
in paradiso!

[*The action shifts to the Matrimonial Birth Home. It is abandoned. They have travelled by car in caravan and Old Zia Ermelinda (Pasqua's other ancient sister) arrives with her adult children. Nicola finds a single fig on the property.* **Canto:** *Il Vagabondo sings a commentary on the beauty of Italian women's eyes. The children are shown everything about their nonna's (Pasqua's) birth home.*]

Maria:
After a time
a car pulls up
We pile inside.
We are going
to the house
I was born in.
The road curves
and curves again
The houses
herd smaller together/
Before I know it
an expanse of fields—
All bearings completely lost.
My Vagabondo tells me
The Castello is back there/
You will see it
when the road bends.
Another car arrives
I wonder who will pour out!
It is Zia Ermelinda
Mamma's other sister, rediscovered/
Angelo and Concetta
Little daughter Raffaella
I am told
they are our new hosts
for this evening.
Sweet beauty
dressed in black emerges/
shaking and squinting
Into my face/
like it is the sun.
We rub long-lost tears
Make way for hugs
embraces and touch.

Vagabondo:
Canto: "In the dialect of eyes"
Buonasera I say
Piacere. My pleasure!
Furtive talking ensues
nodding and glance
O I know/
I am being discussed
in the third person.
The children are now touched
and pinched and kissed.
They are so tall!
For the hundredth time
I hear how much
they resemble Maria!
What am I?/ The chopped liver?
At least the children/
do not have/
my silly genes
I side-step
all unenchanted thoughts.
Buonasera, Signora!
I say grinning/
like the monkey.
Pulled down now/
to cheek level
My eyes are deeply read
It happens so quickly
as if my spirit
is inspected, lifted
turned and put down.
All in a moment
and it is not
unpleasant.
Choo! I gaze back at her myself/
for the Court of Garibaldi
has that effect.
I tell you this!
When you are not talking
Words become like nothing
The dialect of love/
is everything!
There is more time
to observe

to listen
to hear
to scrutinize
to perceive
When you are pulled down
this close to a face
You cannot miss the eyes
and if you do/
you are the fool.
Her eyes are like Pasqua's
All ancient eyes are fluid
and around the corners
you see a little anxiety/
a little worry
Offset by wrinkles
in outer corners
grinning in repose
to multiply/
when pushed
by a smile.
The actual eyes/
green, brown, blue
It does not matter
All appear to be black/
perfectly round
and slightly moist.
Sometimes a dark gleam
deep within reveals/
even more dimension.
Like the sensation
of looking apprehensively
over an edge
into a deep well.
When my own eyes adjust?
I see far past
the circumference.
There are no boundaries/
other than a timeless space
reflecting enough light/
to suggest
depths of meaning.
Once I see this much/
I am too close/ must step back
Focus to find/

the Divine view.
A moist blackness/
reveals many things
Maybe I know/
and maybe I don't know
You can never
really be sure
of what we see!
But I can see
and what I do see/
Is how much they love
How much they forgive
the foibles/
of their men.
How hard life has been
How utterly tired they are
How much they know/
about the Order of life
How much they
are not telling.
Day after Day/
of endless giving
stirred around forever
like the spoon
in steaming pasta
or gyres of olive oil/
slowly upon salad.
These eyes share/
the communion of knowing
that all women keep/
with other women.
I catch myself thinking
It is like flames/ rolling
up the sides/
of my mountain.

Maria:
Now we see the house
behind a tall hedge
bramble pretending to be trees
yet wild, unbeautiful.
The grass is long
The wood so dry
It could be a face/

that we look into.
The door is intact
But the window tells us
no one has been inside/
for years.
Ermelinda points her cane
to the second floor.
That's Momma's room
My children look up/
Complete the chain of command
with open mouths.
This is where Zia Linda stayed
when Zio Giovanni
came over to Canada/
Filomena was here too!
Carefully we pick our way
along overgrown side
In the back
Old vines beg at our cuffs
imploring us
not to rush.
The land rolls deeply/
down to the left
fields swell below that
To the right
I see a stand
of what appears like bamboo
The children have gone
to touch it.

[*The scene segues to Vagabondo and Garibaldi sitting vigil at the downstairs kitchen back in Canada. Garibaldi is despondent while Vagabondo serves him dinner and tries to distract his grief. It is a prophesy of the next Act. The libretto slowly becomes playful and awakens the Man.*]

Vagabondo:
My mind flows back
to the sad time
when I work hard
to distract Garibaldi.
It is evening.
I remove a stack of veal
from downstairs fridge

pry the pieces apart
that Giulia, his neighbour/
has left him.
They lay like
salt cod in rigor mortis
I finish frying
a pair of veal
in a tiny bit of oil.
They cook so quickly.
I pat them dry
serve them plain/
with Molisano sausage
bathed in oil
so difficult to fish/
out of the jar.
I will tell you
there is a technique
to putting one-two tines
of your fork/ to shimmy a sausage
out half way.
Remove it with your fingers
then the rest/
will be easy
If you get the oil
on your shirt
there will be the trouble.
There is a half-eaten
dish of green beans
sitting bereft in the fridge
and I rescue that, too

Garibaldi:
She left me.

Vagabondo:
Si
I say quietly.
We eat alone
in silence/
to give time
for our eyes to dry.
Garibaldi I say!
You are slipping.

Why did you not tell me
about the bamboo guards
you slip over your fingers/
when I am working
the sickle in your
Castropignano fields?
Did you want me
to cut off my fingers?
We call them cannello/
I am not sure
if where you come from/
you used them
but if you listen
I will give you my lezioni.
Eh! I have/
his attention now
Shadows slip from his face
and he looks at me.
You see?
It goes like this:
You slip the cones
over the fingers
of your left hand.
You grab the—how do you say it—
the grain, like this.
You take the sickle
and you make the cut
Perfetto!
Are you listening?
The young
must always/
take the time
to teach/
the old.
He grins now
He is coming back/
from the sad place.
And did you know?
I say triumphantly
We used to put the sheepskin
over our arms/
to protect our tender skin/
from the barbs of the wheat.

Garibaldi:
Ahh, you think you know
But you do not know.
We had those.
We used them for the grain
and for sheering the sheep too!

Vagabondo:
Violetta at work
showed them to me/
when I told her about you.
I am so surprised
you forgot to tell me"
You remind me/
of what my father
used to say:
"I taught you all that I know
and still
you do not know a thing!"
The only way you learn/
is when I listen!

Garibaldi: *(grabbing Vagabondo's hands and pretending to grip hard)*
Eeeh, ehhh, ehhh, ehhh

Vagabondo:
We stand
I clear the dishes
We go outside/
to pass some time.

[*Vagabondo tries to describe to Nicola, a story of making cloth told to him by Angelo. He stumbles and blusters and ends up tired and frustrated and feeling stupid. Immediately, as reflected by his grousing to Maria, he gets an insight on Garibaldi, playing the "dumb Italian" with fast talking English-speakers, back home ... and he understands something beautiful and new about his father-in-law.*]

Vagabondo:
The children and I
rub our hands
along the bamboo

Feel its hardness
its shiny texture
the ridges at each joint.
An old thresher
melts into the soil/
Unspooled sharp, rusty circles
transform to sculpture
a thing no longer of use.
I look off in the distance/
See the river far below
The moment is expansive.
Nicola? Did you know
about the mangina?
(Eh, don't ask me/ *(Vagabondo turns to the audience)*
how to spell it!)
And the tell-eye-oh?
In the old days/
we used to cut
a certain reed
with its hard stalk
,and fibrous core.
We took the reeds
in bundles/ to the river
and set them under water.
You must/ put a rock on top
so the current/
won't sweep it away.
In two-three days pull them out
and use a machine
to chop the reed
and protect the fibres.
Now you have a textile
that women spin together/
roll up on wooden spools
to take to
someone in town/
who knows how to do it.
How do you call it?
The tailor, yes the tailor
He will make you the shirt
or a pair of the pants.
We have such a big sheet
in the garage/ at home.
My translation is so rough

I look in desperation/
but my wife is off
walking with her two Zie
The evening arrives
There is no time to panic
I must pace myself!
Do you remember the mangina?
I point my finger to my temple
Make a chopping motion
with an imaginary handle/
held by right arm
brought smack down
upon my left/
I am so pleased with
the fluid rhythm
of my Inglese,
international sign language.
Even the children/
so puzzled
stop to watch!
O my geezis!
Nicola looks at me/
Head cocked in avian inspection
Holds out his arms
In helpless not-knowing.
Frustration shudders through me
I am so dumb
An idiot some might whisper
So unable to explain.

Vagabondo: *(to the audience of the living opera)*
I hate it when Garibaldi
Plays the dumb Italian
It is an expression/
I sometimes utter
When I take the Old Guy to shop.
The look of impatience/
the wince of contempt
on store-people's faces?
I know what they think
I want to throttle them all!
As Garibaldi grows
older and unsure

I want to protect him.
This man is a King
in his own household
The engineer
the carpenter
politician and grower of food/
mechanic and artisan
He can weave
plastic gauge wire/
around gleamy green demijohns.
He is everyone's friend
on the street/
and at the club/
he makes them containers
out of cereal boxes/
to hold their
scopa and briscola cards.
But when I am
in the store with him
He acts like the bumpkin/
They think he is stupid
Gawd I could kill them!

Maria: *(as if she has overheard)*
What do you expect?
He is old
And they talk
too fast anyway!

Vagabondo:
The children fly off
Chase their attention
Like the butterfly
Later, tug one another
Turn in gladiatorial circles
and put one another
through a mangina machine.
My enchantment/
has not yet passed.
I remember Garibaldi
telling me about
his first job in Toronto.
He is young/

with two kids
He and Pasqua/
are sponsored by her brother
They have the debt to pay
for the trip over/
There is the rent
There is the food to buy.

Garibaldi:
My first job?
My first job/
in this country
did not work out.
I did not know
how to speak
your language.
I did not know/
where anything was.
Somebody told me
about the job in Scarborough
Picking the fungi—how do you call it?—
the mushrooms.
I got up early/
they showed me how
to ride the streetcar
All the way out/
from Montrose at College/
It was where/
we used to live.
When I got there/
they told me:
"No there are no jobs, here"
Then I had to
find my way back.
It is hard/
finding your way back/
when you do not
know the way.
I had my address/
on a little piece of paper.
A lot of pressure
a family to feed
bills to pay

the debt for the room
the furniture and the boat
The TTC guy helped me get home/
That was our life, then.

Vagabondo:
O I understand his lesson
It is so hard
to be alive inside
So happy
so full of the things to say/
Wanting to let people know
How you think and how you feel
—about them, about what you see—
Wanting to converse/
Such hunger to be understood
to give and get the joke/
to feel sharp and shine-y?
not dull and blurry.
Non poi giudicare,
il libro dalla copertina!
You cannot/ judge the book/ by the cover!

O Maria!
I feel like
the dumb Inglese/
trying to talk with Nicola.
I try to tell him
about the mangina machine/
and I feel like a monkey.
Maria listen to me
O my geezis
At least I can speak "scopa"/
Can't I? Hon, can't I?
So trying to salvage/
my pride.
"Yes and you can speak benzina"
she tells me
With eyes/ that look/ like wells.

[*Finally, the day's tour over, they return to Dinnermass at Nicola's home with Pasqua's side of the family. The lovely obligations are complete.*]

Vagabondo:
Canto: "Melodies of prone dreams"
Nicola seems to understand
the moment.
In his hand/
a single green fig.
It is what he went/
to search for.
Fig season I am told
Came early this year.
The tree/
had one straggler
just like me
hanging on/
for dear life.
He presents it to me/
Gestures with his hands
for me to eat.

Maria comes around/
a stand of breezy trees
She walks slowly
arm-in-arm
with her two ancient aunts.
The sun turns honey-gold
I see it in their squinting faces/
the orange and red around them.
The play of white and shade/
on the house behind.
These two generations:
Two sisters and a daughter/
loved by a mother
who is no longer here/
taken so young.
I see a moment so revealing/
A prophesy so sweet
I see how my wife/
will look
in thirty years/
I cock my head
rub my chin/
I am made happy/
by this angelic vision.

The feminine parade/
picks its way so slowly
along the side/ of the house
tugged by vines
pausing before arriving
at the front.
The children notice
dart back
to emerge
in front of us/
laughing beside the cars.
Ancient Zie are coaxed carefully
into front seats.
The resolute slam of car doors
The turn of engines/
We drive back down
the winding road.
In a moment/
there is wine and chicken
meat and pasta
orange pop and pane
lasagna and the beans
meloni e espresso
liquore and benzina
A full tour/ of the modern home.

And in the dark
at an unknown time.
La Famiglia Vagabondo
wind their way up/
past pizzeria, past monument/
around corner to piazza/
up steps/ through narrow courtyard
to our little home.
I fumble with the lock
fumble again and soon
the libretto gives way/
to melodies of prone dreams.

[*The day ends and the next day arrives. There is a caravan
to the train station in Boiano. The red Canadian suitcases
are packed. Domenico takes la famiglia Vagabondo. They
are standing on the platform and suddenly, the entire family*

arrives, en masse, with espresso. The sound of a train's horn blast and a **Chorus of Fond Farewells,** *a kind of* **song of the Family.**]

Maria and **Vagabondo:** *(Duet)*
Vagabondo:
All at once
It is too soon!
Big red Canadese suitcases
somehow fit/ into Domenico's car.
Biago will take Maria and the kids
I go with Domenico
To follow with the luggage.
We take the back way/ to Boiano
From there/ the train to Rome
find a hotel
fly home the next day
Domenico the expert/
weaves his way
over and around
He wears no sunglasses
It does not seem to matter
He takes each turn
Miraculously, without fear
it is a gift (I think)
Dio, Domenico
How the hell can you see?
Choo! He replies
with a mischievous grin.

Maria:
O too soon
we are in Boiano
There is the flurry
of bags and clicking handles/
a procession to the platform.
The Station is deserted/
it has that war-movie feel
The kids go to explore/
while we stand around
with the downcast hesitation/
that leaving brings.
Suddenly to the left/
there is movement and colour

Noise and happy song.
Nina! Salvatore!
Marica and Enrica,
Noemi e Gabriele,
Kristina e Valentina
with little Ester in tow.
All spill out laughing.
There are hugs
There are kisses and touch
Salvatore leaves to return
with tiny cups/
of espresso for all.
Chin Chin! We cry
As train announces arrival/
Suddenly wheezes to a stop.
SSSSSSHHHHHHHHHHHHHH.
There is no time now
We all cry
hoist red bags high
A whistle trills the chill of departure
through our sorry hearts.
"See you again!"
Biagio calls

[*As the chorus fades, a single stage light comes on and reveals* Il Vagabondo *and* Garibaldi, *at a table back home. Vagabondo is describing the trip and the goodbye in Boiano.*]

Vagabondo:
In the cantina/
I take a hard pull
from the plastic siphon/
completely fill my mouth
I remove the tube/
slide index finger off end
The wine fills
the old whiskey bottle
to the cap line.
I return to the table
to sit with Garibaldi/
and tell him my tale.
I cannot believe/
how kind everyone was.
I could not

pull my wallet out.
I tried it once/
Nicola got cross with me.
I had to sneak away/
to buy treats
for the kids.
Nicola and I/
beat Domenico
at the scopa.
I gave him
the set of cards
in the little
homemade cereal box case/
that you gave me!

Garibaldi:
That is good
I am happy.

Vagabondo:
But I tell you this!
It frightens me to think
what a loss it would be/
if we did not/ take the children
to your Hometown.
A man/ should not miss his chance
Do you not see?
I only bang the table/
to give you the lesson!

Garibaldi:
Yes, now you know/
Have some more wine
Then we will go/
to pass some time.

Vagabondo:
We are both/
smarter/ than I look

ACT III

ACT III: Scene 1

Canto Primo

(Il Vagabondo meets Garibaldi for the first time. A scrutiny of eyes. He crosses the threshold of garage to meet the father and kitchen to meet the mother. The enchantment of boiling water, the pasta, oil, vinegar and salt revealed.)

The Players:

The English-speaking guy
The Italian-speaking guy
Maria
Pasqua

[*The English-speaking guy arrives in the driveway of North York, the "Pre-Court of Garibaldi" and is watched by neighbours on both sides. The Italian-speaking guy is puttering in the garage.*]

Vagabondo:
Canto: "The First Scrutiny" *(languid, adagio)*
I turn onto Rita Drive/
in the North York
The first thing I see
is the church/
where we/ will be married
next year.
The road curves sharply/
past the house
with the little jesu shrine
on the front lawn.
next to the house/
where no one is ever home.
Another set of dwellings:
I won't remember a thing/
about the couple
two doors down.
Beside them, a Black Madonna
She is aware/
that I am slowing down.
I wheel into the driveway/
open fully in wonder
to the dark, inquisitive scrutiny
A penetrating, slightly worried gaze
that signals a presence/
of the stranger!
I am sure/
when I get out of my car
If there is a dog
on her property
It will kill me.
I look up/
to say hello
But the Madonna
she has gone.
Later/
I will understand
that she has gone/
to get a better look!
The driveway looks pristine
No oil spots, nothing to suggest debris
A clean, white apron of concrete
Multipurpose threshold/

to garage and to cantina
O! One day, I will sing to you/
about all the mysterious
cantinas I have known.
An efficient van stands
parallel to a red brick wall/
bordered cleanly by cement.
Tiny pink flowers
bobbing snapdragons
and scratchy red roses
proudly cascade
like a waterfall
kissed by perfect hedge.
Everything is presided over/
by a royal plastic lion in repose
And two plastic hens/
seem to squabble and cackle
in laying form
Geraniums grow out of their backs.
A garden fork
rests its tines
in a jaunty,
well used angle.
Shade hovers over steps
to front door
Reaches around corners/
to a side yard
I will later see
opens to backyard/ and garden/
yard barn and compost.
A grape vine/
curls and reaches
towards the sun.
Later I will meet
the other back yards/
crowded around gaily
like they are all
at the feast.
And this is where
I will spend:
all of my springs
all of my summers
and all of my harvests
So that soon/

I will not really
wish to spend/
any time indoors
except the downstairs kitchen/
to eat.
There are three trees/
Thankfully, I can easily tell
the large one grows pears.
Later I will be told
the second grows the peaches
and in years to come/
our children will eat cherries
like robins in safe bows/
of comfort and freshness.
To the left/
I suddenly notice/ a woman
guarding property next door!
She gets up/
descends stairs
to walk slowly
and look.
How do you do?
I call out nicely.
She smiles, nods her head
kneads her hands/
in an apron.
Leaves to go indoors
to see me better/
through glass.

[*His gaze takes in the Old Guy. The English-Speaking guy crosses the threshold of the garage and shakes Angelo's hand. The Old Guy returns it.*]

Vagabondo: *(recitative)*
I am aware now
of a third pair of eyes/
They watch me
from inside the garage.
He is at the work bench
when I drive in/
busy with something.
He looks over his shoulder/
then turns his back on me.

He looks again.
I can see/ he is setting/ something down.
He reaches for one of those/
red-orange gas station rags.
Something has registered.
Like I have driven over a black hose/
tripped the imaginary bell
There is no rush.
He turns/ and in a subtle moment
Faces me/ without moving.
Like the execution.
He wears blue overalls
a solid pair of work shoes
Already his deep tan/ Is made deeper
by the whiteness of sleeveless undershirt/
framed by unbuttoned blue vee.
He has/ a prominent nose
Not unlike his daughter's
A healthy outdoor look/
that old guys/ sometimes get
Along with a fluid paunch/
that grows bigger in the winter
when there is less to do
And flattens out in the spring
when there is everything to do.
Because I am standing still
I see moods
cross his Italian face
with the speed of clouds
moving across a bright blue sky.
First I see/
the imposed concentration of work
then he focuses/
realizes what he is seeing
and the first opinion
moves out to see
what will happen next!
"How do you do?" I say
and step across his threshold/
to offer first my hand
and then my name.
He says Hello
and returns my hand.
There is silence.

Later I will say to Maria
O my geezis/
between Maddalena and Margherita
and the Old Guy
I might just as well
have yelled out.
Hi everybody!
"By now/ you can tell
I am the complete Stranger
I am not Italian
Certainly not a Catholic
Some sort of English guy
Arrived to see/
the daughter of the Father.
How the hell/
is everyone doing today?"
Maria will laugh/
hide her face
in both hands
And the more I come around
the more I will see/
this exact gesture.
It translates in dialect as:
I-hope-you-will-still-be-here/
when-I-open-my-eyes.
Lesser men might look to be rescued/
run away or be angry
By the time
Maria saves me
(O God, what took her?)
I will be able to tell her
That the second tree
is a peach tree
The wine press is solid/
but one of the slats
needs replacing.
A demijohn/ holds about
five cases of grapes/
depending on the year
and how much juice
you get from them.
Do you not know?
You will need
to top them up/

to keep the cork moist!
I am pleased to note/ *(turning to the audience of the Living
    Opera)*
that the Father smokes Export A's
I am able/ to communicate
in the dialect of nicotine
Once enough time has passed/
and I no longer/
stand at attention.
Several years later/
Garibaldi will announce
he has quit smoking.
A package of cigarettes
will migrate to the garage
I will find it unopened/
when we are packing him up.
But for now?
I am somewhat at ease
for it is a little-known fact/
you can cover a lot of ground
sharing a smoke/
quietly, silently.
I am careful to finish mine second place
So I can see where/
he is going to put his butt.
I follow him out to the road/
and return with him
to the garage.

Maria:
Daddy, this is the one
that I was telling you about!
We go to school
together, downtown.

Vagabondo: *(turning to the audience of the living opera)*
She helps to turn me/
into an entity
in her Father's mind.
I can actually see him/
put the idea together
like the hose on the faucet
trying it out/
examining the threads.

Couple it
Uncouple it.
Couple it
Uncouple it.
Set it down/
walk away
It is a strange thing
to be with these Italians!
At first you don't have a presence
It is as if/
you are not there
or will not be there/
in a second.
Later when you are there
And the enchantment pervades
you will be both
visible and invisible—
loved either way.
You are alternately there
and if you are not there/
they know where to find you.
I think they call it/
La famiglia!

Maria:
Mamma says it is time
to get ready
to wash up for lunch.
Brace yourself/
My love!

[*The English Speaking guy goes inside to meet The Mother,
Pasqua. There is a recitative about the beauty and strength
of her eyes.*]

Vagabondo:
Quietly I brace myself/
for the next meeting
Before I know it/
I am inside the house.
Somehow I have slipped off my shoes
I am given a pair of slippers
an oddly informal gesture/
that chips away

at my tension.
I am shown how to wash up/
at the utility sink
near the furnace
Where to hang the towel/
on the line strung indoors
across that low-ceilinged room/
Finally I am shown
where to sit
at the downstairs Kitchen table/
This geography of the love and the purpose
Is where I now meet
Pasqua, The Mother!

Maria: *(in Italian)*
Mamma this is the one
I was telling you about
where I go to school!

Vagabondo:
Buongiorno Signora!
I say getting the time of day/
off by an hour or so.
Ha Ha! It is/
very nice to meet you! *(turning to the audience of the living
     opera)*
She is small/
with a beautiful smile
and gray hair/
that becomes her.
Her eyes/
are worried in the corners
wet-black/
and I can see
that I have been
taken in, fully/
quietly inspected and returned
smoothed out
and a little less wrinkled.
It is not unpleasant/
to be returned this way!
I sit next to Maria
across from the Mother/
somehow comforted

by a sense of intimacy
when all else around me/
the sight
the sound
the smell
the tastes/
are so foreign
Behind me is where/
the plate from the Bahamas will go
brought back proudly for them/
as a souvenir
from our honeymoon

[*The English Speaking guy meets The Brother.*]

Vagabondo:
To my left/
at the opposite
head of the table
like the bookend/
is the Brother.
He is amused/
by the whole thing
alternately serious
and grinning
I have a sense/
that I am passing
an early muster
He lives at home/
but will triumphantly
move to Brampton
as I begin to come over/
more and more.

Carmine:
Later I will have
a word with you
when we pass time
in the garage.
You will know
that my sister
Is important to me
And it is equally important—
how do I say it?—

that she does
not get jerked around
by wrong-meaning guys.

Vagabondo:
O my geezis
I say to Maria
Later on outside
when she removes/
her head from her hands
to stop laughing.
I can see/
that they love you!

[*Il Vagabondo, unnamed, sings and enchanted* **arietta:
"You Can't Escape Your Parents"**]

Vagabondo:
It is one of the lezioni
from the early days
before I enter
the Court of Garibaldi
Well before
all insights into
the ancient Order
and the systems
of hillside flames!
Later I will understand
that even the young
think they know
but they do not know.
They think they are free
or need to be free
of the Ancient Order
but it is turning in gyres
within them, slowly
Like the languid airborne
twist of the hawk
Like the deliberate
squeeze of a wine press
or the oil-and-vinegar
salt-toss-rhythm
of preparing the salad.
You cannot escape your parents!

Go with the motion
and you will feel/
your stubble burning off
offered up like white smoke
in open air cathedrals
on hillsides in the sky
Go against it
and you will suffer
because you reject the way
you are meant
to follow.

[*The song segues to an address on 'felice'—the first reference to the living opera and the enchantment within it. The beauty of a pot of boiling water extolled and the sublime magnificence of preparing pasta and a salad.*]

Vagabondo:
Canto: "Felice"
My stomach
turns my mind to the stove
and I must be under
a certain spell
of two motions:
Two motions
I will copy
again and again
Until I enter
the state of gusto.
When you feel
the languid enchantment
You already understand/
the word felice
in your heart
It rolls off your tongue
like meat sliding off the rib
into a pool
of bubbling thick red sauce
on glisten-y steaming pasta
smothered in dry grated
asiago cheese/
sprinkled against
unbelievable protest
with the salt

and the pepper
for you are their Inglese
heart and soul/
loved forever
in Garibaldi's Court.
No! You hear them say.
Sale? Pepe?
No, No No!!!!!
Dio, Mother of God!
Felice *(to the audience of the living opera, together)*
Fe-lee-chay
Fe-lee-chay
You say it
Over and over
to yourself
You breathe in fully/
Put your left hand
upon your heart
You throw your right hand
with abandon/
out into
the operatic life/
and you sing
the libretto/
in the dialect of love.
There is a silver beauty
to a boiling pot of water
The waiting
The awakening hiss
Molecules heat up
soon to begin
their tumble
The first bubbles
pass the tipping point
and the whole thing
speeds up
now boiling fiercely
with spatters
escaping to shish
off the burners
I tell you this!
Then you will know
It is time
to slide the pasta in

Penne rigate!
Penne rigate!
It heaps stiffly
at the bottom
quickly quiets the surface
of that happy sea
Steam rises
in anticipation,
there is the hissing
and then Presto!
The whole thing
takes off again!
This is when
you pour the salt
at first into the palm
of your left hand
Later when you
know the lesson
pour it directly
into the steaming boil
I Do It/
The Way She Does it
I Do it/
the way I have been taught
You are a fool
if you put the lid on now
and walk away
Don't you see?
you will boil
the whole damn thing over:
Reluctantly pull
the burners out
the pans they sit in
and scrape off the mess
No it is the precise moment
to stay and watch
and enter the thrall
of the enchantment
Pick up the plastic spoon
Slowly, lovingly
begin to turn your pasta
Watch them soar around
in scalding bliss
Watch them grow

happily thicker.
They swirl and swirl
hypnotically
and soon you will notice
you are stirring them
absentmindedly/
gently,
lovingly
while your mind
blends into warm steam.
It is like
being read to
when you watch it being done.
Then, when you are ready—
there is no rush—step back.
Pull off
the green leaves
of the lettuce.
Tear them into
jagged shapes
Let them tumble
into the bowl.
Run your fingers through them
Lift them
Turn them
Cut up the wet tomatoes
into irregular cubes
place their moist weight
onto the leaves.
The cucumber is next
spilling into cracks
left by the tomatoes
and haughty radicchio.
Always slice the onion
into thin,
curving petals
Wipe your hands
on a tea towel
and return
to the pasta
to maintain
the fluid, spinning motion.
This next part
is the best!

Pick up the bottle/
of extra virgin olive oil
Bertozzi, Colavita, Rastrelli
if you can find her
Pour it on the salad
in a slow
steady
circular fashion
from center to circumference
and back again!
Pour it again
Step back!
Remove the lid/
of the wine vinegar
and circle your bowl
in the opposite motion
Unwind:
erratically shake salt
over the whole thing
Stop!
Circle with the vinegar
Stop!
Toss the insalata now
with spoons
Stop!
Add more vinegar/
and because you are
Inglese and possessed
More salt!
Taste!
If you do it right
you will be enchanted
If you close your eyes
and say Felice
like you mean it?
You will notice
that your right hand
comes together at the tips/
that they will
turn towards your heart/
to gently match
the rhythm of its beat.
It is—how do they call it?—the gift!

[*They have dinner together. (lighting fades to dark)*]

ACT III: Scene 2

Overture to a side yard
(Garibaldi holds court. Lovers pass time and zucchinis grow
wild to embrace a thousand back yards. Confrontation at the
click of a gate. Tales of courtship told in a mist of grief.)

The Players:

The English-speaking Guy (Il Vagabondo)
Maria
The Italian-speaking Guy (Garibaldi-The Father)
Pasqua (The Mother)
Pasqua's voice
Pasqua's Father's Voice
The Children (briefly)

[*Seque/continuation from Scene I, as imaginary light opens*
the stage of the 'downstairs kitchen.' The magnificent meal
has concluded. The English-speaking guy offers to help but is
shooed away from the dishes. The Italian-speaking guy takes
him out to have a smoke and observe the neighbourhood.]

Vagabondo:
Dinner is done.
Like a true Inglese
I get up/
to help clear the plates!
There are protests
from Maria's mother.

Maria:
Ma! It's OK!

Vagabondo:
Incredibly, In-cred-i-bee-lay
some might say
I start to rinse/
the plates at the sink
Before I know it
Pasqua is beside me
She gently but resolutely
takes the tea towel/
from my grip.
I sense that/
she is teaching me something
Silently, Maria joins her/
to take my spot.
The quiet ring of fork tines
The efficient clack of porcelain
pronounce the end/
of dinnermass.
I make it up
as I go along/
sort of take it
that I am to leave the kitchen
and follow the Old Guy
outside.
It is all unspoken/
there is no rush.
Carmine has disappeared!

[*Garibaldi and Vagabondo have a cigarette outside and watch the comings and goings on the street. Vagabondo realizes he is getting a first lesson at "passing time".*]

Vagabondo:
Outside in the garage
I try to think
of something
to arrest the silence.
I offer him a smoke
Thankfully, he accepts.
We stand/
at the mouth
of the garage/
exhaling strongly.
Our eyes sweep the street
first up and then down
I feel him/
standing beside me
The silence/
seems to create
an electric current
in the space between us
I know I will get a shock/
if anybody speaks!
I put my hand
in a pocket/
to ground myself.

Old Woman: *(passing by, on the sidewalk)*
Ciao, Angelo
Come sta?

Garibaldi:
Non c'e male

Vagabondo:
A small man and women
in tweed and shawl
head north waddling/
weighed down by
yellow bags of groceries
from Valencia.
Valencia is a beauty
South of the church
at the crossroads.
She is so mysterious
I go there on my own/

for the roast potatoes/
the meat and the cheese
It is—how do they say it—
It is everything!
The Old Guy eyes/
the couple intently
They look over
He waves back.
The women's eyes/
take me in/
I see her turn
to look at the husband.
We walk out to the road
and pitch our butts
into the gutter.
A horn beeps
There is Rocco driving by/
grinning.
Reflexively, I wave
Garibaldi offers me/
an early lesson
at passing time/
but I don't know it yet
and neither, does he!
Later when I learn/
to sing the libretto
of his Court
I will realize/
that it is my first introduction
to his street
to his neighbourhood
to how he
makes his life.
But for now?
I could be anywhere/
I cannot hear the music
of North York/
or sing the libretto
nor can I see flames/
on the side of its mountain.

(to Maria):
He is showing me things
even then!

Maria:
Don't you see?
This is because/
he cannot help it!

[*The door opens and the men are called inside for a sacred trinity of espresso, the fruta and cookies.*]

Pasqua:
It is time
to come in!

Vagabondo:
We come in/
slip off our shoes
I put on the brown slippers/
for a second time
It is a good sign!
Bravo!
I see small oranges
rosy nectarines
apples and green grapes
in the bowl.
A plate of
strange looking cookies!
Hard round ones
with nuts sticking in them
Mamma Mia!
Ridged ones
in the shape of an "S"/
A faceted steel pot
sits on an oven mat
I am poured thick coffee
into a tiny cup.
I watch the old guy/
take the baby spoon
and put some sugar in it.
I follow suit
The thick, smooth taste
startles me/
It is perfect! *(to the audience of the living opera)*
It tastes beautiful/
I tell her/
not even getting

the English right!
She will smile, nod
Nudge the cookie plate/
in my direction
Later when I am enchanted
this offertory will take on
the legendary proportions!
Only because of her/
time after time after time
I will/
pass the plate
to my dinner guests
I will/
look deeply into their eyes
I will/
intrude upon their personal space
And with a proud and dramatic/
inflection in my voice/
With a seriously pained
frown upon my face
I will /
gesture/ and simply say:
For Me/
Take One/
For Me!
O my geezis!
We will laugh!
out loud/
Maria will shake her head
and I?
I will profess my love/
in proper order
for my two Italian women/
and for them alone.
It is the way/
of Il Vagabondo!
Cosi sia.

[*The Lovers escape and pass time in the side yard being careful to dodge the watchful scrutiny of the neighbours!*]

Maria:
Happily
Unbelievably some might say

We are excused
from the kitchen.
"Ma, we are going outside."

Vagabondo: *(recitative, rapturous)*
The front door/
sighs open/ and seals shut.
We turn quickly right/
go up the cement steps
underneath the pear
and the peach trees/
lift the latch
to swing open the gate
to the side yard
There is time/
to hold hands
There is time/
to laugh
There is time/
to kiss
so, we do!
By the time/
we reach the side door
and the window
to the kitchen
Ha!/ We are cleverly
walking beside one another.
Only then/
Does Maria remember
to look back
to Maddalena's side window
to see/
if the coast is clear.
Our hands clasp over our mouths
We hunch over, giggling/
to make our careless way
towards two lawn chairs
spread out by the garden/
We put up our feet.

[*Maria and Vagabondo sing a loving* **duet** *on the Wonder and Beauty of 'passing time' in a side yard. They observe the order and symmetry of the painted house foundations. The personalities of all gardens are beheld and Dante's huge* *zucchini plant, stretching along the fence line, embraces all backyards in a verdant hug.*]

Vagabondo and **Maria:** *(duet)*
It is here/
in Garibaldi's side yard
next to the garden
in the back/
that I am seriously taught
how to pass the time.
I will show it to you!
In order to pass time/
you must be sitting.
it is better/ if your feet are up
but it is not/ totally necessary
There is no rush!
If you do it right/
you will enter
a precise space—
a space where there is/
no immediate memory of past
no immediate thought of future
There is nothing
to do next!
Unnecessary to speak
or engage in anything useful.
We have passed time
with as many as
six people at once/
and not one of us
said a single word.
If you are lucky/
and there is a cherry tree
in your back yard/
You can pick
an entire handful
of gleaming berries/
fire the pits off into oblivion
between thumb
and index finger/
of your right hand
Later if you have children/
you can spit pits
at each other

from your chairs and laugh/
till you cannot
take it anymore.
If you do this
to pass time/
It is unhelpful
to wear the white.
Trust us on this!
it is possible/
to pass time
for up to two hours
but/ if you have to count
or when you get up/
if you feel guilty
or worried about the time/
you are not enchanted
You have not/
passed time properly
So try to do it/ again!
This is all there is
to know about it/
It is a hard lesson
to learn
and an easier lesson
to forget
especially for/
the young/ and the modern

Vagabondo:
I recline now
There is time to gaze
Maria and I talk/
and then we do not talk.
It is the aimless cadence/
where we are growing
comfortable
with one another
and love/
takes its first gentle hold.
My eyes sweep across/
the clean concrete patio
I will later learn/
it is poured perfectly
by Orlando, next door.

He is Calabrese
He is intense
Sometimes I see/
his distracted, troubled look
when he concentrates/
and yes
there is a seismic shudder to the man/
But at least?
You can feel it coming.
To me? He is friendly/
I like him
The concrete pulls everything/
into clean and tidy definition.
Ribbed rebar/
not already put to use
in the garden
is stored so carefully/
beside the yard barn
All foundations are painted grey
Next door, behind, over there
As far as my eye can see?
the grey never peels
It always looks/
freshly painted
It is the way/
they do things.
The movement of my eyes/
from foundation
to foundation
to foundation
unlocks the magic
Suddenly I see carefully/
each enchanted garden

Garibaldi: *(voice off stage)*
"Everyone does it/
their own way"

Vagabondo: *(recitative)*
Vincenzo's tomatoes
are supported by/
six-foot tripods
of wooden stakes/
He has an oven

and later/
I will taste
his pizza!
Zumbareta will give me a jar
of hot red peppers/
bathed in the oil
stuffed with the olives!
Dante is a maestro
at growing zucchini
There is one plant/
She grows from two doors down
to travel along
all the back fences/
She throws her arms
around every yard/
in green embrace!
Between Margherita, Franca
Pasqua and the rest?
I will bring home
hundreds of zucchini.
O my geezis!
Each one tenderly given/
graciously accepted
but years later
I will confess to Maria *(Vagabondo turns to the audience of
the living opera)*
"You know Maria?
I never really knew/
what to do
with all those zucchinis—
We never ate them/
and they are
not that good raw"
(Mockingly)
"And you ate/
canned spaghetti too!"
She will remind me

[*Enchanted, the recitative shifts to song:* (**"You will not die
from this"**) *It is a capricious cultural commentary on what
to do when Italian women give you bag upon bag of zucchini
along with a 'dimostrazione' on how to make Zucchini soup.
(In the opera buffa style as in ... silly.)*

Vagabondo:
Canto: "You will not die from this"
My guilt at looking
into so many beautiful
Italian women's faces!
Accepting Ferlisi bag after Ferlisi bag
of foot-long
two-foot long
three-foot long
zucchinis ...
Mamma Mia!
It tears me apart
(Ferlisi is our other store) *(to the audience of the living opera)*
Just across the road/
from Valencia
on the north side.
She is importante/
like someone from the Hometown
Like a—how do they call it?—
like a paesana)
"Dio! Grazie signora
Grazie, no, per favore,
Grazie, no.
Please God, no
Prego, Prego, Pre-go
arrivaderci, ciao!
You will not die from this
It is the early lesson
I am taught
Later I will attend
My zucchini Soup School
as the penance.
With Pasqua/
as my professore?
I will not drop out!
But I tell you this!
My guilt at looking
at so many beautiful
Italian woman's faces!
Accepting bag upon bag
of zucchinis from heaven
Dio Mio!
It tears me apart.

Pasqua:
Canto: "Now, you know!"
Observe/
This is the only way to learn:
I will do my best
to pass it on to you/
First you must find
the paisley apron
that zips up the front/
Put it on
while the frying pan
is heating up
You want
to protect your clothes/
Add to the pan
the thin layer
of the olive oil
Rastrelli, if you can find it/
Finely chop the chipola—the onion
and sauté with—how do you say it?—
the string beenz/
Slice your zucchini thinly
Leave the skin on
Dio it is not a cucumber!
What were you thinking?
Place your beautiful zucchini
in the pot
cover with water
bring to the boil/
Finally cut
the potate
e sedano
e pressemolo/
You say:
the potato
the celery
the parsley/
You will be amazed to learn
there is another
kind of parsley/
It is not Inglese.
It has always been there
but you have not seen it
When you are enchanted

you will see it/
Salt to taste
Now that it is boiling?
Add the chipola
and everything else
Perfetto!
Now make a chopping motion
in the air
next to your cheek/
Purse your eyebrows
Lean in close
and repeat after me:
Abbi pazienza!
Abbi pazienza!
After twenty minutes
There is no rush/
Crack due uova
The eggs. The eggs!
You should know this by now/
Do not be the testa dura!
Give it ten minutes
to mix with the zuppa
You are the burlone/
if you do not add
the pepper now/
You serve it like this
with crusty bread
and a cheese we call
the asiago/
You are the good student
Have some wine/
Now, you know!

[*Suddenly, the gate clangs shut! The shadow lengthens and Garibaldi approaches Il Vagabondo and Maria, reclining in lawn chairs. He is very serious.*]

Vagabondo and **Maria (duet):**
There is a breeze
The sheets are drying
Everywhere air conditioners hum
Bees fly by
and like our love
accelerate off

into oblivion
Margherita uses the branches
to stake her tomatoes
They bring new texture
to this open-air fresco
O we are expertly
learning to pass time
Suddenly
We hear the gate clank!
We look up to see/
The Father entering
his side yard.
He walks toward us
His tanned handsome face
looks so serious
The shadows grow longer
He towers over us
And then stands there.

Maria:
Hi Daddy!

Vagabondo:
Ha Ha! Hello, Sir!
Your garden
It looks beautiful!

Garibaldi:
There is some things
I have to say

Vagabondo:
I sit up in my chair!

Garibaldi:
My wife and I know

Maria:
Daddy, don't!

Garibaldi:
My wife and I know
That you are coming around now
But I have to tell you

I don't know if I like you
I don't know if I don't like you
I just don't know you
That is all

Maria:
Daddy, Please!

[*The action (through the use of the light of imagination)
quickly shifts to the Cancer Narrative and a micro-scene of
Garibaldi and Vagabondo, who has dropped in to check up
on the Old Man and mend his grief. They are sipping wine at
the kitchen table. It is a veglia, a time to remember. Pasqua
is dead. Garibaldi shares the tale of how they courted in the
Old World. The ancient ways of dating are shared.*]

Vagabondo:
I have arrived!
You never know
when you will see me!
That way I will be sure
to find some food.
Do not look so surprised *(to the audience of the living opera)*
Garibaldi is so sad
I drop in
to talk with him
around the kitchen table
Ask him things/
to cheer him up
How did you first meet Pasqua?
I ask the Old, defeated man.

Garibaldi:
It was different then
then it is now.
In Italy
when you got engaged/
it was not like you go
to the girl's house
pick her up/
and go around
Over there?
You went to a girl's house
You sat there.

Her mother sat there.
The father sat there
and the girl
sat over there/
so far away from you
There was no way
you could get
close to her
to talk
If you had to talk
you had to talk/
through the parents
to the family/
where everyone was sitting
That's the way it was

Vagabondo:
So how do you know
if the girl likes you?

Garibaldi:
Ehhh
You found a way/
to figure that out

Vagabondo:
And? ...
(I say tumbling my left hand
around in front of me) *(to the audience of the living opera)*
This is not an Italian gesture
I use my hand with Garibaldi
In the Inglese dialect/
to encourage him
to pick up the pace
It is a fault of the young,
I know.
But Garibaldi ignores me/
He speaks the slow gait
of memories being called/
over to talk.

Garibaldi:
You see, over there
what you did was/

You wrote a little note
to the girl/
to tell her about
your feelings
When she got the note
She wrote a note back/
to say if she agreed
with you or not
Most of the time
the girl would say:
"No. I am too young/
for that"
So then/
you would say
"That's Ok"/
and you wrote a note
to someone else
What happened to me
was this:
I wrote a note
and gave it to a girlfriend
to give/ to her
The girlfriend
told her boyfriend
to tell me
she already had
a boyfriend/
that they were engaged
and I should have nothing
to do with them/
The same story
was going around
in town
So I sent a note
directly to my wife/
to see what she
had to say
about it
The answer I got/
She told me
she was too young
and could not
get engaged yet
She was/

seventeen years old
So I said:
OK, OK
forget about it!

Vagabondo:
Garibaldi claps his hands
and makes a motion
like he is wiping them off
I can see he is using/
Molise hand dialect
So I slap the table/
to tease him.
it is/
the dialect/
of love
No!
It is impossible
that she rejected you

Garibaldi:
But how I really
got engaged
was through
another friend of mine/
that was engaged
to my wife's cousin's daughter
They were family
So my friend/
he came around
to tell me
If maybe
I insisted/
I would get engaged
But I had/ another problem
My in-laws/
They did not
like me

Vagabondo:
This is
not possible!
Why?

Garibaldi:
Because they had/
some property
and we had
nothing!
That is why
That is the reason!

Vagabondo:
Did they tell you
they don't know if they like you/
they don't know if they don't like you
I have the memories/
too, you know

Garibaldi:
No
It is not that
they didn't like me/
It was a difference
of the position!
The position they were
and the position we were!

Vagabondo:
How did you resolve it?

Garibaldi:
The friend/
that was engaged
to my wife's cousin's daughter
started something going around
He said to me again/
Angelo, if you persist
you might get something/ there
He was giving me a tip
But O, I am stubborn!
I have been stubborn/
since I was born
So I said: No!
To heck with it
I don't want/
to do anything about it!

But my friend/ he persisted
He said to me:
I tell you/ what you could do
There was a feast in town
with a band
in the piazza
in front of the church/
I was going around
with the people/
to have a good time
My friend said to me:
Watch!
She is looking after you
Everywhere you go!
But I said to him
When I get something refused?
I don't push for it
So forget about it
Angelo! He said
"Can't you see it?"
He got between me/
and my stubbornness
He forced me to try

Vagabondo:
Come ti chiami?

Garibaldi:
Donato Macoretta!

Vagabondo:
Well then/
Donato Macoretta
is my friend!

Garibaldi: *(ignoring Vagabondo)*
So I speculated on that
I told Donato:
You go and tell/
your girlfriend to tell her
If she wants to
talk to me/
she has to come
behind the church

Vagabondo:
This sounds more/
like a side yard, to me!

Garibaldi: *(ignoring Vagabondo)*
So she met me
and I asked her/
if the answer she gave me
was because
she was too young/
to get engaged or
she was engaged/
to that guy

Pasqua: *(from off stage)*
No!
I am not engaged
to that guy/
but my parents
don't want me/
to get engaged
with You!

Vagabondo: *(Looking around stage for Pasqua's voice)*
Why?
How could this be?

Pasqua:
My parents/
got a little more
than what you got/
because you haven't got
anything!

Vagabondo: *(Looking around stage)*
You/ said that?
Signora!
How could you?

Garibaldi:
So I asked her
What about you?
Do you/ want to get engaged
with me/ or not?

Pasqua: *(off stage)*
Yes!
but my parents ...

Garibaldi:
Tell your parents
that I am going to come
and see you/
at your home
on the farm

Vagabondo: *(triumphantly)*
It was a Saturday night!
People were busy/
every other night
but on Saturday/
you could go.

Garibaldi:
That is right!
When I went there/
I knocked
and both parents/
came to the door

Pasqua's Father's Voice:
What do you want?

Garibaldi:
So I told them/ about it
They were on/
one side of the door
and I/
was on the outside

Pasqua's Father's Voice:
So
What have you got/
to offer her?

Garibaldi:
Well.
The only thing
I could offer her/

is my love
Other things/
I haven't got

Pasqua's Father's Voice:
Well
I have/ to think about it
You go home
and we will talk about it/
another time

Vagabondo: *(laughing)*
Wow!
Now I can see/
why you put me/
through the ringer!
So when did he say/
Ok
you can marry ·
my daughter?

Garibaldi:
That was later on
About two-three months
I went there/
almost every Saturday night
The first night/
I couldn't get on the farm
Then they told me/
You sit here
The mother sat there
The father sat there
And she was sitting/
way over there!

Vagabondo:
Bravo!
This is so beautiful
And do you remember
Garibaldi?
What I said to you
When you came/
into the side yard
and spoke to me?

Garibaldi:
Yes!

Vagabondo:
I said:
Well Mister Molinaro/
I am going to make sure
that you like me!

Garibaldi:
Bravo!
Yes!

[*The scene ends quickly with a tale of Vagabondo asking Garibaldi for Maria's hand in marriage with a quick story to The Children about their grandfather's love.*]

Vagabondo: *(to the audience of the living opera)*
And later/
when it is time
—there is a rush—
and I am nervous
I will seek him out
alone in the garage
Maria will be inside
with her mother/
In a choreography
of love and respect
I will tell him/
that I believe in God
That by now/ I hope
he should be able to tell
that I am a
—how do they say it?—
a good man;
that we go good together
that I would like
his permission
to marry
his daughter
When I go inside
I am careful to see
there is more twinkle
than worry

in Pasqua's eyes/
and I see in a moment
I am
a rich man/
The old ways
are good enough
for me!

Vagabondo: *(with the children, on the imaginary stage in
the light)*
I tell you this/
Nonno's mother-in-law?
loved him to pieces
One time
when he was married
There was a really bad snowstorm
They had not heard/
from Nonna's parents
for a week!
There were no
telephones back then
So he walked/
all the way over
to the farm
The snow was so deep/
He could not get through
So he wrapped/
his long coat
around himself/
and rolled and rolled
all the way
down the lane/
Like the snowball landing
on their front door/
When they saw him
shake the snow off
like a dog
They came alive again!

The Children:
Bravo Nonno!

ACT III: Scene 3

The Garage. A Winemaker's Tableau
*(A lezione of peace and within that, the silence of being
entirely yourself, within each moment, usefully: Nothing
more and nothing less. It is a good way to live.)*

The Players:

Garibaldi
Il Vagabondo
2 Neighbours (help with the wine production)
Piccolo Coro (Small Chorus)

*(Stage Note: The Scene opens with Vagabondo in recitative
making an acute observation and inventory of the Italian
garage. The action takes place entirely within an exact
imaginary replica of an Italian garage with a working garage
door that opens and closes to demarcate micro shifts in
action and punctuate the intimacy of meaning: a working
curtain within a curtain on the imaginary stage.)*

[The Piccolo Coro *begins with a recitative on the contents
of an Italian garage and the use and re-use of objects: this
notion of ancient order—recycling before it was fashionable.*]

Piccolo Coro: *(with Vagabondo, observing)*
Time after time
I enter/ the perfect place
The smooth floor
has a clean shine
The smell/ could be called
an aroma/
for there are wisps of the cantina
wisps of fresh air
wisps of grapes and pears
and finally wisps/
of clean, unused motor oil
and the faint breath of Varsol.
Along one side/
hang ladders
assorted chords
restrained bundles of rope
against a clean backdrop/
of concrete block.
Homemade brown cupboards/
huddle in the corner
They protect soldering irons
propane bottles
drills
a skill saw
a small working motor/
affixed to a board.
There is a table saw/
tucked underneath
next to the back seat/
of a van
Dio Mio!
the seat is in exile/
from what I affectionately call
—how do we say it?—
the Italian pick-up truck.
It is covered/
in rough white cloth
made from extracted reeds
cracked open by
hometown
mangina machine/
spun from loom.
"Garibaldi, how can you use

something that important
that historic
brought over from the old country/
on something that will
so certainly/
destroy it?"

Garibaldi:
Ehh. We do not
have much use
for it/ now

Vagabondo:
It is like that
with them/
Everything is used
and then re-used
Recycled and then used again
in ways
that make it/
even more useful
Or else it is given away/
to someone next door
who has a better
use for it
After that/
there is the poor to think about
Someone at the church
or at Goodwill is called
Finally, when the last use/
is squeezed out
like juice from the mosto
It is discarded/
thrown out
and there are no more/
second thoughts!

[*A deeper* **"Observation Song"** *on the contents of an Italian garage with an* **arietta ("Rule G")** *about wives going to neighbours to retrieve their husband's incessantly borrowed tools.*]

Piccolo Coro:
My eyes roam/

to the back of the garage
I see/ the detailed beauty
of a homemade work bench
primitive drawers/
that open smoothly
and never jam!
A pegboard is draped/
with clusters of tools
mysterious ones
store bought ones
and hybrids
The mysterious ones/
are used once a decade
I like to think/
of what they were used to fix
when they were purchased
and why.
But it is the hybrid tools/
I love to touch
Works of art/
marvels of engineering
I see
homemade screwdrivers
used to reach
some long-forgotten place/
Back in the days
when you could work
on your own car/
and fix it
Ancient hammers/
with new handles
Curious-looking awls/
grafted into warm
pieces of wood
Concocted saws/ strange thin blades
screwed into stranger
pieces of steel
Long, smooth shovel handles
attached to everything/
that can possibly be used
to scrape or dig or shift or move!
My favourite is the one
with a wafer of metal
grafted to smooth

piece of oak
Used with precision/
to remove ice
from the front step/
by the cantina

Vagabondo: (Arietta) *"The Rule G"*
If you are back
at your house
and you need
a pry bar
to remove a stump?
There are two
in the corner
to choose from/
If you need
a toilet-snake
to unclog
your plumbing
take this one
coiled to the right!/
It is longer
and more functional
than anything
you will ever find
in Inglese stores/
You can always borrow
the orange pruner
or the shovel
that will reach deep
into post holes/
But I tell you this!
Just be sure
you return it
or you will violate
the Rule G!
The husbands will fuss
complain to their wives
for weeks/
Assertively the wives will go
retrieve the tools
and make peace/
And the amazing thing is
if the same neighbor

comes to ask
for another tool/
He will get it!
for it is the husbands
who do not
want to cause
the problem/
I tell you
I have seen it/
This is why
they need
the sons-in-law!

[*Vagabondo's Singspiel about the concentration it takes to solve 'problemi'.*]

Vagabondo:
The garage
in Garibaldi's Court
is a place
of pure solution
You can feel
the sphere
of concentration there:
The problem
the tinkering
the washing up for lunch
the return
the tenacity
the next day
the talking about it/
with a neighbour
The eureka moment!
when the thing
is fixed
and it is time/
to down
a glass of wine
in one go/
The sequence
is all there
inside the garage
singing and dancing
like spirits

at the feast/
I can
see them!

[*Enter the wine press in full view, fully lit, an object of Art. A
Michelangelo statue.*]

Vagabondo:
Canto: The Wine Press
And in the corner
with its slats
its cogs and bars/
The stained dark blocks
of wood
for ratcheting/
The wine press
stands stoutly
on cast-iron base/
Michelangelo's work
right down to
iron indentations
at the toes/
to keep
the macchina stable/
It is an object
that must be touched
must be turned
must be set up
and used
Spirits are made
from this truly
masculine piece/
There is no
tug-of-war
no competition
No foolish
infertile
argument/
It stands
like a fruiting body!
Below/
a mycelium network
of web and fibre/
weave into the soil

the daily cycles
and the life and the love/
all the way
back to textured hillside/
by the Castello
It is planting
It is harvest
It is the burning
off of stubble/
Carefully the tendrils
stretch across the valley
inch up the hillside
grow into the town
Branch this way and that
linking family to family
men to men
ending and beginning
exactly beside
Rosie's stall
and the ancient
wine press/
back home
The Alpha
and the Omega/
Yet it takes two
to make a life/
Because the women
see it all strongly/
They know
what they know
and what I
will never know
and can only
guess at.

Maria
There is romance
to the hard life
It is born
from the unity/
that a division
of labour creates
Have you not
seen it?

[*The old ways give way to the new. Garibaldi and Vagabondo
go to look at the grapes.*]

Vagabondo:
It is late September
We go now/
to the corner
of the Jane/
and the Sheppard
Garibaldi and I/
to look at the grapes
It is morning/
cold and bright
Yellow jackets float
from crate to crate/
completely uninterested
in you/
So Intoxicated/
in the land
of uva per vino!
The place/
is filled with Old Guys
They are small and wrinkled
Some of them smoke
There is laughing/
and loud talk
One or two young guys/
run the giant press
or move crates
around silently/
with propane forklifts
The crates/
are piled
high as your chest
Get close to grapes!
Smell them
Try each one:
The Muscato
The Carrignane
The Alicante
The Multepulciano
The Ruby Cabernet
and the Grenache!

Pull a brown leaf/
wedged in purple sea
and rub it/
with your fingers
See the new demijohns/
in plastic baskets
See the beginning/
of the end
of an era!
They look too stylish
no wicker, no mildew
no ten gauge/
electrical cord
red, white green
like Garibaldi's got/
Plastic tubing
smart oak wine presses
atop metal bases/
painted green
for the urban set/
Stoppers
airlocks
jugs of unknown volume/
It's all there.

Garibaldi:
Observe/
These are the kiki
They must be
close together/
Tight-like
This is what/
you want to buy.
Ehh! The white powder/
is the medicine/
They put on them
to keep your grapes from
going bad/
They are all green
when they ship them/
It is not/
like we had it/
back Home.

[*Nonna-food. An enchanted vignette by Vagabondo on breaking for lunch. He goes to get wine and singspiel's an* **Observation Song** *about the cantina in Garibaldi's Court. A dinner of gnocchi presides.*]

Vagabondo:
Later/
when we are back home
having lunch/
with Pasqua, Maria
and the kids
I will ask him/
about the Old Days
but first/
I will wash up
It will be cold/
the furnace will rumble on
The Children/
will watch the TV
or play with little toys/
we brought over
and left there
When they are little
I see Nonna
enchant them
and bring out
the little clothes pins
for them to line up/
stack and drive about
like cars on the ceramics
She will put
a little carpet down/
so the cold
cannot seep into
their bones/
Nonno will make a ball
out of stockings
wrapped tight
Nonna will get them
a 'bit a luce'
the little bottle/
of apricot or pear
She will toast some bread/

make a mortadella sandwich
with provolone cheese
Another day/
they will have
a beautiful yellow
polo zuppa
with little pasta stelline
a few pieces/
of soft tasty carrot
Whenever they want it?
There is the Nutella
thick chocolate lubrication
between bread
Mamma Mia!
Nonna-food is their
intimate tale/
of gusto and enchantment
spun with hugs and kisses/
only Nonna can give!
"I love you too much"
She will say/
Not quite getting
the English right.
"Thank you Nonna!"/
the kids will say
out of the side of their mouth/
smothered in squeezes
I enter the kitchen/
before it is time
to watch the water boil.
O my geezis!
We are having
the gnocchi
So I volunteer/
to fetch the wine

Piccolo Coro: "The Cantina of Garibaldi's Court"
The steel door of the cantina
opens with a suction sound
I emigrate into/
a new world of smell:
The scent of vino
the scent of fruit

The scent of stained two by fours
smelling vaguely of must/
Small blue barrels
sealed tight/
Their contents
slowly fermenting
in hisses and boils.
If it is too cold/
maybe a heater is going
on the top, wooden shelf/
An old "Bubble Up" Seven-Up opener
hangs against the wall/
if you need it
to drink outside.
The empties are gone
The yellow six-pack of Mio/
white six-pack of Brio
Tells me that the Sicilian man/
in his truck
made the delivery
this morning!
Before me/
at eye level
A full gallon jug/
I don't have to change it
It is misfortune
to change the jugs/
when dinner is ready *(Shrug shoulders, here)*
I am alive/
in the cantina
Pull the plastic tubing out/
let the wine
fill my mouth
O there is nothing like it!
Another quick, guilty pull/
then I fill up the bottle.
It is important to carry it
with one hand
under the base/
It is the way
I have been taught
So I can
teach you.

Maria:
Finally the gnocchi
rise to the surface
Papa sits in his spot
Does not need to be called
The children
take their seats
While I help to serve/
Vagabondo took his time
getting back
from the cantina/
Mamma looks so happy
intent upon her work
Lifts her luscious pasta
with a ladle
to drain the water/
Slides the luscious pieces
into a large shallow bowl
covering its flowered pattern
with a measured determination/
to make sure
there is enough/
She spreads the sauce
in loving circles/
On the top
Steam rises/
Wine is poured
and Mamma protests/
if you pour too much!

Pasqua:
Abasta, Abasta!
Enough, Enough!
You have not
left enough room
to put in the Mio!

Vagabondo:
Ehhh Ehhhh Ehhhhh!
Signora/
you will not die/
from this!

Maria:
O it is a ritual!
to dust the cheese on top/
Nice and dry
the drier the better
Then there is
more taste!
The children sit still
Suddenly alert
when the bowl
is set beside them/
All motion is slowing
Meatballs so large
filled with onion
and basil and oregano/
Sit in a separate bowl
with pork ribs
whose meat
is barely
gripping the bone/
Pane is placed
in the basket
Mamma wipes her hands
on her apron and sits/
Hand to hand
heads bowed
there is a peace
that gives way suddenly
to laughter and smiles
Chin chin!

[*And in the garage, The 'uva per vino' await!*]

Vagabondo:
In the garage
the uva per vino await!
30 cases Carignane
30 cases Muscato
10 cases Alicante
stacked at parade rest
The Alicante/
makes the wine
nice and dark/

not too light
Wasps and more wasps/
buzz and dance
They must be delirious!
singing Volare
like Dino Martinelli/
hopping from kiki to kiki
We go outside now
to new fresh smells
Someone is burning wood!
Garibaldi stacks
his fifty-gallon drums
on cement blocks/
to give the spigots
a little elevation
The insides
are rinsed and wiped clean/
The only medicine
he uses is fresh air!
His systems improve each year/
By now he has the motor
and his crusher
mounted on a frame/
It fits perfectly
over the drum
to catch the grapes
Underneath?
Aluminum flaps/
flare out to guide
the grapes down/
His modification
You must be careful/
not to slit your hand
along the edge!

Garibaldi:
You do it once
and then you learn!

Vagabondo:
Yes, but will
your motor work
this year?

Garibaldi:
Ehhh!
It will work
I fixed it

[*A* **song/speech** *about The Technology. Duelling tales between Garibaldi and Vagabondo. He is becoming literate in listening and tells Garibaldi's stories back to him and wins. The mutual affection continues to grow.*]

Vagabondo:
Technology! Dio!
You Old Guys
Always on the go
You cannot be satisfied
by the Old Ways.
Always have to
—how do I say it—
always have to
improve on the situation!

Garibaldi:
Ha! You think you know
but you
do not know!

Vagabondo:
Ha!
I am smarter
than you look
I am surprised
I have to remind you
that you have
forgotten already
I tell you this
In the Old Days
we used to have
a cement vat·
We dumped the grapes in
And by the way—
they were better then!
Did I tell you
about the blight
in your country

The disease
that destroyed
all the grapes
of the Mezzogiorno?
in the 1920's
Everything was wiped out
We had to start over
Weren't you listening?
Dio Mio!
We would dump the grapes
in the big vat
And all the kids
and everyone
would go in
start pressing them
with their feet
There was a little trough
and a tap
to catch the juice
We did not make this much then
We made more!

Garibaldi:
I remember!

Vagabondo:
And do you know?
The wooden cask
we used to put our wine in
We call it centrali
It is so huge
They used to send
you inside
with a mop
when you were a boy
to clean it.
Must I teach you
everything?
Back then
we made
enough for us
but we had
to sell the rest
in town.

Garibaldi:
You are a Vagabondo!

[*They begin to crush the grapes, load them into the wine press and squeeze to make the juice. The banter is in the opera buffa style, silly some might say. Vagabondo is stained and dirty and feeling proud. Garibaldi starts to whistle as he enters the work-trance. Enchanted, Vagabondo starts to whistle too. Vagabondo sees a Lesson.*]

Vagabondo:
It is a good press
with banded slats/ three feet tall
It stands evenly/
on its cast iron base
You can get them bigger/
or you can
get them smaller
The cogs are well oiled
All the wooden blocks?
are accounted for
This year?
Garibaldi made
a new slat
It stands out like me/
against the dark stained lines
of the old ones/
The metallic ratchet
tooth by tooth
makes a good solid sound/
When you pull
the steel bar
It is/ reliable
The Old Guy
starts to whistle
to himself
He is happy!
It is time
to get into
our work clothes/
He into his
Toronto Transit Commission
overalls and I/
into my father's white

Field Aviation coveralls
Garibaldi look!
In my perfect white/
I am working
without the net!
It is a daring feat/
If you don't get stains
you can be loud
and brag
If you fail?
You must brace yourself
What is/ the matter with you?
Your wife/
she does not have time
to do the laundry
all day!

Garibaldi:
First you have to
take the leaves out/
and throw them
over here
You turn
the motor on here/
to get
the crusher going.
You pick up the grapes
like this/
Put the crate
on your shoulder/
Pull the grapes in
to let them fall/
like this
Make them fall/
into the crusher
Do not put your hands here/
or you will
crush them.

Vagabondo:
Soon/ I have/
the rhythm down
It becomes/
a matter of pride

to do the job/
efficiently
perfectly
in the repetitive cadence
of the hard work
We laugh
at the growing stains
on my white coveralls
I look more and more/
like the well-used slat
It is cool in the garage
Garibaldi checks the tension/
on the fan belt
Inevitably we will pause
and turn off the motor/
Giuseppe or Rocco
will walk by
or some old fellow
from two streets over
I have not met/
They will call out merrily
above the din
to enter the enchanted winery
of the Court on Rita Drive/
Like all Italian men
they will see immediately/
that there is work
to be done!
They will go/
to the job
that needs doing
first.
It is their gift
They are so friendly to me/
Say something in Italian
to Angelo
Look at me/
and then laugh
"Joe/
your wife is going to kill you
for working
with your good clothes on
Aspetta!
Let us do it!

But he won't listen/
they never do
He has quickly shifted/
into his work-face
hoists a crate of grapes/
like it was nothing
He does not/
even get his shirt dirty!
Suddenly, the work is done
The motor is off
The rasp of the crusher stops
and we stand there/
laughing
Magically the door opens/
Presto! There is a beaker of the wine
The correct number of glasses
sit on a tray
and I am thirsty!

Joe and **Rocco:** *(from off stage)*
Buongiorno, Pasqua!
Come va?

Pasqua:
Bene Grazie!
Ehhh!
Why do you work/
in your good clothes?

Joe and **Rocco:** *(from off stage)*
Ehhh!
It is nothing!

Vagabondo:
I work hard/
with My Italians
I drink wine
on early fall days
with crates stacked high/
Their thin lids
tied with twine
in bundles
You will never find/
a better kindling

for your fireplace
After a time
the men leave/
We begin to press
what we have
crushed

Garibaldi:
Observe:
You take
the crushed grapes
from here/
and put them
into the press
When it is full/
you put on this part
and then the blocks
and then the cam/
The iron bar/
goes through here
Every oncewhile/
You give it a good turn
like this/
Now you are ready

Vagabondo:
I notice/
that you give me
all the hard jobs!
You send me/
back with the wasps!
You make me/
lift and pull
this over here/
that over there
You are/ what do we call it?
A supervisor
Why do you do this?

Garibaldi:
It is/
the only way/
to learn!

Vagabondo:
In time—there is no rush—
we are called in
for the caffe and the "S" biscuits
Maybe there will be
some almonds/
As many as you want
Take more/ for me!
Have some frutta
It is always there/
We return
to the garage/
to finish the work
We run the mosto/
through a final pressing
stems and all
Drain that/
into a separate container
to make the vinegar
Some people/
omit this step
It depends/
how you like to make it
The debris/
we cart to the boulevard
Some/
not too much
will go in the compost
Nothing is wasted!
Together/ we tie down
thick sheets of plastic
over each drum
Later?
When I finally
figure out/
what to give him
for the Christmas?
We will carefully cut/
the plastic
attach a new air lock/
in each.
See?
I will tease him

I have improved on your
—how do you say it?—
on your system/ Your sistemi
The Instruction/
not the Education
Makes me smarter/
than you look!

Garibaldi:
Ehh! Maybe

Vagabondo:
Finally, we will be done
We peel off our overalls
I am made to leave mine/
against protests
in the laundry room
I examine my hands/
with a satisfied look
So red, so stained
Wrapped around/
beautiful mortadella-filled bread
the crumbly cheese
and always/
a last glass
of robust red wine/
that I will hoist
and drain in one go/
With my Old Guy
we will stand/
share a wink
and I, Il Vagabondo
and mia famiglia/
will go home
Take your time goin'
but hurry back!
I will teach him to say/
in the Inglese dialect
of his Court.

Vagabondo:
Canto: "An idea of how a thing should go"
The garage door
shrugs open

with a mechanical jerk
He has modified it of course/
To open
with the push
of the button
(It is like that/ with them
but I told you that already/
what is the matter with you?
Weren't you listening?)
If you plant/
a seed upside down
It will eventually/
right itself
If you plant/
that same seed
in the shade/
It will outsmart you
and find its way/
to the sun
If you do something/
a hundred times
there is a point/
where you will stop
tilt your head and say/
How can I make this
easier?
I do not know/
how you say this in Italian
but I have been there/
before, during and after
the question
It is something to watch/
if you find yourself doing it/
you have truly crossed over
into Garibaldi's Court!
I tell you again
First/ you see the problem
Then you must inspect it/
and think about it
This may take/ a day/ maybe two
Then take a day?
to go to the hardware store
to buy the part
If it does not fit?

—there is no rush—
You take it back
(shrug shoulders here)
When you get the right part/
you might glance
over the instructions/
But it is more importante
that you get
the idea in your mind/
of how the thing should go
Once you see how it works/
try the pieces with your hands
to get it working/
In your head
You can install it
If you have to/
chip a little concrete
or chisel out/
a little two by four
The modification/
to make it fit perfectly/
It does not matter
that you are old/
and go up the ladder
by yourself
when no one
is around
Dio, you make me nervous/
but when a job
needs to be done/
you have to do it!

Vagabondo: (with mock contempt)
Ha!
Back in my day/
we did not have
all these—how do you call them?—
these devices/
You had to open
the garage by hand/
with your legs and your back
Now everyone is lazy
You call this ... Progress?

Garibaldi:
You can open it/
next time

[*In the intimacy of hard work, Vagabondo pauses to ask Garibaldi about his childhood. Garibaldi begins a* **canto picalito** *(a small song in dialect) on tending sheep and as they start a new job of braiding green tomatoes to hang and ripen in the cantina, Garibaldi segues into a* **Memory Song** *about the war and a tale about his father being shot and wounded.* **Canto picalito: "When the war passed, we had nothing."**]

Vagabondo:
The day is cold
everything shivers/
the peach tree,
the cantina,
the grey sky
Me!
Quickly we are back inside/
The door clanks down
hits the concrete/
with a practiced clunk
I hear/ the warm-wet sizzling
It is steady/ amplified in series
across six/ fifty-gallon drums
The percussion of fermenting wine
hits your senses/
like no other sound!

Garibaldi:
You have to keep/
the temperature the same
If you leave
the garage door
open too long
the temperature will drop
It will get cold/
the juice will stop boiling
It disrupts the process
We want/ to keep/
the temperature
nice and steady

Vagabondo:
I follow him over
to the first drum
We untie the chord
and lift the edge
so he can show me
how it looks, inside
Curiously/
It has the wet black depth/
of Italian women's eyes
but not so much/
for there is boiling
and pink foam

Garibaldi:
It goes like this/
for a while
and when it is finished/
it will stop

Vagabondo:
I want/
to taste it

Garibaldi:
You can

Vagabondo:
It is/
the only way
to learn!
(turning to sing to the audience of the living opera)
The interior light
in the garage
makes everything gleam
in a sacred twilight
I feel like I am in
Ali Baba's cave
Surrounded by treasure
Hidden from the outside
Garibaldi checks
each fifty-gallon drum
Goes over to the work bench
He whistles quietly

I start whistling too
To see how it feels
He has entered the work-trance
Inviting me in
only when there is an obvious lesson
to be learned
But I see a different lesson
it has to do with peace
and deep within that
the silence of being
entirely who you are
where you are
usefully
Nothing more/ Nothing less
It is a good way/ to live

Vagabondo: *(to Garibaldi)*
Nonno?
What was it like
when you were a kid?

Garibaldi:
Eh?

Vagabondo: *(to the audience of the living opera)*
I repeat the question
He does this sometimes
He gives the impression/
that he has not heard you
and wants you to repeat
but I know he has heard me/
the first time
You see, he is translating
Making the jump/
from Inglese to Italiano to memory
It is why/ I always say
Scuza? Scuza? Scuza?
When I am in the piazza/
in his Hometown
It is a good way/
to buy the time
Ripete per favore also works
when you are in the pinch
and don't have

all the words collected/
of what/ you want/ to say

Garibaldi: (Canto Picalito)
We did not have
much to do
with playing
When I was a kid
There was always
work to do
Right from the time
You were young
Even Carmine
when he was little
and we were on the farm
His job/ was to/ feed the turkeys
When we first got here
Even when we would
go for the walk
He would collect twigs for the fire

Vagabondo:
What were your jobs?

Garibaldi: (Canto Picalito, continued)
When I was a kid
about six-seven years old
I had to look after
the sheep
We did not have too many
About ten
My job was to take the sheep out
To a little piece of land
One day I sat down
and fell asleep
The sheep went
Wherever they wanted to go
They ate a little bit here
a little bit there
They went over to a guy's land
into his corn and into his beans
The way they went in
They destroyed everything with their feet

When they were full
They went back home by themselves
When they got back to the farm
Everybody wondered what had happened
My uncle came out
to see where I was
When he saw the damage
the sheep had done
He thought Oh-oh
there is going to be a lot of trouble
He let me sleep a little longer
So he could walk around and take a look
Then he started to wake me
Nice at first
Angelo, Angelo wake up, he said
Angelo, Angelo wake up
When I was wide awake he said
Where are the sheep?
I started to look around
Oh-Oh I said
They were here a moment ago
But it was more like an hour
My uncle told me
the sheep went back to the farm
So we started walking
He got behind me
He got his belt off
I was wearing short pants
Not like you have now
Mine were different
One had a leg
up to here
and the other leg
was to my knee
All of a sudden
Bang! And I jumped!
Like a sheep
From here to there
I started running
but he was a young man
about seventeen-eighteen
and he caught up to me
Bang! Bang! Bang!

All the way back to the farm
That was the punishment I got
Next morning my legs were black and blue

Vagabondo:
You can tell/
when he is back home
It is subtle/
but you can tell
With the men/
It is not so much the eyes
But the movements/
around the eyes/ over the brow
or maybe/ something in the cheeks/
or the way a nose and mouth pick up
when you are squinting through the fog
He moves his head forward/
as if to see back in time
When he does this?
I know he is in/
the full flight of memory
and there are pictures/
in his mind
We move over to the workbench
hard green tomatoes on top
By now he has pulled the plants out
and salvaged as much as he could
before first frost stakes its claim
I see beautiful onions/
a basket of garlic underneath
and smell their earthy aroma
Our job now
is to tie up the green tomatoes
and hang them
in the cantina
When it is time
—there is no rush—
He will use them
for the salad in December
The last joy of summer
to reach his table
I ask the question/
and he begins

Garibaldi: (Canto Picolito)
When the war came
We had to leave the farm
Move away to live
On another piece of land
The Germans came first
Took over our house and farm
My father and I came back
To watch them from the corn
We had nothing to eat
So each morning
we had to sneak back
to try and find something
After a while the Germans let us come
We made them to understand
through signs
That this was our house
They got used to us
and let us come
My father and I in the mornings
I was fourteen-fifteen
After a while
It got dangerous to go
My father told me every time
I hear an airplane/ to lie on the ground
And all of a sudden
Bong! Bong! Bong!
Bombs were falling
I saw a tree get cut in half
When the Germans had to go
they left one or two behind
to guard the back
I forget how you call it in English
One day my father was coming back
A German told him to stop
He started to run
The German guy shot him in the leg
My father was so wounded
He had to stay in bed for two years
Little pieces of bone
Kept coming out of his leg
You see, my father had a long army coat
that he got when he was in Spain

That made the German guy
think he was a soldier
At that time Mussolini
wanted people to go to Ethiopia
But he made a deal with Franco
and my father was sent to Spain
He was there six-seven months
and never got a scratch
Then he came back to the farm
and got shot

[*Garibaldi finishes with his tale of his family setting sail on the USS Constitution and immigrating to Toronto.*]

Vagabondo:
Was it hard/
to come to Canada?
I ask the Old Guy/
keeping my questions short
For he is in full stride now
woven a vine's worth/
of green tomatoes
Measures their weight
Standing with outstretched arm
They gleam/ in the twilight

Garibaldi: (Canto Picolito)
When the war passed
We had nothing
The land was ruined
There was no future
At first I wanted to go to Europe
But we had nobody there
To sponsor us
Adamo went to Argentina
With my sister
and her husband
They wanted me to come there
But Pasqua's brother
was already in Toronto
He agreed to sponsor us
And we came over in March 1957

[*The scene ends with Il Vagabondo dramatically (and with bombast) declaring he was conceived and destined to marry Maria the moment they set foot on North American soil. He cries: "Open Sesame!" and the garage door opens with fanfare and the light clicks off to end the scene in darkness.*]

Vagabondo:
And did you know?
That the very second/
you got off the boat
on this continent/
The very second Pasqua/
stepped off the SS Constitution
onto the docks of New York
On that fateful day/
I was conceived
and destined/
To meet Maria
The rest is/ of course/ now history
Do you not believe me?

Garibaldi:
Yes, I believe you

Vagabondo:
Open Sesame
Look how I make/
the garage door open
It is the magic
Lets go inside the house/
wash up and get warm.

PRIMO
INTERVALLO

*(Il Vagabondo addresses the audience with things that are
importante to know.)*

*The Intermission is meant to be used in new ways.
Il Vagabondo's address is spritely and fun. The recitative ties
everything together with the activity that engaged the audience prior to the opening of the imaginary curtain. This is
really a tongue in cheek "advice-giving" not unlike a standup
comedy—improvisational, and casual, intimate—by an English-speaking guy to a dominant Italian culture or any other
culture. It is advised that the audience of the living opera:*

1. **Know where to buy veal, chicken, cold cuts
   and cheese in the Court of Garibaldi using
   the technique of "Paesano-by-Association"
   (Go with your mother-in-law to buy the veals)**
2. **A treatise on Veal Wars with Vagabondo's
   Italian friends**
3. **The importance of religious calendars at
   Christmas**
4. **Learn to play Scopa and Learn to play Bocci
   at Wasaga Beach**
5. **How to buy presents for Old Italian Guys …
   with praise and homage to the Italian
   Canadian writers: Zucchi, Gabori, Iacovetta,
   Paci and others …**

*(Stage Notes: The young and old participants in the living
opera are invited to play Hi Lo Chik-a-low during the intermission or any other hand-game they know. An imaginary
demonstration will take place on stage before the light dark-
ens and the curtain comes down. Imaginary Volunteers are
standing by in the lobby to play and continue teaching the
hand clapping game.)*

Vagabondo: *(to imaginary musical accompaniment, the accordion, the saxophone)*
Eh! It depends how
you like to understand it
but there are a few things
I must tell you
We get our veal's on Eddystone
and our chicken at the Jane and Sheppard
Go before 5 pm
if you expect to get
the roasted potatoes
If you go after
you will be crushed
There is no use
But if you go before 5
ring the bell
The woman will come
out from the back
You will want
two containers of roast potatoes
in oil with rosemary
Look happy when they
are preparing it for you
They will put
so many potatoes in
It will be hard
to get the cardboard lids on
I tell you this!
Do not buy your bread there
Buy the sausage and the pizza
Now go to the meat counter
and the dairy section
at the back
You are used to
the bologna, the cooked ham
In those convenient
vacuum packages
So live it up!
Try the exotic cold cuts
and learn how to say them
Capicollo, Mortadella, Genoa salami
(picante, per favore),
the Calabrese salami
So hard and flat

like a dog biscuit
sliced thin
By now?
If you have not had prosciutto
you are a fool!
Ask to see it first
Nod like you know
it is a good one
Ask them to trim the fat
They slice it thin
so buy lots
Trust me on this
I cannot tell you
how many times
I came out
thinking I had the feast
On the way back
You can go to the bakery
to buy the bread
It is not too busy
and they will
cut it for you
Check to see if they have
Rastrelli olive oil
but they won't have it
Nobody does
After that?
Maybe once every six-seven weeks
Go to the Eddystone
back to the hot table
It does not matter when
Somebody is always there
If you can go
go with your mother-in-law
They will see you with her
And know immediately
you are Inglese
However it will be a case of
—how do we say it?—
a case of:
the paesano-by-the-association
Later when you go on your own
You won't have to say
three times

that you don't want
your veal on a bun!
You are coming out of there
with eight veal's
Get a small container
of the mushrooms in oil
(uno piccolo fungi
ripete like me:
uno piccolo fungi, Bravo!)
For the rest
you are on your own
Go to the back
and get the buns
They tell you
to use the tongs
Do not use the tongs
They cannot tell you
if the buns are fresh
Just do not hesitate
Pick them up
like you know
what you are doing!
Look like you are ready
to yell back
If anybody says anything
They will leave you alone
The buns are good
but it depends on how you like them
If you eat the veal to much
They will lose their enchantment
Like the meatloaf
Eat them immediately
when you get home
Like I say
once every four-five weeks
I am hungry
Just telling you
Try to get
some homemade red wine
and pear juice for the kids
You are now fully prepared
for the veal wars
with your friends at work
who may be Italian

O my geezis
They think they know
but they do not know
It will get heated
Everyone thinks
their veal joint is the best
If you want to win
mention the calendars
They are exquisite
Not the ones
with the girls on them
or the cars
The religious ones
and get one
for Nonna and Nonno
Gitto di Bondone
the Resurrection of Lazarus
Caravaggio
the rest on the flight
to Egypt
Now you will have names
for the peppers you skin
so skilfully in September!
It is a gift
Abbe pacienza
Learn scopa quickly
when you are indoors
and bocci
when you are outside
Bocci you can play anywhere
especially between the trees
at the Wasaga Beach
After, when you are tired
there is no rush—
feast on lasagna
or penne rigate
Oil, vinegar and salt insalata
prepared al fresco
with as much watermelon or cantaloupe
that you can eat!
Try to play bocci
with an old set
of rust-red and black balls
and a white ballino

Dio, the plastic ones
are tourist class
Scopa is easier to learn
than Briscola
Observe:
Three cards, four in the middle
goes to eleven
Once you know, you know
Because you are enchanted
You can go anywhere
with your deck!
If you are lucky enough
to be invited
to the club
Be prepared to lose
a lot of quarters
The old guys are very good
They are so good
they will invite you back to play!
This is good
because when you see them
at the feast
give them the hard time
You must get to the festa
There is so much food there!
Too much food
Try the fish
There are many kinds
Thankfully you are not
at the wedding
There is no sweet table
at midnight
You will have no room, anyway
Brandy goes good
with tartuffo.
I have kept you too long!
you are all so patient
Now go and have some fun
Have a rest
The lights will call you back
*(after 20 minutes the imaginary lights flash) (on stage, blue
    demons, in gossamer, dance languidly)*
Ah si! Welcome back!
Did you get the chance

to play Hi-Lo-Chicka-lo?
I can see
that it is time
to come back
and take our places
in the tales of gusto and enchantment
I am rushing now
I have taught you
everything I know
to get around
in the New World
I will tell you one more thing
What you do at Christmas
Do not go to the hardware store
What are you—a testa dura?
Every tool you will ever need
is in the garage, Remember?
Go to every used book store
you can find
Go to the Italian Canadian section
Try not to get
the ones the modern guys write
with the sex in them
The Old Guys
will not wish to read it
They like stories
about the immigration:
Zucchi, Gabori, Iacovetta
They are so beautifully written
Highlights during winter months
in Garibaldi's Court
when there is nothing to do
and you cannot
work in the garden
There are things
Italian men absolutely don't need
Which is why
they won't have them
You are
smarter than you look!

(Vagabondo exits)

ACT IV

ACT IV: Scene 1

La via Rita. Song of the Street
(The young guy and the old guy pass time
and survey the neighbourhood.)

The Players:

The Young Guy—Il Vagabondo
The Old Guy—Garibaldi
Maria—off stage, end
Piccolo Coro (Small Chorus)

[*The scene returns to the clean cement 'hem' of the driveway*
in the Court of Garibaldi. The action is simply a walk around
the block, the "enchanted passegiata" and the acute beholding
and observations of the song of the (Italian) street.]

Piccolo Coro (Small Chorus):
It is such a curious thing!
Time performs differently
on Rita Drive
It is first thing in the morning
Midafternoon—
early evening before supper
or after supper
when the light is softening
It could be any Saturday
It could be any Sunday
Maybe even a weekday
in the summer
It is cool and moist in the shade
or the sun is beating strongly
pulsating bright white
off the cement
It is just like the Hometown
The street lights wink
and then they come on
People are going to church
or people are getting married
They are dying
They are going to the store
They are walking up
or walking down
This side or that
You can feel the threat of frost
Or the promise of spring
in the air
Our part of the stage
is just past the bend
same side as the Church
six doors down
We see a procession!
Middle aged men proudly hoist
a Saint upon their shoulders
The sacred figure
rocks back and forth
The people move like flowing wine
fluidly and in colour
Their performance is enchanting
Encore! Encore!

[*Vagabondo reflects out loud, to himself and to Garibaldi, the tale of his wedding reception. Memories conjoin and they begin to "talk stories."*]

Vagabondo: *(a long call and response duet with Garibaldi, sung interspersed with solos)*
I look left/ and see
Alleluia
I am inside St. Jane Francis Church
This split second/
it is eleven o'clock
I am getting married!
Lamb of God
you take away
the sins of the world
Have Mercy—on me
There are/ forty or so
Inglese on this side
and thousands of Italians/
on that side
The bridesmaids/ have walked
with Maria, six doors down
to the church
People stand/ in their own garages
on their own balconies/
to wave and to clap
Lamb of God
you take away
the sins of the world
Have mercy—on me
Ti amo amore
There is an aisle
We walk as one down it
loved in chorus/
this side and that
The doors burst open/
like petals on a flower
We are outside/
under a blue sky
Everyone spills out/
behind us
into the sun
Lamb of God
you take away

the sins of the world
Grant us/ peace!
Cars start their slow shuffle/
out of the lot
We sidestep them/
make our way
six doors up
to the threshold
of Garibaldi's home
This memory/
is given to me
every time I stand here
An eternal bonbonniere/
from the neighbourhood

"Auguri" *(a chorus, from offstage)*
"Grazie, prego!"
Garibaldi?
Do you remember/
all the old guys
looking at you
in our reception line?
To see/ if you and Pasqua
were happy?
I think once they knew/
you were Okay
then I was Okay too/
Don't you agree?

Garibaldi:
You are right/ on that!

Vagabondo:
The sweet table/
was too much though.
Do you remember?
It is before midnight
I send word to Rizzo's people
not to make the fuss
out of the mammoth table
tiered with sweets/
I sense that they
are going to turn it into
a spectacle!

Music plays/
the night sings triumphantly!
Suddenly a microphone cuts in
Our eyes are directed loudly/
to the bella tavola
I look to see/
who else is getting married
only to wonder why
we are applauding
the food!
I don't know/ how you say it
in Italiano—a molto extravaganza
In English it is ...
too much of a muchness!

Garibaldi:
You will not die/
from this

[*The two of them are "passing time." In a languid observation, Vagabondo enters into a singspiel about the street looking like a tidal pool and the gridlock after church if you go the wrong way.*]

Vagabondo:
When it is time for the Church/
you should sell
parking spaces!
Each Sunday Rita Drive
becomes a tidal pool
Cars sweep in/
Doors slam shut
some walk stately/
others running lately
struggle through
the undertow of time
Coats go on quickly/
Dresses are adjusted
at the hips
The children are led/
like sheep
while the young people/
aspire proudly
to a grown-up world

Always, the self-conscious teenagers/
obedient enough to attend
but on their own terms
In jeans
gold chains
and track suits
It is lecito
—how do you say it—
It is/ permissible
In an hour
the tide goes out
I watch the procession/
the good navigators
and the ones/
who get it wrong
time after time
I tell you this!
Never turn right/
and go up passed the house
You will be trapped/
in the gridlock
of purgatory
Sunday after Sunday
motions speeds up/
and for some reason
probably lunch
everyone is vaguely late
and slightly put-out/
You can see people/
already starting the list
for confession
The holy water
still wet/
upon their fingers
Their snarling faces
The husbands
in frothy pantomime/
Behind the windshield
Their wives/
looking cold and bitchy
Silently proud/
of their men
goddammit!
"You are right/

to live so close
and be able to walk
to the Church"

Garibaldi:
I think that is true!

[*They enter into an enchanted trance. Garibaldi tells the story of his first house and how they eventually arrived on the street.*]

Vagabondo:
It is a beautiful thing
to stand here next to
my old Italian guy
His street is before us
It goes up/
and it goes down
And I never know why
It is time/
to wonder with him
again

Garibaldi:
When we came here
There was not much
north of the Finch/
First we lived in Montrose
in a single room
rented by Zio John
He bought some furniture
a bed
and sent for us
from Italy/
Then we lived on Blackthorn
with Zio John
Joe and Pina/
Domenico and Rosina
lived beside us
Finally we got
our own house/
on the Hope Street
We had somebody/
stay with us

The lady who cleaned
the Church/
to help us
with the mortgage
We worked hard/
And when the house
was ours
We were happy
We knew that people/
were going to Jane-Sheppard
So we decided/
to go too
when houses
were being built
That/ was in 1973!

[*Garibaldi takes Vagabondo on the Divine Passegiata. The recitative duet includes a series of iconic, cultural observations. (There is a call and response to the audience of the living opera)*]

Vagabondo: *(to the audience of the living opera)*
The key to talking
to the old guys/
is to learn
to keep up to them!
On the one hand/
they walk so slowly
On the other hand/
they cover decades of memory
in leaps and bounds
Try going around/
the block with them
at 7 pm on a lazy night/
when the light softens
it is getting cool/
and not yet dark
It is the only time
in your life/
when you will
put your hands
behind your back
to rock slowly
from side to side/

When you stroll
There is no rush!
Dio! It is unbelievable!
It is a—how do they say it?—
a passegiata!
Say it slowly/
Pas-seg-i-a-ta!
Such a beautiful word
Say it like me! *(call and response to the audience)*
Pas-seg-i-a-ta!
Pas-seg-i-a-ta!
See?
You are passing time too!
Bravo!
When you make
two right hand turns/
you are on
a new side
of the block
There is another/
row of houses
in the Court
of Garibaldi!

Garibaldi:
Take your time/
Wrought iron railings
Curl up magnificently
around perfectly poured
concrete steps
rising up, to balconies/
Notice how clean
the balconies look
They are like the mirror
to the one attached
to the next house
Planter after planter
of green leaves
or red geraniums
Pots cascade down steps
big ones
small ones
ceramic bears
plastic lions

The lawn is small, yes
but observe:
They all have
trees to make the fruit
Blessed by a statue
of the Holy Virgin
All rocks are painted white
Flowers border everything
There may be a stand
of the mulberry trees
or the ones with
the serrated leaves
I forget how you call them
You will notice
them immediately
in the spring or fall
Because they
have been
Italian pruned
denuded so drastically
you will marvel
that they did not die!
Cut them short
They will not die

Vagabondo:
I don't know
how they know
but they know
I tell you this!
It is one
of the mysteries/
in Garibaldi's Court
it runs/
through the blood
like the sap!
Our neighbours
stand around
while Maria and her father
prune our trees
You should see them
the disbelieving rabble
looking at one another/
nodding their heads

like they know/
but they do not know
Some of the wittier ones/
bring nursery fliers around
with the prices/
of the spruce
the maple
and the mulberry
circled and underlined
in red!
I collect the glasses/
when it is time to go in
A week later/
they beep their horns
and taunt
"Vagabondo Vagabondo/
did your trees/
die yet?"
Spring comes so nice
—there is no rush—
First green buds/
push off their husks
shoots come out/
then green branches and leaves/
and we stick out
our tongues
Ha Ha! I say/
These pruners are legendary
and next year/
the neighbours politely ask
"Vagabondo/
When is he/
coming up again?"

Garibaldi:
The side yards
have a row
of more fruit trees
Onions grow somewhere
along the edge

Vagabondo:
Always, you are able/
to make out two flags

Take bets
More often than not/
The Canadian flag
she flies on top/
The green white and red one
she flies so proudly
just underneath
Trust me on this/
and you will win
most of the time/
in North York
They know where they live
They know who they are
and they know/
where they come from
It is the sacred trinity/
of the second wave
And I sometimes wonder/
If their children
understand it!

Garibaldi:
If the garage is open
someone will be inside
You nod and it is good to know
how to say
buonasera, signore or
buonasera signora
If you cannot say it
Just nod and they will too
You see the same things
but different
as I have at home
The fifty-gallon drum
is black instead of blue
The white ones
had the vegetable oil
Depending on the season
You see the sauce machine
a bigger or smaller wine press
different pots and pans
colanders and sieves
Remember when I tell you
Everyone does it

their own way
It depends on how
you like to see
the thing done!

Vagabondo:
Canto Picolito: "Making a life"
White haired women/
shell beans
Small hard looking men/
braid garlic
If you are lucky/
and the sky
begins to paint itself/
variegated red over wisps
of dark clouds
You can see/
the husbands and the wives
putting the garden to bed/
together.
It is probably/
the most sensuous scene
I have ever seen
Not sensuous/
the way the modern guys write
Sensuousness/
slightly out of view
swaying to the rhythm
of tasks to be done
In the proximity/
that love creates
and gives away/
so freely!
It is called/
Making a Life!
And when you see it/
nothing else matters
and You
will want/
to make a life too!
A hose is coiled up/
garden tools collected
A pail is carried/
to the back

While a rake is placed/
in a yard barn
Sheets come off the line/
Dried flower heads
pinched off
It is breathtaking!
Like flames/
on a Castropignano hillside
you see/
scores of fields like this
patched side by side/
stitched gently
by enchanted streets

Garibaldi:
Slowly, you keep going
rocking this way and that
There is no need to talk
only to be
or to see
or to listen
or to watch
Children play in the field
beside the Church
behind the school
Splashes of blue
yellow and orange
Chase black and white
checkered balls
The priest's garden
now in shadow
Is growing robustly
Someone like me
swings by each morning
to grow it

Vagabondo:
Turn the corner
It is not like it was then
Past the garbage dumpster
the orange pizza shop
The glitter and litter of cars
Neon blink of signs
Begin to open and close off/

the enchantment
Garibaldi pays no heed
Takes the same thoughtful gait
Around the gentle crescent
Past the aluminum cross
A silver blessing
on the urban life
To return to the driveway
And la casa di Garibaldi
Cosi sia.

[*Vagabondo realizes the conversation is not unlike being invited to walk out to one of the pieces of land in the old country.*]

Vagabondo:
When you learn to walk slowly/
to keep up with the old guys
You realize how quickly/
they tell their tales
of Gusto and Enchantment!
Rich, ripe stories/
span decades of time
in a moment
Slow down your mind
—there is no rush—
Be with them
Listen/
Listen again
Each image/
Each word is a gateway
to a new place
With a little practice
you will soon be able/
to speak their stories
back to them/
in the dialect of love
They will comprendi!
It is not unlike
being invited to walk out
to one of their
pieces of land!
They want you to come/
but be careful

It is not always easy
Go when you
are not tired
For their ground is uneven/
and the distance tedious
When you finally arrive/
and old guys take you
into one of their fields/
to pick the corn
to cut the hay
to watch the sheep
You will work hard/
harder than you thought
for they have/
opinions.

[*Garibaldi and Vagabondo have an argument about parent-ing. Vagabondo is harsh with the old man. A recitative on "hand dialect" and slapping your palm down on a table. A translation of what love is in the enchanted place. Some re-alities of the hardness of Italian life and living; themes of anger, of hatred, of domestic violence, the old, nervous women. The two are stirred up but soon the wind is out of their sails.*]

Garibaldi:
You are making
the children nervous
He has to learn
from his mistakes
If he falls
then he will know
La planta si deve
piegare quand'e tenera
che quando s'indurisce
si rompe e no si piega

Vagabondo:
What does that mean?
Is it another
foolish lesson?

Garibaldi:
We say
the plant you have to bend

when it is tender
because when it gets hard
it will break
but it won't bend

Vagabondo:
O my Geezis!

Garibaldi:
The children of today
are not respectful
If I talked to my father
in that way
I would be hit
Bong, Bong, Bong!
Again and again and again

Vagabondo: *(to the audience of the living opera)*
I admit/
there are one-two times
when I forget my place/
in Garibaldi's Court
There is no gusto/
in rancour
There is no enchantment/
to anger
There are times/
when old men
must listen to
young men
There are times/
when young men
must listen to
old men
It is usually/
the same time
The women/
do not like to see the men
get this nervous
They will pat them/
on the shoulder
make Choo sounds
Abbi pazienza
Abbi pazienza

Enough
Have patience

(addressing Garibaldi)

Garibaldi
What are you
a testa dura?
You make me nervous
Since I have known you/
you have not once said:
"You are a good father/
You are a good man"
Never not once!
But/ As I smack my hand
You are so quick
to correct me
and give me the Lezione!
All this buh bee buh bee buh bee
All this
I don't know if I like you/
I don't know if I don't like you
It is nothing to me/
Do you finally know today?
Did you know yesterday?
Why did you not/
tell me then?
Did you forget?

Vagabondo: *(smacks his hand on the table and turns to the audience)*
I must teach you/
something now
in the dialect of hands
Smacking the table/
with your palm
Is different/
from smacking the table
with your fist!
When you smack the table/
with your fist
to make your point
It usually/
springs back up!

Usually, not always/
the fist shakes
the index finger/
he points for emphasis
suspended firmly
in midair
This means/
that you are in control
still capable of listening
But I tell you this!
When you smack the table/
with open palm
this means you are exasperated/
Dio Mio
The conversation is over!
Ended, finita!
This is followed by/
a sitting back action
A signal that both parties/
or one of you will stand up
and walk out
I don't know/
how you say this in English
Everyone does it/
their own way

Vagabondo: *(to Garibaldi)*
The way I see it/
your father treated
you kids like animals
Probably gentler with/
Rosie the Mule
than he was/
with you and your sisters!
Have you ever thought/
about that?
When are you/
going to tell me
when I do/
something right?

Garibaldi:
Okay, Okay, Okay!

Vagabondo: *(to the audience)*
He holds out both hands/
over the table
as a gesture/
as a sign of peace
I am sure
if I sit closer/
he will grasp my hands
and hold on to them
It is the way
it is with Garibaldi/
It is the way it was
with my father
Time creates distance/
between ages
For a time
the translation of experience/
is lost
I see them weep
I see them explode
I see their humility/
when they adore jesu
I see them be silly/
and tease their women
I see them kiss
I feel rough hands/
pull my neck down
and scratchy beards/
against my cheek
Between the young and the old/
there are dialects of love
that are different
from one region to another
You can still be in Italy/
and not understand
the guy next to you
No comprendi!
Sometimes
even love
must be translated/
in the enchanted place
I think I can comprehend it
It is there/
slightly out of view/

unspoken
It looks like
a blessing on our marriage
a silent judge of character
a patriarch's leap of faith
into God's will/
All the food
I could ever eat
Money if I need it/
anything and everything,
forever, Amen
It is that simple
—how do they say it?—
In their building?
The Ministry of Presence?
Put away your
Mondolori Pocket Dictionary
your Berlitz Self-Teacher
your Collins Gem
your ES Teaching Cassettes
The SeeItSayIt in Italian book/
that you keep
in your car
with the CD for Dummies/
You have to listen
to find common ground
It is always there
Sometimes?
there are no words
If you put your palms down
and walk away/
You are a fool
Be smarter/
than I look!

Canto: "Vagabondo's Lament"
There is
any combination
of struggle
lying under
variegated shades
of anger
I have seen/
Italians hate Italians

On via Rita I heard/
that an Italian woman
is slapped/
on the side of her head
like the dog
The women know about it/
and then men drink wine
slap your back and laugh/
like your best friend!
These are my friends
Sometimes they hurt themselves
Sometimes they hurt each other
I hate it
Morte!
Italians dead to other Italians
Old nervous women
who make the problem/
anytime and anywhere
They are not right
They screech/
and all of it, for what?
For nothing
I too/
have screeched in the court
Pulled my Inglese sword/
to defend mine in-laws
from the spirited onslaught/
of smug eaters-of-cake!
En garde!
And like I say/
keep your palms up!
When you learn to speak/
the dialect of love
Are we not all
paesani?
I do not know/
how you say it
in English or Italian
but I tell you this
It is the one thing/
that I do know

(to the audience of the living opera)

The wind/
is out of our sails
like it should be.
By now
we are working too hard/
I have made
you all too nervous/
It is time to quit
Walk back/
from the fields

Garibaldi:
It is not
that I think
that you are
a bad father
No. You are
a good father
I don't tell you that/
because my father
never said that
to me/
I am not
used to it

Vagabondo:
You know
that I respect you/
and that I love you
Garibaldi

Garibaldi:
I know that

Vagabondo:
But you know
I will really be sure
that you love me/
if you let me take
a big bottle of wine
from the cantina/
Not the little picalito ones!
Io sono Vagabondo!
Grande vino

non piccolo vino
Dio No No!
(I say shrugging/
tilting my head
my hands out/
palms up
for effect)

Garibaldi:
I am out of wine ...

[*Garibaldi* sings his **aria ("When we need help, we ask for it")** *A tale of how early in his marriage, he was hospitalized and the family suffered. Pasqua rose to the occasion and travelled for hours on the bus to visit. She declined offers of help and quietly went herself.*]

Garibaldi:
A few years
After we arrived
I got sick
It was the pneumonia
They say
one of my lungs collapsed
For thirteen long months
I was in the ospedale
The hospital—in bed
My wife
would come and see me
with the kids
There was no one
to look after them
where we lived, then
I was not working
We had no money
Nothing but the welfare
When I got out
they gave me a huge jar
of the pills
I started taking them
But after a while
I say; to heck with it!
I got better myself
We did not have

all that medicine in Italy
Back then my wife
took the bus
like it was nothing
The bus driver helped her
The cleaning lady down there
was a paesana
She suffered but it is the way it is
We do not complain
When we need help, we ask for it

[*The scene closes with Vagabondo saying farewell. He is plied with wine bottles and pasta and bread and zucchinis. He arrives home and expresses his contentedness to Maria who is heard off stage.*]

Vagabondo:
The sun has come and gone
We can see the glowing interiors/
of cars driving by
It is mostly/
just shadows now
The yard barn is shut
The gate clangs
and the latch is down
I trip the switch/
inside the garage
Hesitate for effect/
and dive out of the way
As garage door
lumbers down/
with a shuddering thump
Technology/
I sneer!
I am in the car now/
Wedged behind me
An old whiskey bottle/
filled to the brim
with thick red wine/
A white grocery bag
with a glass dish
of penne rigate
sits on the floor
Held tight/

by rubber bands
Next to it/
another bag
filled with the bread
Another day?
Perhaps it will be a zucchini
or a clean balsa basket
of the tomatoes
Maybe even a clear plastic bag
of salad leaves/
atop a tray of figs
We are between tides tonight
It is not Sunday/
so I go north
Sweep by Rocco's place/
three doors up
I see him in the shadow
He watches me pull out
So does Joe
Four doors up/
On the same side
as Garibaldi
I beep and wave/
now left and now right
The three of us laugh
and soon/
I am home!

(to Maria, off stage)

I had/
a wonderful day
today

Maria:
You always do
Now what did Mamma/
send back with you?

ACT IV: Scene 2

Lament: Come back, Come Back to Rita
(The street is changing.)

The Players:

Vagabondo
Garibaldi (off stage)
Maria (off stage)
A Priest (off stage)

(Stage note: The action takes place on the veranda, over-looking the driveway and the street.)

[*Il Vagabondo opens the scene with an address to the audience of the living opera having to do with the first Italian couple to emigrate from the street.*]

Vagabondo:
Franca and Luciano
were the first to leave
our street for Woodbridge
Rita was a branch then/
on a tall tree
When the two of them left/
it was like a hawk pushing off
I felt the branch dip low/
the leaves around it shiver
The branch sprang back
wobbling slightly/
in a rhythmic return to its place
Quietly it changed tempo/
to join the gentle sway
of a spring breeze
It was a motion
that was somehow different
Different/
from the ancient Madonna's
creeping towards church
Different/
from the sons and daughters
coming by for lunch on Sunday/
Their sleek new cars
pulling into clean driveways
The young bald men/
letting themselves go
Their wives ever so slightly/
past bloom
The little ones spilling/
out of back doors slamming
Different/
from dark skinned sinewy Orlando/
In his sleeveless white tee shirt
ridding his truck
of bags of cement
rebar
and a wheelbarrow for the garage
Different/
from the expectation
of peach blossoms
We touch their twigs/
inspect their buds

and anticipate their annual promise
And in a moment/
a stutter
The misstep releases/
the vague premonition of unease
I feel it.
We all do.

[*He asks* Garibaldi *why everyone is leaving.* Garibaldi *replies but the voice is off stage.*]

Vagabondo:
Why is everyone going/
up to Woodbridge?

Garibaldi:
They are young
the houses are nice
they are going
to make a life

Vagabondo:
I wonder
who is going/
to move in?

[*In opera buffa style,* Vagabondo *launches into a recitative speech concerning aspects of Italian micro-culture: the hardiness of tomato seedlings, turning empty wine crates into furniture, the myriad uses of the vin bon pail.*]

Vagabondo:
Garibaldi has gone/
to his makeshift greenhouse
to check his tomato seedlings
At the end of every May
I am in gracious receipt
of Styrofoam flats
of tomato plants
for the garden
Started in the garage/
moved to the furnace room
transplanted to the greenhouse/
where the sun is warm

planted after the last frost
They are robust
like the people who grow them/
with sturdy firm stems
and good leaves
Plopped in rich, black earth
you can jockey them around
to fit in the trunk
If a wine bottle/
rolls into them
they are tough
the stems won't break
If there is no Styrofoam/
a couple of empty wine crates
lined with green garbage bags
will do.
Remember what I said?
You can also use/
the wine crate for kindling
or if you want to/
turn it on its edge
you will see
it makes a fine table
for the garden
Dio Mio!
We are still/
finding uses for them
It is the same/
with the purple vin bon
twenty-litre pails/
I will tell you the segreto
Listen closely to me
The Italian, twenty-litre pail/
purple (you can get them in white)
is the Inglese duct tape!
It is so true!
Observe:
You can tell who is Italian/
or who is related to an Italian
or who is a friend
of someone related to an Italian
by the sheer number/
of purple pails on their property
For instance/

if they are old friends
the pails will be faded
New ones will appear/
in the fall
If they are new friends
they will only say/
they need one or two
Once they become comfortable/
it will not be unusual
to see ten or more pails/
on their property
I myself/
must have fifty
I never count
Some of them/
are very old
and cut and scraped
Use them/
to collect the weeds
and the grass clippings
But do not stop there!
Leave some in your garage/
You can now wash the car!
Watch out/
for the new construction guys
They could care less
They will go into your garage/
grab a pail or two
to mix the grout
or stir the paint
Why should you mind?
You have so many
They will be careful/
to leave the dirty ones behind
It is not unusual/
to see a new one
in their truck
filled with tools
Why not?
They know
if you have sixty/
you can get more
It is the way/
that things are done

If you camp/
you will need at least four
Presto!
They are end tables/
they are water proof
they are step ladders
Not even the raccoon/
can open them
When your children are little/
they will use them
as drums
Not snare drums/
the entire kit!
Philharmonic orchestra grade drums
They are professionals/
after all/ and so are you
Save the white lids
You can never have too many
They have a rubber seal
Once they snap on/
Nothing can get in or out
The stack very nicely/
and high
But I must warn you
If you do not find/
the little white arrow
on the lids
Slowly open them methodically/
like the face of a clock
You will skin your hand/
pull back a nail
and say the bad words
It is guaranteed and useless/
to try to pry them off
Trust me on this.

[*The door to the cantina opens; side stage and* Maria *can be heard shouting out orders to pour more vinegar for the salad bottle.* Vagabondo, *in a fit of curiosity, asks his wife why everyone is moving to Woodbridge.*

Vagabondo:
Buongiorno Maria!

Maria:
Mamma needs you
to go inside
and pour more vinegar
for the salad bottle

Vagabondo:
How come/
everybody is moving
to the Woodibridgi?

Maria:
Because they are rich

[*The Church is changing next.* Vagabondo *singspiels his admiration for the Priest who marries him and Maria. Segue to a different priest, during the time of Garibaldi's grief who said he would see the Old Man but forgot.* **Canto: "The priest who married us"**]

Vagabondo:
The priest who married us/
is going to another parish
We used to make a point/
of swimming through the current
faithfully exiting the church
To go to Father/
to shake his hand
I can tell/
that he is glad
we are together.
He tolerates that she ...
—how do the modern,
young devout call it?—
She is a holiday Catholic
and I, the Inglese?
Probably a good man/
who believes in Jesu.
We go good together
He can see beyond/
He can tell
that we are
making a life.
I respect that

and because I do
I am not condemned/
to enter his building
I enter it freely/
mostly at Italian mass
and other times
because I want to/
It is part of how we
make a life
in Garibaldi's Court:
It does not matter
that I cannot speak the language
It does not matter
to quibble with ritual
I leave my judgement/
to sing and smell
and feel and believe
A universal libretto/
beyond dialect
spoken by acts/
of love
It depends how you do it
Everyone/
does it their own way!
I suppose/
you could call it
my religion
Still/
the young people
who show up/
Sunday after Sunday
to play in the band/
are growing up
Their hair is shorter/
they are growing plump
New musicians arrive/
to fill the gaps
Suddenly/
all of the regulars are gone
It is our spirits/
that begin to fade first
and then our bodies
Later/ that particular building
will be dead to me/

when I go to the new priest
to ask him
to minister
to Garibaldi
in his grief.
Like the Peter
at Gethsemane
He forgets to!

New Priest: *(voice, off stage)*
Yes, yes yes of course/
I will see him
Yes, yes, I know him
I know who he is

Vagabondo:
Grazie, Padre

[*After the song,* Vagabondo *begins a recitative of for sale signs on two friend's lawns. He notices a tree across the road that is starting to die. There is a singspiel or* **aria** *about how Italian men respond to a dying tree that is iconic to 'Contadini' life or the men of the 'mezzogiorno'.* **Canto: "They grow things. It is what they do."** *(Stage note: sung in a minor key, like a proud lament, like something is fading.)*]

Vagabondo:
One day we see/
a for sale sign
on Rocco's property
Within the week/
another for sale sign
goes up across the road
on Joe's property/
They are going
to new houses
up by Wonderland
A tree across the road
near Pasquale's
starts to die
This is an unusual/
thing to see
amidst men
who are Italian

Canto: They grow things. It is what they do"
I see them
cluster around
a cherry tree
Stake it
Wrap it
Put medicine on it
Bring it back to life
I see them
start new grafts
Gently inspect
their work
in the morning
I see them
pronounce a tree dead
Like checking her pulse
They pull out knives
Skin a little bark
to see if there
is any green underneath
I sense sadness
when all they see
is brown
Quickly, the tree is taken out
a useless thing now
Resolutely they return
from the nursery
within two days
to replace it
The new tree
looks so fragile
Like an immigrant
at the bus stop
It will be tended to
fussed over,
inspected for insects
screened for rabbits
and wrapped for the winter
They grow things
It is what they do.
They grow things
It is who they are
I can see fields
in their eyes

the old hoes
and their bent backs
My Contadini's
sweat leaving
clean trails
on their arms
Donkeys piled with figs
fig tree after fig tree
shaking its fruit
onto the ground
aching to
be picked
Thin-necked jugs of wine
hoisted in the shade
Minds emptied
by tedium
While the pile of corn
that is husked
grows taller/
than the pile of
warm green ones
coming in
from the fields
At night
we will dance
All night
we will dance
If one of these Italians
ever moves next to you
I tell you
you are lucky
Garibaldi's personality
is more present/
in his yard
than in his house
The yard is their living room
And the living room
is a place to go
at Christmas
Their yard
is the al fresco kitchen
an extension
of the one inside
the basement

And if you are
beside them in August
Remember what I told you
About the zucchinis!
They grow things
It is what they do
They grow things
It is who they are

[Il Vagabondo *abruptly stops the song. He begins to lament.*]

Vagabondo: (Lamentation 1)
Pasquale's tree is dead!
It is still
in the ground
The street is dying
It is over
and I probably
knew it
before it happened
Rita is a lament now
I do not see
the sea of bodies
carry the crucifix
up the street
at Easter
Palm fronds
are not fun anymore
We are not coming out
to the sidewalks
on cold September days
to wipe our grape-stained hands
on rags
Fewer people wave now
There are more cars
parked at the curb
and tripled up
in dirty driveways
There is more pizza trash
People change their oil
on the street
Useful things
are thrown out
They sell

Triple X movies
on the corner now
In North York
I have not seen
a Black Madonna
in months
They pick out new trails
to lead them
to the church
The Spanish fellow
does not care
that a case of Carignane
has gone up
by a dollar
But I like
the sound
of his music
Across the street
The Chinese couple
convert their garage
Take the door clean off
Convert the space
into a little factory
Why not?
Everyone
has to make a life!
Did I tell you
Orlando and Maddalena
are gone?
We trade hot peppers
for spring rolls
with the Vietnamese fellow
beside us
He consults with Garibaldi
on the garden
before it dies
The Jamaican house
on the corner
smells good

[*The final sequence begins with an address by* Vagabondo *to
the audience of the living opera. The imaginary blue demons
begin their dance in the dark.*]

Vagabondo: (Lamentation 2)
What can I tell you?
It wasn't always pretty
I know things
that you know
You are smarter
than you look
and so am I
It is la famiglia
Eh? What do you expect?
In our Tales
of Gusto and Enchantment
the demons on the street
come back
So what!
There are demons
on every street
it is why we need the fire
to burn off our stubble

[Garibaldi *can be heard off stage telling a modern-day tale of an old Italian woman going door to door begging for the food but really wanting the money. It is an omen* (**Stage note:** *There is a rumbling of imaginary kettle drums to announce a change in mood.)*]

Garibaldi: *(recitative)*
One day
I was in the house
and the doorbell rang
My wife
she took the bus
and the street car
to St. Clair
She made
a couple of sandwiches
for me
that I like
When I went
to the door
there was an old
Italian woman there
She put her fingers together
and put them

to her mouth
like she needed the food
Ehh Ehhh!
What she really wanted
Was the money
I went to the kitchen
brought her back
one of my sandwiches'
She looked at me
like I was a criminal
She took the sandwich
but when I closed the door
I said: "To heck with you!"
In my Hometown
there was no money
If you were hungry
you asked for food
To get some food
you had to work for it
After that time
she never came to my house
but walked up the street
to go to the other houses

[*As the scene comes to a close,* Vagabondo *is seen on the upstairs balcony, in singspiel, observing* **"The Dance of the Blue Demons."** *The characters are chimera's and represent the reality on a street that is dying now.*]

Vagabondo: (Lamentation 3)
I am standing
on the upstairs
balcony now
My arms are on
the cast iron railings
Pasquale's tree
is directly in front of me
It is cold
and I watch
the demons walk by
They march
through my heart
and I say

goodbye to them
I see
an Italian fellow
who was injured once
He is okay now
He has been
okay for years
He is not working
He does not
want to work
His house is nice
the compensation is good
He is strange
but his wife
is so nice
An old guy
stumbles behind him
They say
he killed himself
I don't know why
There is a pair
of Black Madonnas
They gave me tomatoes once
When I helped them
with their bags of groceries
Behind them
two women
make me nervous
One of them
looks right up at me
Her eyes smoke
wondering the wrong things
They no longer
look like wells
The other is in pain
It drives her
to the distraction
She yells at me
for no reason
Bringing up the rear
is the florid-faced fellow
who drinks too much
Finally,

the happy, stupid guy
who beats his wife
like the dog.

[*The Procession fades into the dark and off stage while blue
demons continue to dance in the shadows.*]

ACT IV: Scene 3

Morte
(The terrible grief.)

The Players:

Il Vagabondo
Pasqua (elevated image, stage-lit)
Garibaldi (elevated image, stage-lit)
Maria (elevated image, stage-lit)
Relatives at a funeral

(Stage note: The action is a dark stage, with Vagabondo, *lit in the spotlight, intimately addressing the audience of the living opera.)*

[Vagabondo *begins a recitative of the family cancer narrative; its onset, how it changed the family.*]

Vagabondo:
How can I tell you this again?
We are one family
It is our turn/
to suffer
Did I tell you it begins
as two tiny lumps?
About a quarter-inch wide/
Maybe a bit bigger
They walk in a little procession
along the inside/
of her clavicle
Paired together like twins
The silver chain of her crucifix
Nestles into the evil valley/
between the two
Yea, though we walk through shadows
Hoping against all hope/
that it is just the unbecoming carbuncles
that old people get
We know it is something more
Garibaldi is not worried yet
Pasqua shrugs her shoulders
Turns to the stove
The water boils
It is time to put the penne in
Wherever her thoughts go
They go deep inside her
I see them fifty feet below
In the pools of her eyes

[*A light comes on at elevation, stage left. Pasqua is standing in the (blue-as in blue demons) light. There is a short duet between Pasqua and Vagabondo. The light goes out.*]

Pasqua:
Panghe, panghe!
Do not make me smack you/
with my spoon

Vagabondo:
Abbi pacienza/
Abbi pacienza

What am I going to do/
with you?

Pasqua:
Ehh/ Do you not see?
There is nothing
for you to do

Vagabondo:
I watch the ribbed penne/
Go around and around
in the pot
Pick one out/
and track it with my eyes
It dances on a hill/
of boiling water
Moves to the side/
slips underneath

[Vagabondo *continues the cancer recitative. He chants quietly,
gently.*]

Vagabondo:
We are all dying now
Garibaldi slowly/
quietly, innocently
Vaguely oblivious/
to the whole thing
Carmine disappears/
into his own world
To die silently/
on his own
He will return the way/
he always does
So practically/
when the business needs doing
accounts to settle
coffins to buy
a paesana to call/
about the flowers
Perhaps the pain is too great/
for the men
They run off/
retreat to a little knoll

Look back to this nativity
to watch and to weep
But a son's stoic soul
Will rise to the occasion
When the occasion
calls hoarsely
Maria is dying
So quietly, so completely
She is as close as she can get
Into the evil valley
Immersed in friendship/
and love towards her mother
Fighting against all hope/
fiercely trying to kill all cells
One by malignant one
Specialista after specialist
One appointment at a time
Until/
there is no time

[*A light comes on at elevation, stage center. There is a short singspiel between* Garibaldi *and* Vagabondo. *Garibaldi tells a Hometown tale about fetching the doctor. The light goes out.*]

Vagabondo:
I cannot stand the dottore
He writes eternal prescriptions/
for pills that are killing her
It is in the papers now
Old women/
should not take
the estrogen pills
forever/
He should have changed
the prescription years ago

Garibaldi:
It is not that

Vagabondo: (*to the audience of the living opera*)
It is years later/
when I finally excavate
his reasoning

Maybe it is a new story
or an old story/
told from the next
piece of land
It depends how you look/
into the tale
Where it is told/
or when it last
got interrupted
Stories are like digs
you get some fragments
you get some pieces
and you lay them out
one by one until/
you unearth a new piece
and put it/
beside the first one

Garibaldi:
In our Hometown
you had to send/
someone for the doctor
There were no phones
like there are now
When he came to your house
You had the hot water
and the towels/
ready for him
He might leave a little medicine
And tell you/
what to do
Back then/
we had no money
to pay him
So if we had a little pig
We would grow it/
to be a big pig
We did not keep/
the prosciutto for ourselves
We gave it to him
At Easter we would give him
A bag of flour/
or some eggs

That is how/
it worked

[*The light returns to* Vagabondo. *He sings about the joy of the last days, the last Christmas of reprieve.*]

Vagabondo:
Canto: "Two more years in the valley"
In the end she has a
—how do I call it?—
a treatment
Another little pill
gives us two more years/
in the valley
We will always be grateful
for our last Christmas
The last time/
we are all together
The last time the cold fresh air/
sweeps in the door
and we stoop down/
to kiss her on both cheeks
I stir the boiling pasta
beside her slowly/
Lift the last lid
of baccala bubbling in the sauce
In the oven/
there is battered cauliflower
I place the bread, the olives, the finocchio/
The nibbling begins
The cantina is cool
and the wine is perfect
I endure the final la tasse
and we rush out to mass
We join the throng
of black leather jackets
fur collars and jeans
gold chains and track suits
The light inside glows
the organist looks so beautiful
the smell of candles and incense
lasts forever
Inevitably, the congregation

starts to cough/
but the stained-glass windows
the lights and flowers on chancel
are breathtaking!
After a Yuletide blessing
the throng sways out
like bells ringing
It is too cold to watch
the cars go the wrong way
We come home to play cards/
eat "S" biscuits and torrone
At midnight we stand vigil
over Jesu with camels and sheep
at the base of the artificial tree
bought in the 60's
We exchange gifts
load sleepy children in cars
and call out Buon Natale/
into the cold, dark night

[*A (blue) light comes on at elevation, stage right. It is* Maria
*calling out to her father, stage-lit, center. She is trying to make
him understand Pasqua is dying.* Garibaldi *looks aged and
is numb in his denial. The light goes out.*]

Vagabondo:
Less than two months later
barely able to walk/
we take her
to the hospital to die
Garibaldi now understands/
what is happening to the life
Already his eyes/
look far away
He tells no stories
no longer shepherd/
He allows events to lead him
Everything must be said
to him twice

Maria:
Daddy I know
you are listening/
Listen to me

Vagabondo:
An insensitive intern
tells us bluntly/
that her kidney is dead
Walks away behind doors
that cowards go through/
when they give up the facts
Maria gathers up Garibaldi
I gather scopa cards
inspect the bella seta/
and curse
We return from the dead house
Who cares when it was?
I have twenty minutes
Alone with My Italian
For me—just for me!
Wise Pasqua
Who knew my eyes
and my soul
Who loved me
for loving her daughter
Ti amo
I touch her cheek
Stroke silver sweet hair
Our eyes share everything
We don't say a word/
but we know
Ti amo

Maria:
Outside relatives gather
Old Madonna Zias/
the brother, the sisters
the cousins, the nipote/
like lambs

[*On the darkened stage, blue lit, Vagabondo sings the final tale of the end of the cancer narrative and the death of Pasqua. The light comes on above him. It is* Maria *speaking to her father.*]

Vagabondo:
Finally, the nativity of death
Presto! Morte!

Later I will wonder/
if they put up a poster
in the Hometown
Garibaldi is ruined
Maria takes her pain/
down deeply into her eyes
It will come up again
—there is no rush—
She holds her father

Maria:
Daddy. Take Mamma's/
silver crucifix
It will/
help you.

[*The light goes out and the stage is bathed in darkness and in silence. There is no dialogue-only activity. The curtain rises and a dim blue light reveals the wall of a mausoleum. It is filled with flowers and relatives. The action focuses on the workman and all that can be heard is the "click-clack, click-clack, click-clack" of the putty gun. The seam is smoothed. The light goes out. Pasqua is entombed. Scores of flowers are left to rot. Vagabondo walks off stage.*]

ACT V

ACT V: Scene 1

Death of a Garden
*(The old guy and the young guy mourn together. Vagabondo
worries that The Depression is winning. Garibaldi resolves
to find someone to take care of him.)*

The Players:

Garibaldi
Vagabondo
Maria
Piccolo Coro (Small Chorus)

*(Stage note: The Action takes place at the downstairs
kitchen table.)*

[Vagabondo, *in recitative, recounts for the audience of the
living opera, the tale of Garibaldi's grief.*]

Vagabondo:
About a month later/
Garibaldi almost burns down
his Court
Lost in his grief/
he places a memorial candle
in a pot of sand
Somehow he falls asleep/
it tips over/ something catches fire/
He extinguishes it
Prophetically, black ash residue/
coats the entire downstairs kitchen
the TV room/ the furnace and laundry room
Everywhere we live/
It is like the shroud
over all the happiest places
in the house
We do what needs to be done/
We clean it. Spotless/
the way She would have done it

Garibaldi:
She was my guide/
and my companion
There is nothing now

Vagabondo:
Over and over/
he says this
Throws his hands/
up in the air with abandon
Claps his hands/
and then shakes them
over his heart
The patriarch has fallen
(to the audience of the living opera)
Nothing holds his interest
The days are hard/
but it is at night
that he suffers
Suffocating/ crushed
by three hands of a clock/
that circle without meaning
The last time/

Mary is down with him
I hear he has been singing
He is singing/
and then he cries
He cries for a tiny moment/
There is a little peace
like the space in time/
before the next wave crashes
Like a piece of driftwood/
I arrive after work
the next day.
Il Vagabondo/
like a son
He never knows/
when he will see me
or where I will wash up/
I have a better chance
of finding some food that way
Otherwise/ he will hide it/
and the wine too.
He lets me in/
but he looks older now
The old joke/
is not so funny
I take off my shoes/
follow his heavy shuffle
into the kitchen
There is dust/
along the edges
of the baseboard
Old spill splotches/
crossing the threshold
They are like/
the slap in the face
She would never/
let the house get this way
A capital offense
A violation/
of the Rule G
To me?
It does not looks so bad
But to Maria
It is a violation/
of how it used to be!

[*Vagabondo's gaze turns to Pasqua's crawlspace and the small chorus recites an "observation" song/speech of its contents.*]

Piccolo Coro:
Underneath the stairs
leading to the top floor/
is a tiny crawl space
with a trap door
First you move the garbage pail
Open the door with a decided pull
and bend down/
to get in
It is easier
if you just give in
and go down on all fours
It is a woman's space
The first thing you see?
Three Raggedy Ann mop heads
slouched on nails/
driven into stair steps
A new slim wooden pole
extra bags of yellow mop heads/
green gloves/ a never-used pail
and jug after jug/ of bleach

Maria:
She is always
stocking up!

Piccolo Coro:
... big boxes of laundry detergent
unopened bars of Sunlight soap
standing at parade rest/
Five orange plastic bottles
of the Ceramica Bella
Do not be fooled/ .
by imitations!

[*Maria sings an **arietta** of her indignation of old ways in a new world—of being made to clean on Saturday mornings, while her brother sleeps in.*]

Maria:
Every Saturday morning
I had to get up early
to help Mamma with the cleaning
Dusting and vacuuming upstairs
laundry to do and to fold
fresh sheets to put on the bed
mopping the downstairs floor
O my Brother was always
in his room sleeping in!
They would not think
to ask him to clean
On Saturday mornings!
An injustice Yes!
But that is the way
that we did it.

[*Vagabondo wonders if a house can be too clean and Garibaldi recites his tale of the dirt floors in the patriarchal home.*]

Vagabondo:
I sometimes wonder/
if it is good to be so clean
or if it isn't, I tell you again:
Stories are like the fragments/
held up to a light
Lezioni are like artifacts
When you see them/
you see them
We are smarter/
than we look!

Garibaldi:
Back then
the house
was not like
we have it now
There were no floors
Nothing like today
There were clay bricks
Maybe one-two chairs
and a big table
by the fire
The fire was where we cooked

where we kept warm
Underneath were the stalls
Where we kept Rosie and the pigs
and the sheep
That was all we had.

Vagabondo and **Maria:** *(picolito canto to the audience of the
    living opera)*
We found the last envelope
with two hundred dollars
in that little crawlspace
down on all four's cleaning
We shifted a bleach bottle
and there it was
After she died
we found envelopes
in the laundry room
in a pot in the back cantina
underneath sheets in the cupboard
on a top shelf/
under a cup
You never know
what life will bring
If you did not work hard
you will suffer more
Waste nothing!
Save everything!
Be prepared!
in case the trouble
comes to you

[Vagabondo *has stopped off after work to be with the Old Man
and distract him from his mourning. He prepares a simple
meal and addresses the audience, directly.* **Canto (duet):
"The Way They Taught Me, Is the Way I Teach You"**]

Vagabondo:
Garibaldi I understand/
why Pasqua/
stocked up
all the time

Garibaldi:
You are learning

Vagabondo:
Did you drink all the wine
or did you pour it down the sink/
When you saw
it was me?
Don't look so smart
Is there any food?

Garibaldi:
You arrived too early
There is still/ some food

Vagabondo:
Canto: "I teach you the way they taught me"
I tell you this
Even when you are sad/
Gusto is in
the simplest of tastes
Do not ask me/
how he makes it
I still cannot/
get it right
On the counter is a bowl/
with some potatoes in oil
Boil the potatoes/
when they are cooked
but still firm/
drain them
and let them cool/
Add some oil
not too much
Rastrelli if you can find it
Colavita will work
Maybe press some garlic/
and mix it all together
Cut up hot pepper rings/
add a tiny bit
of the wine vinegar
Serve immediately/
with crusty bread and
hard sausages
soaked in the oil/
You may wish to open some peas

warm them lightly in oil/
add some onions
It is helpful/
if you are not wearing
your work clothes/
when you eat this
If you are thinking/
Save the oil
from the store-bought sausages
Good for you!
Now/ take the hot red peppers
from the garden
Slice them up/
steep them in oil
It depends/
how you like
to do it./
The more you put in
the longer you let it sit
the hotter it will get/
Dip only the tines
over your fork
into the hot mixture
Repeat three-four times/
if you are crazy!
I teach you/
the way they taught me!

[Vagabondo *knows the old man has been singing to help his sorrow. He brings him a micro tape recorder to record his poems. Later he brings his father in law a simple computer. In a moment of intimacy,* Garibaldi *begins to let go of his grief.*]

Vagabondo:
We hold hands/
across the table
I notice/
that he has not shaved today
We recite the Italian prayer/
say nothing
when our glasses clink
It is obvious who we are toasting/
So I break

the silence
"Maria tells me/
that you are singing now"

Maria: *(offstage)*
I've got an idea for Daddy!

Garibaldi:
Yes

Vagabondo:
Did you know?
You used to sing
all the time
when you were working
in the fields./
(I say, giving him the lezione).
It helped you to pass time/
It made you happy
It was—how do you say it?—la vita opera!
The opera of the life!
Look at him!
(to the audience of the living opera)
He smiles his assent
He loves me (shrug shoulders here)
It does not matter/
that I butcher the language
turn the libretto
into dolce Inglese sausage
Well then/
(to Garibaldi)
I have something for you/
You must take it
Maybe one day/
you will let me
hear you
It is a piece
(to the audience of the living opera)
of the technology/
This man can dismantle
and fix a furnace motor/
design a new piece
for the grape crusher/
pinch of the copper end of a pipe

to get the perfect flow/
of water on tomatoes
But you should definitely
go slow with them/
when explaining
the micro tape recorder:
how it works
how to change the tape
how to talk into it
Naturally/
he catches on
He is like a minstrel
I still hum/
his beautiful grief songs
They are just like/
the Alan Lomax field recordings
of the Abruzzo
Moving in time/
as the sun comes around the back
and you have all/
the red peppers
you can peel

Maria: *(off stage)*
I am worried/
he needs something else
to occupy his mind

Vagabondo:
Garibaldi/
My father in law
You are getting too good
at this technology/
I have something
new for you/
It will simply
amaze you
It is unbelievable!
You will wonder
how it is possible/
that you did not
think of it before/
You will offer me
more wine after I tell you/

Dio Mio! I will
not have to steal it anymore
like a ... like a Vagabondo!
Soon/
there will be food
in this house!
Always ... But ...

Garibaldi:
... a computer! Eh!
What do I need the computer for?
My son-in-law/
At first
I did not know
if I liked you/
Now I know
I do not
like you

Vagabondo:
Trust me on this!
In your stories/
you tell me
you are a peasant/
a farmer, so poor
But this is not true!
You are—how do I express myself
in your language?
It is so difficult—you are—
come si dice?—artistico
Yes/ you are a poet
You sing beautiful songs
It is time
that you write now/
This is your lezione
Abbi pacienza. C'mon!

Thankfully/
(to the audience of the living opera)
Maria has found a machine
that is like the Rambler
he worked on in the 1960's/
You can get underneath
the hood and fix it/

with the long, homemade screwdriver.
when the engine breaks down/
He can re-boot his computer on the back
with this little paper clip!
It is so primitive, I know/
For a minute I am worried
he will take it apart/
to study the thing! Gawd!
This is not for taking apart!
(to Garibaldi, sternly)
It is to write with
It is better
than a typewriter
It will help you/
with your grief
Write stories or songs/
or poems
Whatever you want!
You will never know
when I will arrive
to hear them/
or return
to bring back
my empty wine bottle!
(to the audience, exhaustedly)
Soon, Maria has taught him
how to use the WORD processor:
how to save files
how to print/
His thick Contadini fingers
spring over the keys
like the deer!
We have won
another round
against his depression/
Soon—there is no rush—
his work begins to appear
at the mausoleum/
What we call
her apartmento/
taped to a granite plate
on the wall
We are/
so tired.

[*Unaccompanied by music and like a Hometown Hill song,*
Garibaldi *sings* his **grief poem: "Perdendo La Sposa" da
Angelo Molinaro (reprinted with permission)**]

Garibaldi:
Piangio di giorno
Piangio di note
Piangio di mattina

Piangi di sera
Perche mi trovo
nella dispara

Giacche 'il buon dio
si ha preso la mia consorte,
questa sara'la mia sorte
fino alla mia morte.

It is my solitude
My Depression.

[Vagabondo *realizes that the Old Man's "solitude", his
"Depression" is winning. He reflects on how life is changed.*
Garibaldi *is no longer interested in the Club.* Vagabondo *is
sentimental about "Nonni" time … his children spending
time with Pasqua and Garibaldi when they were little.
Nothing is the same.*]

Vagabondo:
He is not really
going to The Club anymore/
All the men
have to leave by 3 pm/
to pick up their little nipoti
from the school:
Resolutely/ proudly
they get up to go/
Metal chairs slide back
They have a purpose
They are rich men/
It is so obvious
that they are contenti
and in love/
So sweet

to see them wobbling home/
to Nonna
with their little ones
Or patiently waiting
in the park/
For hopping and scooting
little lambs to stop
To race back, giggling
and declare:
He is MY Nonno!
Late afternoon
is Nonni time/
Nonna may be resting
before supper
or maybe she is at the stove
warming up
A little polo zoupa/
with soft orange carrots
and picolito pasta stars/
swimming in it
A little cheese/
sprinkled on the top
Perhaps she is watching
Italian TV:
La Farfalla (The Butterfly)
She is so warm and cozy/
Waiting for the door to open
the quiet transfer/
from Nonno in-the-park-a
to Nonna/
with-a-little-bottle-
of-the-juice
It is The Divine Daycare
of North York.

Pasqua: *(voice off stage, in Italian)*
Nico, Daddy's here
Go to the furnace/
to get your boots
It is time to go home now

Vagabondo:
To my utter amazement/
My son completely

understands/
what she is saying!
I tell you this
it is the magic!

Nico: *(voice off stage)*
Daddy, It is time/
to go home now

Vagabondo:
No. Garibaldi is not really interested
in The Club anymore/
He is no longer interested
in the festas either/
There is no one
to go with him.
I see Old Men
come up and grasp his arms/
They say nothing:
They know
They will look
at one another
and cry a little bit
then they part/
Tender old women
will bring him
a little pasta
or a little sauce
some sausages and lasagna/
He will try a little
but most of it will sit starkly
foreign-looking, out of place/
Like borders sleeping
in an empty fridge
It will be offered to me
or thrown out
It does not matter/
Like everything else?
There is no heart and soul
in the downstairs kitchen anymore/
That living stage
is just a place now
to sit and listen

to bulbs hum or clock's tick/
There is really
nothing to do:
but drink wine
sleep forever on your arm
let the candle burn down
wake up suddenly
fall and bang your head.

[*A telephone call comes from a hospital.* Garibaldi *has fallen.*
Maria *and* Vagabondo *begin to think of the Retirement Home.
A Cleaning lady is retained twice a week. A nurse comes peri-
odically to visit. It is not enough.*]

Vagabondo:
The telephone rings at night
He has hit his head again
This time/
he is at Humber Regional
I will retrieve him/
bring him back
to his Court
and sleep over
Maria and I/
We begin to think
of the retirement home
It depends on/
how you like to do it
But for me/
it is like putting the cat
in the cage
He is an outside creature/
who would not
be happy indoors
Maybe I am wrong
but there is
no cantina
no garage
no garden
nothing to fix
The Institution
Is not the Life!

Maria:
I talk him into
getting a cleaning lady
Every two weeks
Rosaria will come
to approximate a life/
He will have
someone to talk to
someone to visit him/
His home will be clean
We will get a nurse
to come and see him
He will enjoy the company
We know
It is not enough
His solitude
makes time blend
into one long wall
that runs the length
of his life
There is really
no morning
no afternoon
no evening or weekend
Just a wall of time

Vagabondo:
We are outside now
I am about to leave
Garibaldi I say/
on a variation
of our old joke:
Do you think
it would be the good idea/
if I take a bottle of wine?
I must look to see/
if it tastes as good at home
as it does down here?
It is an importante experimento/
I think I should try/
but I must know
your opinion!

Garibaldi:
I know you think
It is a better idea/
than I do

[*Slowly the Court of Garibaldi is crumbling.* Vagabondo *sings about the loss of a culture, of artefacts being thrown out.* (**Canto: "We don't need that anymore"**) The *tale of the steamer trunk in the garbage is told.*]

Vagabondo:
One day Maria and I
pull into the clean driveway
on Rita/
We see on the boulevard
a large brown steamer trunk
Weatherworn/
with wooden slats
and solid hinges
Maria!/ Tell me why
they are throwing
the trunk out
Tell me that is not the trunk
that came over with you/
on the SS Constitution!

Maria:
Ma. Tell me
as I kiss you
on both cheeks
Why you are
throwing out the trunk?

Pasqua:
Eh! We don't need it
anymore

Vagabondo:
Panghe, Panghe
I make the slashing motion
in the air/
with my right hand
Stoop/
and kiss her twice

Garibaldi It is
—how should I say it?—
incredible that you are/
throwing out this
important part
of your family history/
How can it be?
Why do you throw
the trunk out?
This is not right!

Garibaldi:
We do not/
need it anymore

Vagabondo:
I am going/
to save the trunk!

Garibaldi:
If you want to save it/
you save it.

Vagabondo:
I go to the boulevard
inspect the steamer trunk
run my hands
over smooth wooden ribs
open the hasp
lift the lid
inspect the interior
sniff for the mold
I close the lid
and gently place it
Like Moses's basket
into the trunk of our car
I notice a flat iron pan
wedged on top
of the garbage can/
It looks ancient
For some reason
I have not seen it before/
Perhaps it was
tucked under the workbench

A Hometown nest
for screws and nuts and bolts/
The word antique is Inglese?
It does not apply
to what I see/
What I see
is an artefact/
It is "of the life"
So I rescue that as well

(to the audience of the living opera)

Canto: "We don't need that anymore"
Maybe it is because
so many of my toys
found their way
to the white elephant sales
at our schools
So many
of my father's cufflinks
my mother's costume jewelry
lined up
for five cents/ for ten cents
on portable tables
in gymnasiums
In my Hometown.
For some reason
I am enormously sad
almost frightened!
I know the treasures
of the second wave
of Italians
slowly find themselves
in garbage bins
across North York
These treasures are melting
Like the Castello of Castropignano
Back into the rock
that they came from
It is a huge loss
to watch the stories
and the artefacts
melt back into nothing
At least I can rescue

two things!
And before I will go
I will also rescue
the coarse white Telio-made sheet
draped on the van seat
in Garibaldi's garage
Later when the Old Man
does comprendi
He will pull out
a small blue and white ladle
that came over
in the trunk
to help make the Life/
He understands the lesson.

Garibaldi:
There used to be a metal handle/
that went from here to here
on this pan/
We cooked everything
over the fire/
With that piece
we would hang it/
Three is a little hook
that came out of the wall
I don't know where
that hook is now/
We used this
to make the polenta
or to cook the vegetables
like a stew.

Vagabondo:
Why did you pack it
There was so little room
In that trunk?

Garibaldi:
At that time
when we came over
we did not know
what we would find/
We had to eat

so we brought it
We took the plates
and the cups/
Everything we packed
so tight-like
We used the sheets
to cushion it
The sheets were
for the bed

Vagabondo:
Do you not see
we have to save it all
for the kids/
It is part
of their heritage!

Garibaldi:
Maybe.

[Garibaldi *is reflecting at the kitchen table. He sings a lament* **"She was my Guide and Companion"** *(again in solo voice, unaccompanied like an ancient shepherd's song.)* Vagabondo *joins his father-in-law. He sees something has to change.*]

Garibaldi:
She was my guide and companion
You and Maria
You have done a lot for me
But there are some things
that you cannot do
It is my solitude
My depression
What I need
is someone to be with
who can cook for me
and clean my house
I need a guide
I need a companion
Not a companion of the bed
but a companion of the Life
Who can give me that?

Vagabondo:
He throws up his arms
clasps his hands together
with another slap
It is a hard thing
to see!
I am afraid
that his Depression is winning
It is spring
and his garden
is a wreck
It is dead to him
The first thing you notice
is the weeds
They are obscene
Next you see
the ground
has not been tilled
It is hard and unyielding
unhappy
not germinating
devoid of all life
bugless
dry
There are no bees
Behind him
Vincenzo's garden is living
He plants his tomatoes
Stakes them enormously high
Anticipates
the bursting forth
His bean house
is newly rebarred
Same with Maddalena's and Orlando's
and the fellow
two doors down
I forget his name now
Who grew the giant zucchini
that embraced us all
in one joyous hug
The Court of Garibaldi
lies in ruin
There are a few flowers
left in the side garden

Popping up
despite the pain
I do not yet see
the metaphor
in their tenacious growth
I survey death
For Christ's sake
I am weeping
and so is Maria
Eh … What do you expect?
Death turns life
into meaningless
space and time and place
and when that happens
It is easy to be bitter
It comforts me
to be bitter
We are not
getting any stupid
tomato plants this year
I will grow my own
and bring him some
It should not be this way
but it is
We should have had
two barbecues by now
I have not had
the good sausages
from Eddystone
since she died
What can I tell you?
I don't care
if you shrug your shoulders
here or not
to heck with you!

[*In a final act to engage the Old Man and assuage his grief,* Vagabondo *proposes the two of them write a book called "The Things they Carried", a pictorial on Steamer Trunks and what was brought from the Old World, to the New.*]

Vagabondo:
Garibaldi I have
more than one piece of land

to take care of
You know that
It is so far
to get to them all
Sometimes I have
to walk for hours
At night
I build a little house
with corn stalks
Maria and I and the kids
we sleep in it
The next day
we get up with the sun
and work
You know it is the life
But we are happy
I have a little piece of land
in your garden now
but I cannot get there every day
I need you
to keep it for me
A few tomatoes
some hot peppers
some cipola
and that soft lettuce you grow
I have no money
to pay you
but I have something
to trade
You and I
we must make a book!
Yes a book!
That is what I will trade
We will call it
The Things They Carried
An Italian Treasury
It could be like a
—how do you say it?—
like a coffee table book
There could be
a chapter for everything
people brought over
with them to Canada

With a little map in the front
of Molise and Castropignano
and all the Hometown's marked:
Torello del Sanio
Oratino
Montagan
Petrella
Sant'Angelo
Next to that?
A map of the North York
We could set up
two groups to advise us:
The Old Guys
and the Young Guys
The Old Guys
could share their memories
tell us
what everything is
The Young Guys
and maybe some girls
Could do all
the running around
Design the book
to make it ready
It would be a gift
to everyone from Molise
The nonni would love it
We could put recipes in it
Every chapter would have
a saying like
"if you move the compost
it will stink"
We are going to need
a place to store the artefacts
and someone to photograph them
Maybe Johnny Caperchione
could help us
He knows everyone
Mario is president
of the Castropignano Club
He will help us
if you ask him
I am going to email some people

at the University of Toronto
Maybe they could help us
Who cares if they don't
What do you say?

Garibaldi:
Maybe ... Maybe

ACT V: Scene 2

March of the Grafted Limbs
(Garibaldi Searches for a guide and a companion.
The Journey to Eldorado.)

The Players:

Il Vagabondo
Garibaldi
Two Sisters (Giulia & Caterina)
Pastora (Companion audition #1)
Santuzza (Companion audition #2)
Piccolo Coro (Small Chorus)

(Stage note: The Action takes place in the side yard.)

[Il Vagabondo *declares his fascination of the graft of an apricot branch to a plumb tree. It is the beginning of a lezione:* Garibaldi *explains how the thing is done.* Vagabondo *sings an "Observation song" about the problem solving process of an Italian mind.*]

Vagabondo:
It is not possible!
Look at that tree!
You are—what do we call it?—
a mago, a sorcerer!

Garibaldi:
It is possible
I will show you
how it works
Look!

Piccolo Coro: *(with Vagabondo in tow, observing)*
He takes me/
over to the plum tree
I inspect the phantom limb
Luminescent, ethereal/
back-lit by a breeze
gently stirring
the white fluttering
undersides of leaves
It is the beginning
of a lezione/
in Garibaldi's Court
The enchantment of contadini thought/
remember what I told you
First you must see the thing/
gaze at it
Look underneath/
or from the top
You must inspect it
Once you inspect it/
touch it with your fingers
once, maybe twice
Now that you have touched it/
you get it into your mind
Here you can turn it over and over
inside your head/
like you are already
at the work bench
in the garage
Hold it up to the light
Say "Holy Mackerel!"
Turn it to see the problem/

Call on all other thoughts
to share their experience
of past solution
You are—how do we say it?—
consulting the problem
What tools will you need?
Who could do this back home?
Did someone do it once/
at the old place on the Blackthorn Avenue?
No, you don't think so
But you have an idea/
of how the thing works now
Once you have the idea/
you are ready to begin!
Go to garage
Get your tools
Everything you will need
Start to whistle/
You are concentrating
not quite present to anyone/
Vaguely aware
of your surroundings
There is nothing else
to do right now/
but this
Try your first idea
If it does not work
Try your second
Stay with it/
until you get it
When you get it/
stand back and inspect the thing
The light is changing now
Gather up your tools
Bring them back
to the work bench/
Clean them with a cloth
put them back/
Exactly where they belong
Trip the switch:
The garage door bumps down
There is no rush/
Today your song is finished!
You will know it is time?

to go to the utility sink
in the furnace room
to wash up
Have a glass of wine!
It is the education of the Life!
You are the student
and the professor/
all at once!
I tell you this/
What does not work now
is the early stage/
of what will work, later
Abbi pazienza
Eureka!
Chin Chin

Garibaldi:
First you make three cuts
Snip open the skin
Peel back the bark of the plum
Ever so gently
Not too much!
Now you take
a little piece
of albicocco:
the twig
It must be young and tender
You put it like this
Wrap it up with the string
nice and tight
It does not always take
but sometimes it does
When it does
you have a branch like this one
With albicocca
while all the rest are plums
That!
is how we do it!

Vagabondo:
It is brilliant!
Garibaldi you remind me/
of a young me!
Later at the new house

I will see him be
a mago again/
but curiously?
The graft will not take
The magic is not strong there
We are somehow
a little happy about that/
It is unbecoming.

Garibaldi:
You can do this
with a plum
and an apricot
but you can't do it
with a plum and a peach
or a peach
and an apricot

Vagabondo:
Why not?

Garibaldi:
It is because of the bone
The plum and the albicocca
have a similar bone inside
It is smooth
The bone of the peach
It is different
I don't know how you call it
in your language

Vagabondo:
Wrinkled?

Garibaldi:
Yes, wrinkled

Vagabondo: *(to the audience of the living opera)*
He does not know it
but he traded me a word!
To this day/
I never refer to the peach pit
as the peach pit

It is the bone!
The wasps in Garibaldi's Court
pollinate everything/
when they are not singing
like the Dino Martinelli/
It is a gift!

[*The conversation shifts to two sisters,* Giulia *and* Caterina, *from across the road who are becoming more prominent.* Garibaldi *helps them with making the sauce (with* Vagabondo *in tow) and they feed him. He pays Giulia to bring him some food.*]

Vagabondo:
We begin to notice
there is more talk
about the sisters
Giulia is across the road/
beside Pasquale
She was married/
to the Russian fellow
so tall and so friendly
If you saw him/
and did not wave
You are the buffone—a fool
I believe he took an interest
in Garibaldi's half-children
coming to see him on Rita
Giulia is coming/
across the road
a little more
Katerina?
She lives over by the Finch
One day I will go over
with Garibaldi/
Early in the morning
I will help with the sauce
If you throw a potato/
in a huge boiling pot
to seal the jars/
When the potato is soft?
It is time
to pull the jars/

I have never seen a potato
become a clock!
It depends how you like to do it
I do it/
the way I have been taught

Katerina:
You take an interest
in these things
It is unusual/
Have some more sausages
Take as much
as you want!

Vagabondo:
The conversation will pause/
They will look at you
surprised to hear
any Inglese spoken at all!
They look at me
like I just appeared
for the first time
at the table!
The laughter and happy chatter
will resume:
It is/
an international phenomenon
The food is good
Homemade wine/
so different than Garibaldi's
Guaranteed to invite you
to a nap in the afternoon/
Black olives and sardines
such salty rewards/
All part of the trinity
of the morning's work/
in a backyard
The food is good
The work is hard
The company, Merry
It is so simple
What else do you need?

[Garibaldi *speaks of "His Solitude."*]

Vagabondo:

Giulia seems so nice/
I tell him
one evening
after work/
I heat up the frozen veal
she brought over
to his fridge

Garibaldi:

She does not want to live
in this house
And I
do not want to move

Vagabondo:

He catches my interest
I stop patting the veal/
pour some wine
in his glass
and mine
and go to sit
beside him

Garibaldi:

It is not like
I don't miss Pasqua
I miss her so much

Vagabondo:

He claps his hands in the air/
but it does not have
that desperate quality to it/
He is working on the problem:
inspecting it
fixing something
I am silent now
Listening

Garibaldi:

At night my solitude
suffocates me
When I went to the festa
The sisters brought me up

from My Depression
I was happy again
I was happy

Vagabondo:
I start to cry a little bit
around the eyes/
But what the hell!
I don't care/
It is the way
it has become/
in Garibaldi's Court

Garibaldi:
She was my guide
and my companion
but I do not have
my life anymore.
I do not know
how long it will be
before I will die

Vagabondo:
You know I love you
and I will do forever/
what you need me
to do

Garibaldi:
Yes, I know that
I think you are
this way with me
because you miss
your own Father

Vagabondo: *(off stage to Maria)*
There it is
out of the blue!
Like he can see
deeply into wells
the way I can

Maria: *(with affectionate laughter off stage)*
How does it feel?

Garibaldi:
What I need is a companion
Someone who will cook for me
and clean my house
and help me
Not a companion of the bed
But a companion
of the Life!

Vagabondo:
Pasqua is my importante friend
I love her/
You and she
are my heroes/
I can only hope
that Maria and I/
will be like
the two of you
when we are older

Garibaldi:
Yes, I know

Vagabondo:
Picalito canto: "it takes two to make a life"
And he does know it
and I know it
and the thing is
his solution
makes so much sense!
There is an ancient order
an ancient rhythm
to the Life
You can
call me a fool/
but when you look out
across the Castropignano Expanse/
at the valley
up by the Castello/
When you can see through
the grainy atmosphere
of a twilight sky/
the orange flames rolling
slowly in the distance

across textured fieldscapes/
You just understand
Everything all at once
Capisce.
Divino.
For me?
It depends how
you like to see it
It takes two
to make a life
Even memories are a spirit
an entity
a companion
It is okay
you have to fix things
for someone
There is no point
to a garden
if you grow it
for yourself
The wine is for you
and for me
Your flowers
are my flowers
A cherry tree
will not grow
if there is not
another cherry tree
close by
But you do it
the way you
like to do it
and I will too.

Maria: (*offstage, indignant*)
There is no way
I would do
someone else's laundry!

Vagabondo: (*in response to her*)
I know
These are ancient ways
in a modern life

[The Old Man begins to socialize, to fix things for widows on the street, to go to the bingo.]

Vagabondo:
And for a time
on Rita
there is new growth
Garibaldi takes all of the ladies
to the bingo
at the Weston and the Sheppard
New, strange dishes
appear in the fridge
It looks fuller
A zucchini is on the counter, again!
There is more garbage to take out
He starts playing cards
two doors up
Widowed nonnas bring him toys
to fix for their grandchildren/
lamps in need of new cords
appliances that are broken
He gets calls/
to install things
Still
She will not live with him/
but she does take
a little money
to prepare his meals
across the road
She shops for things
he will eat
You can tell he is living
but he is not/
making a life

[Vagabondo continues to acutely observe the Old Man and his need for companionship. He turns directly to the audience of the living opera with his thoughts and insights, to bring them into an intimacy, as if to observe together what is happening to Garibaldi.]

Vagabondo:
Garibaldi is still inspecting the problem

The thing is not yet fixed
I have seen him
weave and entire basket
with branches
then take it apart
at the finale
because something was wrong
four rows down
I have seen him
spend an entire week
weaving green, white, red
(the green is the basil
the white is the cheese
and the red is the sauce)
wire around a glass bowl
working for days
to finish off the lip properly
Why anyone
would want to weave
electrical wire around a glass bowl
is beyond me
I fully understand
constructing scopa card holders
with working lids
out of cereal boxes
but wire on glass?
"Geez are you still/
working on that?"

Garibaldi:
It is not right yet

[*Unknown to* Maria *and* Vagabondo, Garibaldi *places an ad in the community Italian newspaper:* Corriere Canadese. *There are two responses.*]

Maria:
He has placed an ad:
"Fiercely Canadian
proudly Italian"

Vagabondo:
You're kidding

Maria:
Vedovo di 76 anni
Cerca compagnia
Zona Jane e Sheppard
Chiamere etc.

Vagabondo:
Do you know how many buzzards
he is going to get
with that ad?

Maria: *(facetiously)*
No. Tell me.
How many?

[*Interview One.*]

Vagabondo:
He gets a bird of prey
and a songbird
The first caller is an Italian woman
named Pastora
She is down in Toronto
somewhere

Garibaldi:
It is almost like the name
she had ...

Maria:
Pastora telephones
and comes over for a coffee
She says the banks
will not loan her the money
She needs ten thousand dollars
Yes she will cook for him
and clean for him
and do his laundry
... if only he will help her
with her debt
He is smarter than he looks
thinks ten thousand
is quite a lot

and gives her three
He makes her sign
a little piece of paper
that she will pay him back

Vagabondo:
She signs it because she is honorable
She is a good Italian woman
who does what she says
She is dead to me
She soils the nest of her people
At first we plot
how to exact
three thousand dollars
in retaliation
But you never know
how deep the rot is
in her soul
and in her family
Shit!

[*Interview Two: Santuzza.*]

Maria: (*arietta*)
The second caller
is ready to have a new boarder
A nice man
stayed with her
for five years
but he died
Her name is Santuzza
She has a life
but living alone
the house is
—how do you say it?—
crushing her
They talk on the phone
for an hour each day
Later she will
come over for a coffee
He does not
want to leave his house
She does not want
to leave hers

There is too much at stake
It is like that
with Italian couples
when they are married
She loves him
He loves her
Together
the house flourishes
When she dies
He dies
The home dies
To leave the house
is to accept death
You have to be ready
—there is no rush—
to accept death!

Vagabondo:
By now Garibaldi
has built a little memorial
to his wife
Fittingly it is in
the downstairs kitchen
Typically he has constructed
the corner shelf unit
with it four tiers
out of old bedposts
and spare triangular
pieces of the wood
that he cut
in the garage
On it he hangs her picture
one-two of his poems
a few treasured things
pictures of his son
his daughter
his four grandchildren
Before Christmas
he gets a six foot piece
of plywood, paints it white
drills holes in it
Places tiny lights
to spell the words
Alla memoria della mia consorte

Proudly and deliberately
he hangs this on the balcony
for everyone to know
O my geezis
Buon Natale!

Santuzza: *(off stage)*
I see that you persist
in staying in your home
If you see it differently
You call me

ACT V: Scene 3

A Songbird
(A songbird lands on an albicocco branch. Il Vagabondo
and his people row Garibaldi to the new world.)

The Players:

Garibaldi
His Sister
Maria
Her Brother
Vagabondo
Santuzza
Piccolo Coro (Small Chorus)

(Stage note: The Action takes place in Garibaldi's
downstairs kitchen.)

[Garibaldi *calls* Maria *to make an*
announcement. Vagabondo *arrives at Garibaldi's home,*
slightly late (similar to the opening Scene in Act I.)]

Vagabondo:
One evening Garibaldi calls us
to announce the he intends/
to move to Santuzza's house

Garibaldi:
It is for the best
It is what I want to do

Vagabondo:
He sounds distant/
removed
Like someone who knows us/
but is not that close

Maria:
Are you sure
this is what you want
Do you trust her?

Garibaldi:
Yes
It is time you meet her
We are having supper on Tuesday
I want you to come
My sister is coming down
I will call your brother
You can see/
what the situation is like
We will talk

Vagabondo:
Maria is the daughter of her mother
She has vested authority
It is subtle/
but she represents
the ancient kingdom of Italian women
You must be enchanted/
to know about this kingdom
I tell you, it is real!
I have seen it
Slowly, gradually/
by the proxy of Death
Maria is becoming/

the new young matriarch
of the family
She is the rightful heir/
to her mother's throne

[*He views Santuzza for the first time.*]

Vagabondo:
I turn right
off Jane to Rita
Thankfully, it is not Sunday
there is room
at the curb to park
I see by the cars
in the driveway
that his sister
his son
and his daughter
are already present
at our curious summit
I try the door
It is locked
I am slightly irked
The Old Guy has got me thinking/
too much
about the omens
I ring the bell
Carmine lets me in
Shoes go off
slippers go on
I slide my way
to the downstairs kitchen
like a skater/
on thin ceramica
I catch Santuzza's face in profile
as I glance into the kitchen
I don't know if I like her
I don't know if I don't like her
It is hard to know
She is dressed like it is the church
She has a stern formal look
Her eyes are a little hard

[*The scene switches to the silliness of opera buffa as a tension-relieving device.* Vagabondo *fetches the wine and then there is a duet with* Maria *and he recites the full story of their first meal and her refusal to eat canned spaghetti.*]

Vagabondo:
Buongiorno!
(I call out)
(getting the time of day wrong)

All:
Ahh Ciao!
Hi hon'!
Here is Il Vagabondo!
Buonasera!

Vagabondo:
There are kisses
two for The Sister/
one for mia amore
two formal ones for Santuzza/
a slap on the arm
for Garibaldi
an urban handshake for Carmine
Salutations complete/
I round full circle
to the head of the table/
coincidently arriving
in front of my Mio glass
I will get the wine!
I say with a flourish
Resolutely, I tread the familiar path
to the cantina!
I return to the kitchen
The distinct aroma of pesce
—how do you call it?—the fish
The Aunt and Maria/
are serving now
as part of the ancient rhythm
Baccala in red sauce/
with speghettini—Mio Dio!
where are my manners?
—the strange and glorious world
of pasta—how could I forget it?

Vagabondo and **Maria:** *(duet)*
I must tell you again
for that is the way to learn!
When I first met Maria
and we were courting
one day, it was time
for the Lunch
I did not have much
I was a student
cared little for food
nor was it a priority
in my budget
I go to the cupboard/
thankfully, cleverly
I have a can of
the Heinz spaghetti
I will make for her
my specialty, I say
Place a pot on the stove-a
Open a can of the spaghetti
put it in the pot
Heat till bubbling
Place two pieces
of the white bread
in the toaster
Spread with margarine
top with the spaghetti mixture
serve with milk

Maria:
I am not eating that

Vagabondo:
Why not?
I thought you liked
the spaghetti
I am so surprised!

Maria:
That is not food
I am not going out with you
ever again!
She slams the door

with a definitive
Mediterranean gesture

Vagabondo:
O my geezis!
I am flabbergasted/
speechless
I must call her
this evening

Maria:
Yes, I will
see you again

[*The duet fades to Vagabondo's recitative on the various
species of pasta.*]

Vagabondo:
Canto picalito: "The enchanted world of the pasta"
The enchanted world of pasta
the soul of gusto/
is the metaphor for the Resurrection!
It is—how do you say it?—
what heaven, what paridiso
will be like for you
when you die
Trust me on this!
The noodles/
they start off so fragile
so dry and so lifeless
in full rigor mortis
They are laid out flat/
curled or twisted
like shells or like stars
ribbed cylinders or smooth
They are sold in nests
and packages with numbers
No. 86, No. 88
La donna e mobile
Will you buy De Cecco or Delverde?
Loretto e Barilla?
Try them all
and then decide

who you will sing with
For me?
I sing with De Cecco or Delverde
when it is on sale
at Garden Foods
Put on Verdi's *Rigoletto* and repete
repete after me/
Put your heart into it
like you are yanked up
on the stage unwittingly
like a tourist in the Café Concerto
to sing with Paolo Foti, Maria Paola Turchetti
and Pietro Jang
at the Tanagara Ristorante
in Roma
Are you ready?

(Il Vagabondo gestures to the audience of the living opera)

REPEAT AFTER ME
Penne rigate!
Penne rigate
Ditali Tubetti Gemelli
Stelline Puntalette Quadratini
Filini Anelli Gobetti
Tacconelli
Orecchini
Capelli D'angelo
Bravo, Bravo maestro!
Like songs/
This one takes four minutes
That one takes nine minutes
This one takes twelve minutes
Always make too much
Add salt
Watch the pieces
softly resurrect
and fly in circles
It is truly magnifico!

[*The action shifts to the table. The formality of the situation
is not unlike Garibaldi's tale of courting Pasqua. The Deal is
discussed.*]

Vagabondo:
And on this earth
The sister serves baked whitefish
while Maria follows
with enchanted pasta and ... beans
There are two kinds
of olives
a basket of bread
and enough of everything
for three helpings
Have some more
for Me!
There is the sponge cake/
with biscotti/
the fruta for dessert

Santuzza:
You look more Italian than she does!

Vagabondo:
It is because of Garibaldi!
his vino and his food
They have—how do you say it—
in your language?
They have enchanted me
I am like/
the Canadian flyer
shot down over occupied Italy
befriended by an entire hill town/
hidden from the "Chermans"
The war is over/
and I decide to stay
Maria is my war bride!

*(Vagabondo turns to the audience of the living opera to
explain)*

I am triumphant
I try not to look like Il Duce
I never get tired of this story
Don't you see?
It is why I tell it
to you twice

The Brother is laughing
his happy laugh
He is amused by his cake-eater

Santuzza:
Ahh! I see!

Vagabondo:
We say the Italian prayer
led by Garibaldi

Garibaldi:
Signore benedice/
questo chibio
questo chiama
per prendere/
cosi sia

Vagabondo: *(an aside to Maria)*
Maria, did Santuzza ask you/
if you were Catolica?

Maria:
No
She asked if you
were Catolico

Vagabondo:
Ehh.

[Maria *and* Vagabondo *have a micro-scene where they process what has taken place in an intimate duet remembering her mother, Pasqua and the old life.*]

Vagabondo and **Maria:**
Canto: "The Deal"
Suddenly we are talking seriously
authentically and with emotion
It feels very ancient
Maria is sitting/
where Pasqua would have
The Brother is on this side/
next to Santuzza
Garibaldi is at the head/

of the table
I am opposite him
They are going
to make some sort of life
and we are interviewing them
about it/
We are ancient chaperones
They are answering
all our questions/
weathering all scrutiny
We know that
what is going to happen/
has already come to pass
The Ghost of Donato Macoreta/
is in the room and then
I make him go
We talk about widowhood
the suffocation of loneliness
There are some tears
and then the conversation/
shifts to business

Santuzza: *(canto picolito)*
It is not a lot
when you add things up
I will cook for him
and buy groceries
I will clean his clothes
I will sew his buttons on
when he misses one/
In return
he will have a companion
I will go places with him
like to the bingo
if he asks
Believe me my dears
I can get along by myself
I have plenty to do
but I will go with him/
if he wants
There is a garden
in the backyard/
and tools he can use

Maria and **Vagabondo:** *(duet)*
We talk about
the power of attorney
the old tenant
who just died
Garibaldi's four grandchildren
and Santuzza's children
who conduct the same interview

Vagabondo:
I do not want to
disrespect either of you
We love Garibaldi
We want what is best for him
How do you know
that this is the right decision
and that it will work out?

Garibaldi:
We know

Santuzza:
Our generation is different
At our age
we know these things
We want the same things
I am afraid to live alone
in the house at night
Loneliness will kill you
slowly

[Vagabondo *sings a sad, yet resolute arietta about Garibaldi moving and becoming a companion of the Life.*]

Vagabondo: *(aside to Maria)*
I cannot believe
in this day and age
He is going to get
what he actually wants
Wisdom is sometimes forged
from sadness
Your eyes are black
Swept back to your mother
somewhere in the ancient kingdom

I know
It is raining there now
but you know it will clear
You will make it clear
It is called suffering
and we will draw courage
from it
The are both wise innocenti
Dry your eyes
and hear the lovely dialect
of the Court of Garibaldi
They know what they
are getting into
They are allowing us
to get over it
and interview them
to see what goes
It is respectful
All we can do
is shrug our shoulders

Maria:
I know
but I really miss
Mamma

Vagabondo:
Yes
She loves you
and he
still loves her!

[*The song ends, the light on stage dims and the table becomes a silent tableau, fixed in time.* Vagabondo *walks to center stage and prepares the audience of the living opera in preparation for the second Intervallo.*]

Vagabondo:
Canto: My Italians
Maybe in the old days
when you are poor
when you have nothing
all you have
is each other

You have relationships
All the stories
about working hard all day
The women coming to bring food
sleeping over under the stars
in corn huts constructed
in fields
Coming back home dead-tired
to shuck and pile corn
Then sing and dance
Escape the gaze of the old
to be with the young
This is why loneliness
kills My Italians
It is almost a primeval
comfort of presence
Deeper than anything
I can ever know
in this disposable society
of disorder
and runaway adults
They are like our cat
Peach-of-the-Serengeti
Moosh-Moosh or one of the Sister's
unnamed garden felines
They need to be around
each other
They are restoring a life
and it does grow
like grain or like a corn plant
in a fallow field
the year after the harvest
He will fix things
She will cook
They will take meals together
They will go on outings
She has her own place
in the house
He will have his
She is landlord
He is tenant
Together they will restore
the enchantment to the garden
the enchantment to the kitchen

Life has a use
for Italian women
and for Italian men
You need both the heart and the lungs
if you are going to sing
Volare!
It depends on
how you like to do it
Everyone does it
their own way
but set down your troubles
settle your piece of land
Come home.

Santuzza:
Now we will
go over to my house
have a little espresso
and you can look around

Vagabondo: *(walks to center stage and prepares the audience
        for the second intervallo)*
The name of her street
keeps nagging at me
so I look it up
El Dorado
Do you know
the Incas call it "Paititi"?
Doesn't that sound
vaguely Italian?
Everything does to me now
The fabled city of gold
the mystical place the Spaniards
were convinced was the last refuge
of the Incas when they fled
with all of their treasures
If I told you
that one of the streets
on the way over
after you say farewell to Rita
is named Courage:
that you have to
traverse the SpenValley
to pass by

the curiously named "Ladyshot"
Would you believe me?
Would you?
I know you will think
that I am a pagliaccio
Perhaps you will say
Someone has hit me
with the malocchio
The Evil Eye
and you will no longer
believe in the Living Opera
or in my Tales of Gusto and Enchantment
I tell you
It is all true!
You can tell the street over there
is a little richer
than my beautiful Rita
The houses are larger
much like the Woodibridgi
Nobody comes out that much
at least
as far as I can see
The properties are kept beautifully
the trees are pruned to a "T"
or a stolid "Y"
cut in the same
bold Italian
pruning font

Vagabondo: *(to Maria)*
I don't think
I am going to get to know
this street very well
Is it prophesy,
grief or fable that I speak?

Vagabondo: *(to the audience of the living opera)*
But the House?
I know I am going
to get along with it
The driveway is clean
There are flowers out front
There is a side yard
You can see the yard barn from it

The garden is bigger
than Garibaldi's
Three are fruit trees
and a patio table
on clean cement slabs
The basement is painted grey
I see plastic chickens and lions/
migrated from arid Rita
Bringing along their
bright red geraniums with them
There are black and blue
fifty-gallon drums
Purple vin bon pails
hop like rabbits
and when my eyes dry
there are little
systems, Everywhere!
A long time ago
I introduced you already
to the cantina inside
But I do not wish to
talk to you
about this house
anymore
There is another house
that we must
say goodbye to
first!

SECONDO
INTERVALLO

(Il Vagabondo and his people butcher an Italian house.)

The Players:

Garibaldi
Il Vagabondo
A Neighbour

[Il Vagabondo *addresses his audience alone on stage.*]

(Stage note: There is a For Sale sign alone on stage and shadows of people viewing the house and leaving, the blue demons are doing a slow ballet or modern dance in silence on the stage … the notion of dervish or slowly dancing in gyres.)

Vagabondo:
Ahh, you are stretching your legs
Good!
Before you go out
for the glass of wine
and some conversione
Stay for a moment
and I will share
an ancient art with you

(Garibaldi's voice is heard off stage describing the butchering of a pig in the hometown.)

Garibaldi:
When it is time
to slaughter the pig
we waste nothing
You buy it
when it is little
You give it some food
and you raise him up
to be big

We had maybe one-two pigs
at a time
This was all
we had the money for
My grandfather knew the way
He knew how to do it
You hoisted it up
over the branch of a tree
and you cut his neck
so he would bleed
We even collected the blood
and made it like a sausage

(From the darkened stage, a neighbour and prospective buyer is heard.)

Neighbour:
It is a good house
I notice the for sale sign
Is your father moving?

Vagabondo:
My father-in-law
Yes he is moving
He does not want
to be alone

(To the audience of the living opera.)

I want to be alone
to look at the house
a little bit
I can see the neighbour
assessing with a measured stare
into the garage
up over the steps
by the cantina
through the branches
of the peach tree
down the side yard
to the back
I am vaguely irked
say goodbye to him
and turn to busy myself
with nothing.
When he goes away
I come back out
to look at the For Sale sign
framed in metal
resolute in its purpose
For a minute
I think of all he elections
the municipal
the provincial
the federal
I laugh at the image
of hundreds of signs
staked into the front lawn
They represent all the political parties
Garibaldi and his friends in North York
support everyone equally
until it is time to vote
They are flags of convenience
to the Italian gardener
so long as the stakes

are made from good, clean wood
It is a small secret I share with you
Everything has a purpose
Capisce?
But I tell you this!
This metal sign
buffeted by a shivering February wind
is a magnet
Within a day and a half
the house is on the market
Sold!
possession in July
A clean quick stroke
It is deep
The house bleeds out
It is dead
Like the pig
we must cut him up
let nothing go to waste

[Il Vagabondo *extends the metaphor and intimately tells his audience the tale of 'butchering' the family house.*]

Vagabondo: (Lament: "Cutting up the Pig")
So we do it
It is already a barren place
First we cut out a bed
the crucifix
a filing cabinet
the dining room table
the hutch
my precious Mio glasses
some furniture
and other entrails
I rent a truck
Nico and I haul it all
over to El Dorado

Decisively with sharp, clean strokes
The Brother gets his portion
of the inside
Maria gets hers
We leave some leftovers
for the new owners

and the guts
are taken over
to the church

Alone in cupboards
a few pots and plates remain
for our last supper
when the work is done

We cut to the outside
We are in the garage now
The automatic door
shudders stupidly up
and stops with a jerk
Useful things are separated
divided into three portions
A good carcass is left
Some meat on the bones
can be boiled down
a spare ladder
countless jars
of bottled bolts
Irregular pieces of plank and lumber
The good Italian
spine of it.

Curiously it is the outside
We dress with a most tender care
and with the sharpest of blades
It is the choice section
Everything represents "her"
The forsythia is gently pried out
so tenderly we remove
root from soil
We rap the holy bulb
with burlap, moisten it
Slip green garbage bags
over the entire muddy thing
and heave it on the truck
Every rose bush cut out
tenderly lifted
divided in portions
and carted away
Next the tiny organs are removed

the silver dollar plants
the yellow flowers
and the pink ones

I take the purple pails
to stack in my yard barn
it is like I am removing
the feet from the pig

Spring comes, then June
I stand by the grape vine
next to the metal shed
I see the kiki
begin to develop anew
I run my hand
over the hairy central vine
up over my head
to where the reliable bark
gives way to slender new branches
green and tender
I rub the tiny leaves
trail their serrated edges
with my fingertips
Talk to them softly
in a grower's dialect
My eyes catch
a white malevolent cluster
of hard, hidden half-grown berries
Cancerous non grapes
with black spots on the bottom
They shriek at me
I pinch off the stem
with my thumbnail
Crush it underfoot violently
like a Castropignano scorpion

It is time—there is no rush—for a last supper
I am well versed in the art
of making sauce
It is the way I have been taught
It is my gift
But it is the smell I want
to pervade the entire downstairs
one last time

swirling within the kitchen
wafting around the corner
to the furnace room
lifted on wings up ceramic stairs
to tempt the ceremonial rooms
that we spend so little time in
Continuing the sensual flow
across the little downstairs room
where we watch television
and finally out to the entrance
to mix with the age-old musty smell
of the cantina
Like a bouquet of flowers
It is here that I write
underneath the clean, wooden planks
"I love Nonna"
Then I seal the door
to that sacred tomb
for the last time

For dessert we stand and weep
by the cherry tree in full bloom
I spit the bones at the children
We rub our hands
along the smooth bark
to the feel the knots
The tree is too big to butcher
I would cut that out too
but this must be the new owner's portion
His share of the meat
Her share of the fertility
The children climb up into the tree
to relive an older, happier time
We take a picture
to enact when Their Nonna
let them climb and pick
and pick and climb forever
while barbecue smoke
and planes fly over

The nipote understand
that it is a goodbye act
in the Grand Opera of Living

I am pleased

I wipe my brow
The job is done
Nothing is wasted
Everyone now has their share

[Vagabondo *ushers his audience out to the lobby.*]

Vagabondo: *(to his audience of the Living Opera)*
I have kept you too long
Go and have some wine
You are working too hard
You deserve it
It is for you and for me
Pass a little time
and I will
flash the lights
when it is time to ritorno
Ciao!

[*Gently the lights are turned off and then on, off and then on ...*]

Vagabondo: *Prelude to the Final Act*

Perfetto!
Come with me now!
It is time/
to go forward to Eldorado
It exists!
There are treasures to be found
More tales of Gusto and Enchantment
New lezioni to be learned
I will show you
how to make the sauce
and then/
you can go home

ACT VI

ACT VI: Scene 1

The Life in El Dorado
*(Garibaldi is on the far bank. Il Vagabondo hitches the ferry
and decides to stay and stir the polenta.)*

*Gently, the lights are turned off and then on,
off and then on.*
(Vagabondo address his audience: *"Perfetto. Come with me
now! It is time to go forward to El Dorado. It exists! There are
treasures to be found, more tales of gusto and enchantment,
and new lezione to be learned. I will show you how to make
the sauce and then, you can go home.)*

The Players:

Il Vagabondo
Maria
Their Children
Santuzza
Garibaldi
Two Ancient Dinner Guests (Garibaldi's people)

*(Stage note: The Action takes place at Santuzza's house in
the Upstairs kitchen. Time has passed. Il Vagabondo, Maria
and their children are invited to dinner in the New World.
Garibaldi has moved his Court to Santuzza's. They have
recently returned from their visit to Italy and their Hometowns.)*

[Vagabondo *opens with an Observation recitative on buying
bread at the local Italian bakery. He surveys how the
neighbourhood continues to change.*]

Vagabondo:
If you intend
to stop and get a bread
at the Jane and Hwy 7
You must go early
Trust me on this
If you cannot get a bread
Don't worry!
You will not leave
empty handed
Get something else
The bruschetta is so light
The way the oil
soaks into the crust
is so beautiful!
You can get the buns
on the Eddystone at Commisso's
or, like I say
La Stella is your second choice
It is however;
Your first choice
for strange oval cookies
with almonds in them
I forget how you call it
but somehow, they melt
When you snap one
in your mouth
You better go quick
for it is different now
Ferlisi's has been taken over
by the wholesale store!
Valencia emigrated
to parts unknown
She moves aside for
Sieu Thi Vinh Phong-
Yong Feng Supermarket!
You must try
The Uncle Chen's "Chillisously hot" chili
on your potatoes
It is in aisle two
Lamentably Yung Feng
does not stock
Rastrelli oil

[*The phone rings and Vagabondo remembers an old joke with Pasqua about bringing her tomatoes as a gift.*]

Vagabondo:
One of the best ways/
to tease your Italian hosts
the beautiful elders/
is to bring them
tomatoes in August/
It is guaranteed
to start a happy argument!

Pasqua's Voice: *(off stage)*
Ehh?
Why do you bring these?
We have so many
already in the garden
The cantina is full
What will we do
with them now?

Vagabondo: *(to Pasqua's voice off stage)*
Signora
You are making me nervous
You will not die
from this!
I thought you liked tomatoes
It is wrong
to return my gift
How can you do this?
I am so hurt!
(to the audience of the living opera)
I must tell you
that I know
from the experience?
If you bring them a zucchini
they will see through you
immediately/
The women
will give you a smack/
You may wish
to experiment with the thing
But! You have been warned

[*Maria, the new matriarch and Santuzza, talk on the phone.*]

Santuzza:
Maria
come sta?

Maria:
Bene, signora, grazie

Santuzza:
How are the children?
Are they okay?
We are back now/
from our trip
You must come for lunch
Garibaldi's sister will be there
She is bringing
Nunziata
We will look at pictures
from the hometown/
There is nothing to bring
We have everything

[Vagabondo *listens and addresses his audience about passing the time. He remembers a tale of Garibaldi talking about the first days when his family arrived in Toronto. He sees the irony of the moment. The cycle of change and the return to familiar themes of making a life.*]

Vagabondo:
I am always
glad to go there
You never know
what you will find
The company is good
There are Tales
of Gusto and Enchantment
in every visit!
No matter how short
or how long
Yes, I could tell you
more about the trip
across the river

to the El Dorado with Garibaldi
But I do not know
if it is important
Besides, there is
a little
compost in it.
My people and I
do not wish
to move it
Dio Mio! What are you?
a testa dura?
There are other
lessons to learn!

Garibaldi:
Listen to me now
about the first house/
When we came here
It was the win-ter
We took the train
up from the New York to Toronto
and from there
we got to Montrose
We lived in the same house
with two other families/
After the first year
if we had the money
to go back
we would go back
But we had the debt to pay/
There was nothing
to go back to/
After the war
the land, it was ruined
There was nothing.

Vagabondo:
Somehow
I feel the same way
but for the different reasons
I was worried
when you returned
to your hometown/
Saw the life

that they had there
You would regret
that you even
came to Canada
in the first place
When Maria and I
saw the view
from the Castello?
We did not want to
come back home/
It was scary.

Garibaldi:
I am glad
to be back
and it was good
to go

[Vagabondo *sings an aria to the audience about the beauty of
the old ways, slowly fading.* **Canto: "The Court of Garibaldi
is a Wine Press"**]

Vagabondo:
The Court of Garibaldi is a wine press
The Tales of Gusto and Enchantment
are the juice
The old guys know
what I am talking about
There is nothing more satisfying
The press is full with purple clusters
Carignane grapes are authentic
They taste better
if you drop them
on the garage floor
Hands are so cold
Pick up the stained
half-moon blocks
Fit them perfectly
in clusters
around a threaded pole
There is hardly any gap
between the outer edge of grapes
and the smooth inside
of stained slats

Fit the last blocks
snuggly against the threads
Place cam and ratchet
over the stem
Start it with a turn
then spin it smoothly
with your palms
until it is tight-like.
When you are ready
—there is no rush—
Give it solid pulls/
Feel muscles awaken
along forearm and shoulder
while cogs press down
to click tighter

This is exactly where
all time and space stops/
There is nothing
to think about
There is nothing
to worry about
There is only joy
hard work and love/

There is a pause
a magic moment
where juice swells
along the base.
Growing, pulsing, pausing
Aching to begin
this thin red stream
into an orange pail/
It is everything!

But what I tell you now
will be lost soon/
It has to go that way
Yes/
Somebody was smart enough
to bring over the centrali/
the huge wooden casks
that stood proudly
at the mouth

of a nursery
at the Islington and the Steeles/
They are gone now
Nobody crushes the grapes
with their feet anymore/
You do not need to
over here/
It is Okay
You can buy your juice
or you can buy your wine
in twenty-litre pails/
Stained wooden wine press slats
are not replaced anymore
Cast iron bases
they rust and look old
Steel turning bars
hide in the corners
are misplaced
won't be found
Now you put cardboard
on the trunk of the van
If you buy five?
You get an extra pail
Let the young guys
load them in your truck
Make sure they put
the green garbage bags on them
so nothing spills
I don't know how they do it
where you are?
Or if they still even do it!
Where we get the pails?
They puncture the lids
to let the wine breathe
and ferment

It was the wives
that made them use
the green garbage bags/
It does—how do they say it?—
Improve upon the process
and avoid
the fights!

Women: *(voices off stage)*
Mamma Mia!
Why do they do it like this?
Every year you come home?
The van is a mess!
There is a better way
Don't be a testa dura!
Tell them. Tell them.

[*The action shifts to the arrival at Santuzza's. Garibaldi's ancient sister and friend, Nunziata are present. Maria, starving to see her father, immediately sits by* Garibaldi *and holds him and touches his face. Vagabondo is pressed into service at the stove.*]

Vagabondo:
We approach El Dorado
from Driftwood to Spenvalley
Make a right/
You can bypass the Rita
altogether that way/
Forget about the home
we have lost/
Sometimes I go there alone
Remember what I told you:
Do not go
on the Sunday
Avoid the gridlock
and the cursing
I have to tell you/
Most times I avoid
my street altogether.

The doorbell rings
We come in/
There are hugs and kisses
We are welcome/
in this home
Garibaldi's sister
touches Maria and holds her/
Nunziata is blessed with a face
that smiles so happily
in repose

Santuzza:
This is Il Vagabondo
He is not Italian
He is better
than an Italian boy!

Vagabondo:
There is laughter
I look to see
if Garibaldi is happy
If he is happy
Then I am happy
It is a gift/
Santuzza is one of
my Italians now
(to Santuzza)
Eh! You say I am better/
because I bring your plates
and you jars
all your plastic containers
back on time

Santuzza:
You are right!

Vagabondo:
Ciao, Garibaldi
I have two empty bottles
for you now!
I am not sure
what to do with them?
Do you think
I should take them
to the Cantina?

Garibaldi:
No!

Vagabondo:
The children disappear
to drink orange pop
The women begin
their happy catch-up chatter/

Because I am smarter
than I look/
I join Santuzza
at the stove

Santuzza:
Here. Take this spoon
and stir!

[*The* **Piccolo Coro** *sings an "Observation Song" about the process of cooking Polenta.*]

Piccolo Coro:
Stirring polenta
has nothing to do
with delicate circles
of oil and vinegar
It is hard work!
You have to keep
your eyes on it
It is an enchanted food
When it is ready
It is very ready
Do not serve it
If your guests
are unreliable
Here is what you do:
Get a large pot
fill it half full with water/
Heat it until
just before
it is going to boil/
Let it ride the edge
of the tipping point?
Add butter and the salt
You may add
the Polenta now:
In slow, loving circles
that spin memories/
Some use the fine corn flour
But Me?
I do it the way
I have been taught, remember?
I prefer the coarser grain

Begin to stir now
to infinity
Keep adding the cornflower
Make sure
you do not
let it boil!
If you are doing it right
you will begin to see
a fine yellow texture/
Not as consistent
as Inglese mashed potatoes/
It is more moist-like
I forgot to tell you
In another large pot
you are simmering
homemade tomato sauce/
Don't be so nervous!
Soon I will show you
how to make that too!
Magically, the Polenta takes form
It becomes thicker
Turn the heat down now
Call all guests
to the table
(We say
the tavola)
If you are playing
la musica?
This is the good time
to put it on
Put out the large flat bowl
of steaming pork shoulder/
Beside that a smaller bowl
of raggedy sausage
and grande meatballs
You have already thawed
your Caravaggio mudcat
red peppers remember?
from the freezer
Prepare the red strips
in the oil and the garlic
the basil and prezzemolo
(I forget
how you call it)

Pasqua's Voice: *(off stage)*
Ehh! I am not
going to translate
this last word for you/
You should know this by now!

Piccolo Coro: *(continuing)*
Put the prezzemolo
on the table:
beside many kinds of the bread:
Some sweet chard
from the garden/
Mixed green salad
with the home-made dressing
The inevitable
little wooden bowl
of hard brown almonds/
You have already
made room on the table
for orange pop
aqua
the Mio
the wine
and one-two bottles
of benzina,
the birra, the gas!
Afterwards
when it is time
I will set before you
a large bowl of la frutta, you brutta/
Espresso will be on
I have prepared for you?
The sponge cake:
It is like a bird
it is so light
There is a homemade apple pie
And always!
Too many hard cookies
that melt in your mouth!

[*There is banter with the table guests about the life back home,
immigrating so young and learning to cook as women.*]

Vagabondo:
Did your mothers
teach you how
to make desserts
when you were little?

Santuzza and **the Ancient Women:**
Mamma Mia No!
We learned how to make it
when we came here
when we were married
You see back then
we could not afford much/
The sugar and the flour
the—how do you say it?—
the ingredients
that you need
to make these things/
We did not have the oven
like we do now
We just had a fire
some flat stones
to cook on/
Maybe at Christmas
We would trade
a rabbit for some sugar
or some eggs
We would take them to town
to the baker
to have our sweet things made/
If we had a hen
we used the eggs
to barter for things/
Like the cobbler
to fix our shoes

Vagabondo:
How many eggs
would it take
to fix your shoes?

The Ancient Women:
Maybe about
Twelve-thirteen

Vagabondo:
O! A thousand questions
Crack open
in my mind!
Mamma Mia!
Dio Geezis!
I have forgotten
the Polenta!

[*The* Piccolo Coro *finish their polenta observation song and they all sit to dinner.*]

Piccolo Coro:
The polenta
is the perfect texture now/
Turn off the heat
Clean off the long
wooden stirring spoon/
Take a ladle:
place a good portion
on your plate
Flatten it out
with the underside
Like a ... like a Pancake/
Perfetto!
You make a little trough
around the edge/
To gather the sauce
on top of your pancake/
It is important to know this
You do not want to waste
a drop!/
Ladle thick red sauce
atop your yellow wheel/
Dust liberally with cheese
Watch it melt
into beautiful shapes
The children will say:
Reading the cheese
is like reading the clouds/
There are pictures in it
It is part of the enchantment/
Repeat the process

for all of your guests/
So long as they
come to the table
on time!

[*The recitative shifts to Garibaldi's impression of his return
to his hometown in Italy.*]

Vagabondo:
Garibaldi?
How did you like it
In your Hometown?
Was it better
than you thought?

Garibaldi:
No, not really
Yes, I liked to see
my sister
and my brother
and their families/
I had not seen them
for forty-eight years/
Biagio was so amazed
I remembered where
everything was
and all the names
of all the people
It was like my memories/
They flooded back to me
at once!
We went everywhere
and saw everyone
I like that
We went to the cemetery
with Nicola
to see my parents' grave
But I tell you this!
It is not there now
like it used to be

Vagabondo:
How so?

Garibaldi:
It is the food
They grow it
but they
do not use it/
It all goes to waste now
When we arrived
the figs were ready/
Nicola took us
to my wife's house/
The figs fell off the trees
There we so many to eat?
The wild vine was filled
with clusters of yellow grapes/
Not like the ones
you can get over here
They were better!
Santuzza picked them/
We wanted to bring
them all back
with us
But they all
go to waste
Nobody wants them!
It was not like that/
when I left the first time/
If you were lucky
if there was any fruit left/
You had something
but mostly
there was nothing.

Vagabondo:
Did you get stung
Picking the grapes?
I ask him, teasing

Garibaldi:
No.
We walked in their gardens/
They stepped on big cabbages
We tried to save some in bags/
There were too many:
They have more time now

to grow things
but there is too much food
Nobody to eat it
It is not right

Vagabondo:
I understand now
Why it is good to go
and good
to come back

[*The conversation shifts. The ancient ladies joke at Vagabondo's expense. They too, accept him.*]

Santuzza:
Have some more espresso!

Vagabondo:
Grazie, non!
Let others have it

Santuzza:
No. You most have it
I insist!

Vagabondo:
I accept
My tiny cup
is filled to the brim
The pot is finished/
What can I say?

(shrug shoulders, here)

Il Vagabondo is
an honoured member
of la famiglia/
He is—how do they say it?—
He is better
than an Italian boy

Santuzza:
Good!
Now I can make

a fresh pot
for the others!

[*The scene ends with Vagabondo's reflection on all that
Garibaldi has taught him. He prophesizes the time when
Garibaldi will be gone.*]

Vagabondo:
Later when the women
clear the table?
I make a point to help
to purposely disturb
the ancient order/
It is my Inglese Butterfly Effect
Garibaldi and I
are left alone
at the table
I am across from him
We sit
rest on elbows
our fingers clasped in prayer
I suppose you could say
It is the holiness
of the content
A time when old men
will listen to young men?
I have seen it.

For some reason
the wine press/
does not matter much anymore
Yes, it is the beautiful machine?
this sacred Michelangelo
this cast iron statue
of the garage winery of North York/
But I tell you this
It is an importante thing of the life/
but it is not the life itself:
What we do with the libretto
How we love who we are with
Is the thing we must know.

Garibaldi?
It was good

to go with you
to see where
you get the wine
to see
how it is done/
Now I will know
how to do it
when you cannot go

Garibaldi:
Yes
That is the way
it will go.

ACT VI: Scene 2

Venus de Gnocchi
(If it is Giovedi, it must be time again for la scuola.)

The Players:

Santuzza (The Landlady)
Il Vagabondo
Garibaldi
Maria
Zio's niece, Angeolina (offstage)

(Stage note: The Action takes place in the Landlady's Upstairs kitchen, in the Court of Garibaldi.)

[*The scene opens, reminiscent of Act I, Scene 1 with* Vagabondo *arriving late to the Landlady's. He has tried to find the religious calendar but is empty handed.* Garibaldi *sits doing a crossword and looks up when* Vagabondo *raps on the sliding door.*]

Vagabondo:
A quick stop at Commisso's
on the Eddystone/
and still they do not have
The Renaissance Paintings calendar
for the New Year
Mamma Mia!
Sometime in the morning
I arrive empty handed to El Dorado/
The driveway
it is so clean!
I see that Garibaldi
does his crosswords
in the upstairs kitchen/
So I rap on the window
Il Vagabondo is on time!

Santuzza:
That is not true
You are/
ten minutes late!

Vagabondo:
Ehh! So, you say
It is hard for me/
to believe you
but I will do my best!

Garibaldi:
Three across
Seven-letter word
for the Joker

Vagabondo:
Ha!
O my Geezis
That is easy
Do you think I am stupido?
B-U-F-F-O-N-E

[Vagabondo *has come for a cooking lezione. He sings an* **'Observation Song'** "Gnocchi la scuola". *(He mocks the Piccolo Coro)*]

Vagabondo:
I am at the table now
We discuss our health:
the health of our children
the health of my wife
We conclude/
that we get old
and we get sore
Before I know it
I am downstairs
in the basement kitchen
ready for Gnocchi School!
I am given a pair
of the slippers to put on
It is a good sign
Our work table
is right beside the furnace
on a large clean sheet
of warm wood
Behind us the sink:
the air conditioning sistimi
with its valves
and its hoses
the gas burners
pots and pans
ladle after ladle
suspended from the rafters
The bare bulb
of the basement light
sheds a sleepy glow
Beside us
in another area/
Garibaldi is at a workbench
He repairs a drawer
to open and shut smoothly/
I hear him singing
La Scuola begins!
Santuzza instructs me:
Ten medium-sized potatoes
go in the pot
leave their skins on
boil them for twenty minutes
drain and take the teaspoon
to peal their skins/

Mash them in the ricer
The texture is nice and smooth-like/
dump them on your clean board
spread them so they are cool/
Have a banana
Crack three eggs:
one, two, three
and whisk them/
Spread the potatoes
in a donut shape/
On the clean board
put the eggs in the center/
Rinse the bowl
with a little milk/
It depends on how
you like to do it/
Pour it on the eggs
Bene
Prepare two cups flour:
one, two
Sprinkle liberally
over your potato mixture?
Pour a third cup flour
into a bowl/
Place it next to you
for occasional sprinkles
or to dry
your hands
Bene
I tell you this!
Now you must
knead the potato:
the eggs
the flour
everything together/
Learn to say 'farina'
instead of the flour/
Add some more farina
whenever you need to/
Soon you have a beautiful ball
of the potato dough

[*Vagabondo steps away from the demonstration and speaks
to the audience of the living opera.*]

I cannot believe
You take such an interest
in these things/
It is so unusual!
Bene
Pull a piece apart
Roll it out about a foot/
Slice it on an angle
Dust your hands
with the farina/
See?
You are the expert now!
Bene
Take each slice
roll him along the board
until you have
the slender dough-snake/
He is about eighteen-twenty inches long?
The kids like to help you
with this part!
Aspete!
I am reminded
of all the snake stories
I have heard
at other meals?
It is a fact
Vagabondo collects these stories/
They slither around
coil in my memory:
I cannot believe they are true!

[Vagabondo *interrupts his song, to ask* Garibaldi *to share some "Snake stories" he has heard over the years.* Santuzza *joins in.*]

Garibaldi:
A husband and wife they are sleeping
The husband wakes up
Notices a snake sliding down
the mouth of the sleeping woman
He does nothing to wake her
Sees the tail of the snake
go down her throat
She is pregnant

They go to the doctor's
He can do nothing
until the baby is born
The Wife, she must drink the milk
to keep her stomach
out of the turmoil
When it is time for the baby
The snake it comes out first!

Vagabondo:
Tell us/
another one!

Santuzza:
A mother gives birth
to the baby
The baby is so fussy
always crying
She is not gaining the weight
The mother was healthy
but she is not doing well
after her baby is born
People question if it is the snake
that comes through
the little round hole
in the bottom of the door
where the cat comes in
To prove it
They spread ash from the fire
onto the floor
So they wait
to kill the snake
and the baby
she gets better!

[Vagabondo *turns to* Maria *(now lit on stage) and complains to his wife, the way men do, that today is different with The Old Guy. He does not seem involved. The distinctive roles of ancient men and women are made clear, while* Garibaldi *sings and quietly goes about his tinkering.*]

Vagabondo:
When I was working
with Santuzza/

Garibaldi barely
came into the room/
It was like
I was invisible/
I liked the work
but there were no stories
no conversations
no debates
between the young
and the old/
All he did was come in:
to ask Santuzza
if she showed me
how to flip the gnocchi
with the tines
of my fork/
I had to stop his singing
and ask him to tell me
a snake story

Maria:
He never helped Mamma
when she made gnocchi
in the kitchen/
That was her job
not His!

Vagabondo:
There are some things
I do not
I will not
agree with?
I say to Maria
in the dialect of the Court

Maria:
Good!
I will never
let you get away
from not helping!

Vagabondo:
Garibaldi
You sing so beautifully!

Can you sing:
"Over the hill
and far away?"
(It is the old joke
of my father's)

Garibaldi:
No/
I don't know/
that one.

[*Vagabondo finishes his Observation Song.*]

Vagabondo:
Observe:
This is the time
to start a big pot
Get the water boiling
on the large burner
Bene
On the little burner
You have the red sauce simmering/
Take some cooked rapini
from the freezer/
Thaw it under low heat
in a shallow pan/
Now you must add
the oil and the garlic
It is good if you have
some pork shoulder/
simmering in its juices
Before you are ready to serve/
I want you to prepare
a cup of the red wine/
Turn up the heat
pour the red vino
onto the meat/
O watch the smell
and the steam!
Perfetto!
Turn around now
to the table
Take the knife
cut your remaining

snake into the angled shapes
about an inch long/
Take the tip
of your index finger/
gently press below
the half-way line
of each gnocchi/
Pull your finger back
to flip the gnocchi over/
The dent you made
holds a tiny pool of sauce
when you serve/
You do this
to all of them/
Trust me on this!
Bene
Like the pied piper of gusto
Watch all the gnocchi
dive into the hot water/
Bring it to a boil
Stir a little bit/
After twelve-thirteen minutes
Take the ladle
from the rafter
put the gnocchi
in a steel bowl/
Put a little sauce
in the bottom first/
Add more
Dust with cheese
Another layer
dust with cheese/
Cover the bowl
Place it back on your pot
Presto!
You have the double burner/
to keep your Venus di Gnocchi
so warm-like
Come with me now
Let us go upstairs/
to the table

[Vagabondo *turns to the audience of the living opera to explain there is another of the paesanos who is grieving. Maria's ancient uncle. He loads up the car with parting gifts from* Garibaldi *and the Companion of the Life and departs.*]

Vagabondo:
It is mezzogiorno
when I say, arrivederci
to drive south on the Keele
There is another Italian street
that changes beneath
the cycle of the sun
in Garibaldi's Court
Old Zio grieves
His stories weave
his hard life, lived
He came to Welland
to Niagara
to Toronto
to Italy
back to Toronto
with his family
What is it with us?
The women seem to
die first all the time
It is too much!
As I leave
one of his daughters
pulls onto the clean driveway
We laugh
I say hello!
Silver cars never look dirty
Black ones do

Angeolina: *(offstage)*
You know you can put
ricotta in the gnocchi
instead of the potato
If you do that
Get some frozen spinach
Thaw it and cut it fine
Now you know!

Vagabondo:
She is her mother's daughter
It is an ancient lezione
learned easily
and shared freely
in the wind
"Grazie, Angeolina
Grazie, Farewell!"

[*The final scene, stage lit, is a snippet of matrimonial conver-sation between* Vagabondo *and* Maria, *at home. The urban opera is coming to a close.*]

Vagabondo: *(merrily)*
I head west on the Maple Leaf
right onto Jane
north on the Hwy 400
Soon Il Vagabondo
will be an eroe
in his court!
Triumphantly I bring gifts from afar
Like the Marco Polo:
the gnocchi
the rappini
the porco
the pane
the vino
an extra vin bon pail
my Tales of Gusto and Enchantment!
Maria!
I am home
I say with a flourish

Maria:
I thought you said
you were bringing
lots of gnocchi!

Vagabondo:
Choo!
O my Geezis!

FINALE
AND CURTAIN

(Il Vagabondo addresses his audience, gives them something to take home and reveals the secret words on the inner band of Maria's wedding ring.)

The Players.

Il Vagabondo
The audience of the living opera (the Audience)

(Stage note: The Action takes place in an imaginary replica of a (North York, Toronto) garage replete with working garage door.)

[Il Vagabondo *sings a summary to his audience.*]

Vagabondo:
Canto: "Tales of Gusto and Enchantment"
Signore e Signori
Ladies and Gentlemen
We have come
to our close
In our Tales
of Gusto and Enchantment
there are no
dragons to slay
No natural disasters
to flee from
So little compost
to move-a
No, our tale is told now
in the ambling gait
of life approached
of wire weaved
of mosto squeezed
of peppers skinned
Abbe pacienza
A time to pass time
to remember
to perceive
to stir the polenta
In the Court of Garibaldi
lezioni abound!
Gardens will live
and gardens will die
While we sing Cantos
of love and of loss
Wasps, intoxicated
with no thought of stinging
Sing Dino Martinelli
between the kiki
Zucchini spread their arms
in back yard embrace/
Grow wildly in the night
We see the art
in day and place and street/
Interact with it
and create our own compositions
We add new paesani
to our dance

Bring them in/
while others parade past
stumbling
Our streets die
Macchina become obsolete/
Steamer trunks are rescued
from garbage heaps/
The ancient order
is preserved
We pray in faraway cemeteries
Are loved by friends
We eat the figs forever

Houses are butchered
in clean, efficient strokes/
We collect the blood
to make the sausage
In kitchens we sit
smack tables with bare hands/
to stir our thoughts
in the gyres of love
Flames clear away
our hillside stubble/
We graft anew
Through Divine Providence, we meet"
we laugh
we doubt
we suffer
we cry

We think we know
But we do not know/
Our shoulders shrug with acceptance
In acceptance:
we go to God
beyond the barriers of language
back to the old ways
and our ancient order
Into the Living Opera
Arms outstretched before you
To stand on the rich stage
of Felicita
Felicita!
There is no rush

Io sono content
Grazie
Molto grazie

The drama of la famiglia
is the prima drama
It is everything
The wine is for you
and the wine is for me
And because you are leaving
I must give you/
something to take home
Like Il Vagabondo
return to those you love
And you will return always
with tales of gusto and enchantment
It depends/
on how you like to do it.
This is how I like to do it/
It is the way
I have been taught

[*Vagabondo's gift to the audience of something to take home is a recital on how to prepare sauce for the pasta. (An "observation recitative")*]

Vagabondo:
I tell you this!
First, you must remember
your mother-in-law, always/
Then take a big deep pot:
Set him on the stove
Take any oil but Rastrelli:
pour it slowly
in rings
along the bottom/
Peel the onion
slice it gently/
Let the sacred tears
mix with oil
on the low heat/
Let garlic fall
one-two cloves
to join the great dance

watch small bubbles form/
Now you must add
the pork ribs
you have singed and browned
It is time:
for the salt
the pepper
the basil
the—how do you call it?—
the oregano
along with my secret Inglese weapons/
the savory
the sage (Not too much sage!)
You are turning
the ribs now with a fork
or use the tongs
Beautiful
Now remove them
Place them into a bowl
etched with grape vines
or Italian beauties
pouring water
How is your oil?
Add some more
Let it heat up/
It is time to brown the veal
perhaps some lamb
It depends how you like to do it
More savory!
More sage!

Do not have the banana
If it is past 10:30
You may have a Mio glass of wine/
Only a little
There is no rush
Perfetto!
Now you must take
Three mason jars of the sauce
I showed you how to make it
The kids are so fussy
Do not use the jars
with the hot peppers in them
They will be marked

with the rubber bands.
Dio Mio!
One time/
I made the sauce
with the wrong jars/
The rubber bands
they were too old/
They broke.
It was—how do you call it—
in your language?
—the tragedy!
The kids they had hot dogs that day
Maria's aunt puts a carrot in
Some people add sugar to the sauce/
maybe a little anis seed
But for me
I do not use those things.
I put a what Pasqua puts in it/
The dot.
A "dot" is:
non-dialect
non-formal Italian
non-Il Vagabondo-speak
non-Inglese?
I tell you there is slang
even in the ancient order?
A dot is a bouillon cube
Put one-two in
Si, Si!
Now you must spoon in
Three picolito cans
of the tomato paste
to thicken your sauce.
The difference between
the Inglese
and the Italian?
The Inglese will buy
only three cans at a time
maybe six if they are on sale
The Italian will buy
the entire case!
Have them go to the back
to get it/
Okay

You are ready
Turn your stove
up to high
boil the sacred mixture
Now you may have/
a second Mio glass
of the wine
In thirty minutes or so
—there is no rush—
Turn the sauce down low
Let it simmer
for two-three hours
Your house will smell so good!
As my Inglese friends say:
My House/
is to die for
Take the little brown bottle
of the "Kitchen Bouquet"
Remove the yellow cap:
pour a good splash
of browning fluid
into your sauce
If you let them see you do it
You will hear them screech
As far away/
as Castropignano!
A little Inglese Butterfly-Effect/
Never hurt anyone.
You are, after all
the Canadian

[Vagabondo *implores his audience to stay.*]

Vagabondo:
I don't know why
you have to go
Why don't you stay and eat?
Mangia, Mangia
But if you must go
let the sauce cool/
I will pour it
into two pots
use the rubber bands
to secure the lids

You must always
carry the wine in the bag
in case you get stopped
by the Carabinieri?
Make sure the pots lie flat
Do not forget
to return them
if you ever
want to get sauce
again!

[*In a gospel call-and-response, an ancient woman's chorus is heard, off stage calling playfully.*]

Woman's Chorus:
Maria.
Why does he not
learn to speak
the Italian?

Maria:
He is trying!

Vagabondo:
Ti amo amore!
I whisper it to you
Like the ocean
in the shell
(shrug shoulders, here)

[*The Garage door slowly closes.*]

FINAL
CURTAIN CALL

Canto: Take Your Time Going, but Hurry Back
(Il Vagabondo addresses his audience and goes home.)

The Players:

Il Vagabondo
A tableau of la famiglia
Piccolo Coro (Small Chorus)

(Stage note: In the midst of applause, the garage door, slowly opens to reveal Vagabondo bathed in the light. In the background a dinner table in Vagabondo and Maria's home with Garibaldi, Pasqua, Maria, the Children, and a representation of Vagabondo in silhouette. Vagabondo sings his final address called "Making a Life")

[Vagabondo *address his audience for the final time.*]

Vagabondo:
Signore e Signori
The ladies and the Gentlemen
It is too much!
We must part ways
and ritorno
to our own lives
to our own
Living Operas
Piacere
Before you go
I must teach you
one last lezione
Then you must/
take it with you
to teach someone else
how to do it
But only the way
you like to do it
Then you are ready
to sing in the ancient rhythm/
the dialect of love
Per favore
Do it ... For me!

[*Vagabondo leads the audience of the living opera in an Observation Recitative about how to make "the traditional Inglese high cholesterol meatloaf of the 1950's and the 1960's."*]

Vagabondo:
Observe:
This is the way
to make the crown
of Inglese Gusto and Enchantment
If you are married/
Into an Italian family
(Or any other family)
It will make you
an eroe!

Piccolo Coro:
Here is the instruction-ioni/
complete with dialect
on how to make

the traditional
Inglese, high cholesterol meat loaf
of the 1950's and the 1960's

Vagabondo:
It is the way
my mother likes to do it/
so it is the way
I teach it to you/
It depends
how you like
to do it
I must warn you
this meatloaf
is so bene
but it is not
that good for you/
It weighs about thirty pounds
Mamma Mia!
(It is so dense
It is like a free weight!)

Piccolo Coro:
Like the store-bought veal
It will lose the enchantment
if you eat it too much!
For this?
You make it once every six weeks
or at the end of each week
like we used to do/
When you are poor
and running out of the money?
you can use it
for the sandwiches
for the next four days/
If you are a kid?
Take the sandwich to la scuola/
Your friends
will want to trade you for it
Trust me on this:
If you take the thing for lunch
Make it with lots of margarine:
salt and pepper
HP sauce/

or if you are a buffone
like my Brother?
With the green pickle relish
Gawd!

Vagabondo:
I will show you the way
so you can get a picture
of the thing
in your mind/
Then you will know
how to do it
Take a meatloaf casserole dish/
the butter
a little piece of wax paper/
to coat the inside of the dish
Take the sharp knife
and cut a sliver
of the butter
and put him
in your mouth
Perfetto!
Now pour for yourself
a little rye with ice/
This is a good time
not to smoke

In the big green mixing bowl
or maybe the yellow one
if you still have it/
Whisk three eggs, the uova:
Put some milk in
and whisk again/
Get a packet of onion zuppa mix—
He is my friend/
Cousin to the Lipton Chicken Noodle zuppa—
The Inglese polo zuppa mix of choice!
Pour him into the bowl and stir/
Now you add the herbs:
lots of savory
not too much sage
more sage than thyme
marjoram and the basil
Bene

Now you must
chop up the sedano
(It is okay to look it up)
Have a sip of the rye
—there is no rush—
Find your can opener
to open up the can
of mushroom pieces and stems/
Dump him in the mixture
water and all
It is so moist!
Give it a little stir
to blend in the herbs/
Put in some of the bread crumbs
not too much
to help with the binding/
You have already thawed
your ground pork and beef'
Make sure that neither of these
is extra lean or lean/
If you want to do the thing
the way I do it?
Make sure you keep
the mushroom can
to drain off the sea of grease
midway through the cooking/
If your kids are the students
of the Meat Loaf School?
Explain to them carefully
why it is unhelpful
to pour the grease
down the sink!
Teach them the experiment/
Put the grease in the fridge:
It will get hard and white/
You can throw him out
on the garbage day
Bene
Crumble the ground meat
into the mixture
Knead it together
with your hands
Ah! Scuzzi!
Before you do this/

Make sure you have
another little sip of the rye
Your hands will get greasy
so watch it!
The kids will want
to work without a net
but do not let them/
By now, your sposa
has made and up and down motion
with her left hand?
She does not want
to do the laundry/
She has tied the apron
around your waist/
Inevitably, you are wearing
your best shirt/
This is a good time
to kiss
Bene
Your meatloaf mixture
should be nice and moist-like now/
Take a little ball of it
Put it into your mouth/
Remember in the 1950's and 1960's
there was the bogey man
but not the tape worm!
So it is okay
to do it this way
Scare the kids though:
The raw meat is so good
they will want
to eat it too much.
So will you
I tell you this!
If you eat too much
you will get a—how do we call it—
in your language?
You will get
a snake in you/
I have seen it!
By now you have asked
someone to turn the stove to 325/
Your hands are so greasy!

Piccolo Coro:
Use the middle oven rack/
Bake for an hour and a half
and take him out of the oven/
Let it stand
for one-two minutes
Pour your children
some Goofy Grape
Shoo them away/
There is time
to finish your rye
There is time
to have a smoke?
Back then?
Even the dottore
were lighting up/
I encourage you
to do the same/
This is Inglese dialect for:
I cannot believe
we actually lived like way!

[Vagabondo *invites his guests to the table and calls out "Addio" to the audience of the living opera.*]

Vagabondo:
Call your Italians to the table:
Garibaldi
your mother-in-law
the nipoti
your beautiful wife/
The children will have:
mio
the pear juice
or the orange pop/
Maria will be happy
The Old Guy
will look serious/
Slightly out of place
like he is in
an upstairs kitchen/
Put on your recording of
Opera Without Words:
The Barber of Seville/

Rome Symphony Orchestra
on the German Label: Kapp/
Serve with silky mashed potatoes:
the steamed carrots
with process cheese:
(DO NOT use cheez whiz!
Maria will kill you)/
If you are feeling dramatico
sprinkle some walnut crumbs/
on your carrots

Say the Italian prayer/
Begin the new tale
of Gusto and Enchantment/
Make sure you offer
your mother-in-law
at least three helpings!
She of course/
Will look so worried
around the eyes/
Like she is waiting
for the bus/
She is not comfortable:
the chairs are not right:
She is not
in her own home.
But she loves you too much
and that kind of love/
Is more than enough.

The garage door slowly shuts.

[*The curtain comes down to end the Urban Opera.*]

Addio

IL VAGABONDO'S SURTITLES
(shrug shoulders here)

Canto: The Speech (not the Language)
of *Garibaldi's* Court:

[Il Vagabondo *sings to his audience in the dialect of love.*]

Ahh, my friends. You are still here! Perfetto! Stretch. Stay with me a little bit. Return to your seats and then you can eat what you learned to make in our tales of gusto and enchantment. Did you know that you remain for the most importante lezioni and that you are all smarter than you look? Si! I don't know if you agree with me. I don't know if you don't agree with me, but I tell you this: Although it helps, it is not necessary to speak the language to speak to the people. There is a speech in the Court of Garibaldi that is deeper than whether or not you can merely parle Italiano. It is called speaking in the dialect of love. You do not need the lezioni of instruction to do this, no; you need the lezioni of the experience. If you love and are loved, if you can listen and be with and amongst happily, you will be able to comprehend the universal libretto. This I guarantee. You will not need a book to learn it. Yes, all of our green white and red dictionaries are importante but! (shake your closed fist here but remember what I told you) Do they teach you the life? Do they show you how to make the peppers or to stir the polenta at midnight? No, I think not. Sing with Il Vagabondo now, and wander forever into the enchanted speech of love in Garibaldi's Court. It is everything. Ciao. Arrivadello!!

(We speak now, in the dialect of love)

Act I Scene 1.
A Sauce Making Tableau. Canto in Red

How do you say it?: Phrase used to punctuate an important word in the conversation or phrase used to buy time in a conversation when your mind is not working quickly enough.

salsa la Scuola: a school of the experience not of the instruction

old ways: everything before 1957

It is too much: dramatic phrase punctuated by shrugged shoulder, usually left, and tilted head. English translation: what's the use?

Lina: English translation of *Maria Christina Pasqualina Molinaro*, my mother-in-law

comprendi!: complete and utter understanding, similar to the phrase Eureka, I get it!

giovedi: Try to learn the days of the week, they are pretty easy and you will use them a lot. Using these words increases self-esteem.

mia moglie: another easy word to build your romantic vocabulary

"When they are ready, you have to go": usually associated with the ripeness of tomatoes and a prime example of Italian laws of the land.

squeegee: very *importante* outside tool to keep the garage and driveway clean after you frequently hose them down

English tourist: stranger in a strange land

(cock your head to the left, open up your hands at the waist, tilt your face up and bring your mouth corners down): Fundamental body language in an Italian household; easy to learn; after a decade, the movement will become reflexive and natural body punctuation; many variations on this movement, as in dialect

vin bon containers: Italian equivalent of duct tape; come in purple or white

we have time to do it: Italian dialect or code for: "if you don't come now, then forget about it, you will miss out"

Perfetto!: vocabulary builder; easy word to use that makes you feel dramatic

garage: *importante* place in the Court of *Garibaldi*; second in the trinity of sacred rooms

tomato machine: distinctive Italian tool; enchanting object d'art; time slows down when you turn it on

Il Vagabondo: endearing term of affection: the Tramp, the Wanderer, the rogue, the *brigande*

burlone: what you turn into when the language doesn't take after two decades

for it is their way: ancient rhythmic phrase, like plants always turning towards the sun

you just know!: ancient rhythmic phrase associated with gyres and cycles of the seasons

Il Vagabondo rescues his audience!

Ahh, you are still reading! It is so kind of you. You have such a passion to learn these things but ... I must tell you the segreto. If someone had only told it to me. Then ... I would not be such a burlone. (shrug shoulders here)

It depends how you like to do it, but do not work so hard. You are making me nervous. There is no need to read all of this. You are not in language la scuola. After all, does anyone read the dictionary all at once? No. Aspetta.

Eh, there is nothing to memorize in the Court of Garibaldi. You must simply be there. When things are ready to be done, they will be done. You will know. It is the Experience, not the Instructione.

You can come back and read this in the winter when it is cold and there is nothing to do outside.

So, for now, you must go. Make a life! That is the lezione. It is the way I have been shown so it is the way I show you. Everyone does it their own way. Remember?

la prima lezione: the first lesson of the morning; you are much more sophisticated when you learn to pull more than one word together; trust me on this

Inglese: genteel word for cake, aka *mangia* cake

bushels: Italian garden furniture

Garibaldi's Court: enchanted place of gusto and *felice*

Garibaldi: beloved leader of the people

Never do yourself what the machine can do for you. Italian measurement for the I.Q. quotient of hard work and experience; giving rise to the maxim: the less you strain yourself, the smarter you are

Macchina (ma-key-na): Phonetics are incorporated in the text to make you smarter than you look see **Carmine**

"that is the way she makes it.": translation: there is no use arguing with her because her mother taught her to do it this way

Mezzogiorno: In the dialect of the *Court* it means: my beautiful people south of Roma

yellow jackets: frequent guests at sauce making, pepper skinning or grape crushing events; often heard singing *Dino Martinelli* songs with abandon possibly due to fermentation of natural sugars

huge silver pot: *importante* Italian outside tool; may be borrowed and used for *Inglese* corn roasts

Auguri: vocabulary builder; easy word, well used

basilica: key Italian spice used on everything; later, you will be surprised to learn that there are sixseven different varieties and that they are not all green

dimostrazione: six syllable word; makes you feel like you have mastered the language when you use it; excellent word to *dimostrazione* (i.e. show off) your accent

malvagio: face it, some Italian words are just fun to say

systems; also, sistemi: spontaneous and remarkable engineering feats of an Italian mind

bocci: see **scopa**; if, for some reason, the language doesn't take, learn the games and you will be fine

fagiolini: seasonal word, remarkably easy to forget; summer/fall vocabulary, start practicing it in the spring; it means green beans

rebar: popular ribbed metal garden structure, excellent for building *fagiolini* houses

tomato plants are gigantic: implied and redundant usage; I have yet to see one of my *paesani's* tomato plants under five-six feet

zucchini: not a cucumber; tougher; from the country; they say you can do a lot with them; frequently thrown out by non-Italian family members or friends of Italians

the frutta: south central Italian dessert; always present after meals; ripe, green figs (*frutta*) will change your life

importante: (im-por-tan-tay); easy word to learn; see self-esteem builders above

the Education and the Instruction: excellent subject for cross cultural debate; gender debate; tradition versus modernism or the merits of the young versus the old (guys)

small plastic bowl: there are at least fifty thousand of these; any size; any shape; in any room, in the Italian household; you rarely need to return them, but you should

Hometown: said as one word; constant reference point for all memories and spiritual space filled with stories; very *importante* to take your kids there or to go with your wife

Valencia and Ferlisi: beautifully named sisters of strange and interesting food in the Court of *Garabaldi*

uva per vino and **'thirty cases':** begin to understand that you are making enough red wine to last approximately one year and that you never, have to buy store-bought wine again.

Carmine (Car-me-nay): should never be translated as Car-mine; what are you? A *buffone*?

contento: complete and utter feeling of peace linked to gusto, hard work finished and eating; see **felice**

Mio: distinctive drink used to cut potency of homemade wine; good substitute for orange pop for the kids; glasses are getting hard to find

drinking (vino) at 10:30 in the morning: hard work trumps time of day and Anglo guilt

the wine is full and warm and primitive: an acquired taste; every one of my Italian's *vino* tastes different depending on the grapes or the natural yeasts; deceptively strong and a guaranteed nap summon-er

I am a rich man: Italian currency associated with love, respect and happiness in family

gusto: more than an enchanted word, it is a way of life; usually associated with the emergence of appetite it evokes ancient rhythms; the cycle of seasons; lilies considered and *the living opera*

fifty-gallon plastic rain barrel: distant cousin to vin bon pails; essential garden and garage tool; no one knows where they get them but if you need one, I can get it for you

a plastic tube: a relative of the garden hose; you can never have too much of this around

you just get them: mysterious phrase used to acquire rebar and fifty-gallon drums

muscato e carigane e alicante: life skill: if you can't speak the language, study the grapes

the warm sizzle of fermenting wine: exquisite Italian sound of nature working

Lezione cinque or sei: life skill: learn how to count to ten, at least

Canadese-ize: when you make something Italian and incorporate what your mother and your mother-in-law taught you, you enter into the old rhythms of your own culture; translate: the beautiful graft, or; it is a gift; may also be associated with *Inglese* butterfly effect when you are mildly irked.

curious way of speaking in the third person: the accent of conceptual thought; really quite beautiful to hear

testa dura: or hard head; perfect word to use on your wife during squabbles

improved on the process: Italian measurement for the I.Q. of hard work and experience (i.e., the more you study the process each year and find ways to do it better, the smarter you are; see **never do yourself what the machine can do for you**)

Like an old guy who shouldn't be bending down: curious practice of the old in all cultures; very frightening

"Holy mackerel": obtuse English phrase adapted by old Italian guys who worked for the Toronto Transit Commission (TTC) for twenty-three years

These men know when the woman is right: no definition or explanation required

"It is time to eat now": Feminine usage; equivalent to an order; separates work-time from rest-time, like a reflex

Mangia: use this word when you are serving your mother in law meatloaf

zucchini lasagna: something you can use a zucchini for

cooked sausages all raggedy at the end: unbelievably good and never enough

oregano: beautiful little sister of *Basilica*

potato: ancient timepiece

a small piece of hose: Essential garden repair/engineering instrument

art of siphoning: Life skill: useful in the *cantina*

espresso e biscotti: translation: strong coffee and exotic donuts

"Grazie senora e senore per lezioni salsa la scuola": *Il Vagabondo* on a good day; sometimes the language just all comes together

Act I Scene 2.
Variations on Red Peppers.
The Dance of the Mudcat"

"if you can make the time, you come": The dialect of meaning; same as: 'when they are ready, you have to go' and 'we have time to do it' You are smarter than you look.

incredible, magnifico ... a miracolo: vocabulary builders; okay, I had to look up the word for miracle

Come prima: greatest love song ever written; may be sung with utter abandon at the back of a gondola for full effect

violate Rule G: ancient *Canadese* rhythmic phrase; in Italian: *violare regola G* if you must know

"Emmmph": translation unknown

"Eh, eh, eh": see **Emmph;** probably **tsk tsk tsk?**

Come si dice?: proper usage of: *how do you say?* If you are fooling around substitute: how do you say it in your language? or I don't know how you call it, in Italian; otherwise the formal usage is better practice

Mamma Mia!: dramatic phrase mostly used by women or in the company of women, slightly gentler than the blasphemous, Dio!

yakker; to yak: incessant talker involving things of various and questionable importance; Canadese phrase

flattened cornflake box: recycled Italian tool; frequently used on the top of sauce jars, before you close the top; keeps boxes uniform and stackable (i.e., never make just one box of sauce)

"You don't want to waste anything,": ancient Italian *lezione* and maxim in *Garibaldi's* Court

... like old, bent red men in the *piazza*: how we all feel standing up in the square after an afternoon of playing *scopa* and drinking *benezine*

bella giornata: vocabulary builder; usage: after you greet a neighbour, say "it is a *bella giornata.*" If they see you first and say *"e una bella giornata"*, the correct response is: *Ah si, si!* and then go inside the house quickly in case they say something more in Italian.

I feel the Order: vaguely like the feeling at a car wash of having your wheels grabbed, your steering wheel turned and your car pulled forward. Not unpleasant

It is a gift: full translation: it is God's gift of happiness to you; see **Felice**

banana: *frutta* used to signal a break in hard, repetitive work. *Vino* may appear in lieu of banana if the work is difficult

"Si, Io sono molto contento": I am happy (that I can say an actual sentence in Italian)'

It depends how you like to do it: The dialect of meaning; translation: others can do it the way their mothers taught them, I have no quarrel with that, but I will do it the way I was taught by my mother to eternity; see also: **'that is the way she makes it'**

add some oil and a little garlic: *Canadese* equivalent: 'salt and pepper to taste' Note: a little garlic is an oxymoron

This one is a Caravaggio: clever and sophisticated way to speak the culture (translate: show off) as opposed to being bothered with the mechanics of language. Another good reason to get the advent calendar at Commisso's

A jet flies over enroute to the Airport: incessant Italian-like phenomenon typical to North York

"La bella tavola!": Vocabulary builder; use frequently

"It is nothing.": modest and becoming phrase used after a compliment to an utterly life-transforming every day Italian meal, usually accompanied with only a hint of a smile

"poco poco vino senora?": etiquette lesson; you never just pour for an Italian matriarch-the patriarch, yes-the matriarch, no. Suggested *experimento* if you are feeling like a *burlone*: try pouring a full glass of red wine for any Italian woman over, say, fifty and see what happens

Chin Chin: casual toast of affection among friends

Io sono: hugely functional Italian words to learn, trust me

Homemade pizza: with the exception of pizza *margherita* (the green is the basil, the white is the cheese, the red is the sauce) of Castropignano, everything else store-bought is reduced to a can of *Canadese* spaghetti. Ancillary translation and maxim: It is impossible to have a bad homemade pizza in an Italian household

when it was hard: i.e., until the grandchildren started appearing

The first job: fascinating story to listen to and collect; see **snake stories**

But we were glad to do it: ancient rhythmic phrase symbolizing the passage from sacrifice, to suffrage, to making a life and owning your own home

scuzzi: vocabulary builder; impossible to forget, fun to say

cantina: *importante* place in the Court of *Garibaldi*; third in the trinity of sacred rooms

Dutch Boy Carrignane, Sapore Dolce etc. …: another interesting Italian artefact to collect, and/ or build garage furniture with

… the wine bottle, pressed into service when its contents of rye are finished: why would anyone throw out a perfectly good glass beaker with thirty cases of grapes fermenting in the garage? Etiquette *lezione*: it is a sign of knowing and cultural respect when you bring some empty bottles over for the old guy's cantina, preferably, forty *ouncer-es*. People tend not to return them. This can be a *problemi* when it is your turn to decant some wine to take home.

a happy problem: you can start an *argumento* at the kitchen *tavola* within thirty seconds anytime you complain about not having a luxury item…which is basically anything not serving a functional or practical use and curiously, anything luxury is often hard to recycle

Rosie: any 'named' animal played an important role on the farm and was spared from being eaten or sold

Alan Lomax Treasury of Italian Music: very authentic and a beautiful gift to give to the old guys; at face value, they won't understand what you are giving them until you put it in the machine, play it and keep quiet. Watch them begin to reminisce and talk with one another…it is how do you call it, a tableau

shade!: reflexive place, constantly sought Most of my *paesani* have a solid base on their tan by end May, early June anyway so sun doesn't matter except for growing things

This was how we passed time: passing time is an ancient Italian art; see section devoted to same in Act III, Scene 2

We had to make our own fun: making our own fun is another ancient Italian art; beautiful to ponder and listen to how they did it

too much of a muchness: all utility *Pennsylvania* Dutch phrase of my mother's; dialect for *Mamma mia!*

Zinca: curiously, *Il Vagabondo's* father had the rare Rome Symphony *Opera Without Words* Recording of Rossini's: The Barber of Seville (on the German label, Kapp) and mia madre was an opera aficionado; maxim-of-the-land? *The snob doesn't fall far from the uh, tree.*

"the man who needs nothing": i.e., all *old guys* who own their own home; see music, books and wine airlocks for advice

clank of metal on porcelain: common al fresco sound of summer

Italian men being silly: the only time they are like little kids

stanco: dialect vocabulary builder; as my father used to tell me: "the only way you will learn is if you look it up yourself"

"Senora, I cannot go until the work is done ... you know this is the true lezione": the measurement of 'a good man'

"I am smarter than I look": witty statement not that far off the mark when a fellow still doesn't "speak the language" after oh, twenty years

The taste of espresso is everything to me: you really have to have been there to understand the authenticity of this enchanted *Canadese* declaration

When you love someone, you do not always take the black peppers even though you want to: An ancient *Canadese*-Italian truism that can only be discovered through the experience not the *instructione*

More kisses: that's amore!

orange pop and chips: local and international staple in Italian households for the *nipote*

mia figlia: I don't know why but I still have to look this up; lament: try to learn all the family names: brother, father, sister, uncle, daughter, aunt...they come up a lot in conversation

squeezing the remaining juice out of the mosto, you will always find something: this is the beauty of the Italian influence on *Il Vagabondo*...a maxim in the making, it is worth watching and then applying to life, the way nature and its metaphors are in the soul of the men and women who know the land

Act I Scene 3.
Dinner al Fresco

Michelin map of Italy: tip; if you can't speak the language, don't just sit there, study the map! It is fascinating to learn: a. where everything is in relation to Rome and b. where all the provinces are in relation to the hometown

benzina: cultural exchange; *birra*, gas; You will never call it "a beer" again and neither will your *Inglese* friends

scopa: life skill; see **bocci**

not companions of the bed but companions of the life: Does anyone else see the utter beauty and wisdom in this phrase, juxtaposed with the modern world?

It is foolish to argue with the weather: Italian measurement quotient of a man or women's patience

"You will not die from this": phrase used to ward off "nervous" spirits; a truism

my good fortune: see; **I am a rich man**

a Globe: Italian atlas

click-clack, click-clack, click-clack: exact sound of the caulking gun used to prepare the face plate that seals a body inside a mausoleum or tomb in-the-wall

"that was our life": phrase used to signal the end of a story, usually accompanied by a sigh and a fidgeting motion (clear plates, get up to go outside etc)

"we never see each other anymore except at funerals and weddings": common usage and lament of the children of Second Wave Italians

dead to her: abject, generally old-world phrase used to denote an eternal unwillingness to ever speak to or think about a living person again; frightening; in ancient Egypt a similar practice would be to chip a person's name off an obelisk, rendering them unknown to eternity

nervous: active, all utility descriptive phrase used to describe a person who is either being: anxious, or fussy, or complaining, or angst ridden; or making someone feel anxious, fussy, complaining or angst ridden; very unpleasant state of mind

"If you move the compost it will stink.": as in, or pertaining to family matters

field-mass al fresco: any meaningful or intimate conversation that occurs outdoors

There is a time to talk and a time to stop talking: simple truth; usually learned the hard way

Arrivedello!!!: passive: formal, useless, butchered, never-used-in-real-life phrase taught in Italian night school classes; dialect for *arrivederla*; avoid using because you will think you are getting at least that word right but you will repeatedly hear the response: "No, we say *arrivederci* or ciao in **our** language" Active: if you are 'being the *buffone'*, use it as a-how do I call it- an *esperimento* to yield predicted results; good phrase to bet on with another *Inglese*

Act II Scene 1.
The Hometown Aria

veglia: late night *yak*-session

Castropignano: Hometown of *Garibaldi*; i.e. About three or four hours southwest of Rome in the province of Campobasso, Molise region

"Well, if you are hungry, you eat": simple and logical ancient Italian law of the land usually accompanied by a shrugging gesture

Bar-bar-ah: beautiful and enchanted way to pronounce *'Barbara'* in Italian with a perfect old world accent every time; good linguistic callisthenic to warm up each morning in Europe

Americanos: *Io sono Canadese!, Io sono Canadese!"* Ah! Si! *Canadese!* (repeat to infinity)

lemon yellow Mediterranean walls: as opposed to unenchanted beige-bland *Canadese* walls

some other things pickling that I do not recognize: frequent Italian fridge and *cantina* observation; in my experience the odds are 80/20 that it will taste good; hence the ancient culinary maxim: 'it is worth the risk'

a beaded curtain: Italian screen door

saying everyone's name phonetically a thousand times, over: trust *Il Vagabondo:* life goes better if you do this

the rest will come later: ancient rhythmic phrase loosely translated as: 'don't worry, tomorrow comes after today; see **'you won't die from this'**

Italiano notte la scuola ... dropout: of and pertaining to the instruction not the experience

la tassa: regional and shiver-inducing concoction served before dinner; acceptable excuse for kids to drink wine at *la tavola*; monitor ratio of wine to hot water closely

an idiot: What *Il Vagabondo* feels like at night school in the early days and uh, later on

lizards: Italian grasshoppers

scorpion: Italian rattlesnake

a three-act play starring a large slug: see **'we had to make our own fun'**

la bella sette: highly desirable card in *scopa*; worth one point; causes groaning when lost by opposing player

just go around: Italian slang for hanging out

"Grazia senora ... Io sono Canadese. Mia moglie e Italiana da Castropignano. Figlia di Angelo Molinaro": *incredibile* and mile long specimen of Italian conversation spoken by *Il Vagabondo* (with only a trace of accent)

I feel tall: common and not unpleasant sensation experienced in south central Italy

elemental loyalty, primitive and instinctual: perpetual, enchanted experience of being amidst my Italians

chickens milling about: backyard suburban creatures fantasizing that they still live on a farm

the Grand Garden: of or pertaining to the Court of *Garibaldi*; enchanted view from the *Castello* in the Hometown

Abbi pazienza: frequently used rebuttal statement in *Garibaldi's* Court; vocabulary builder

bell tower: ancient Hometown clock

piazza: any language friendly, non-threatening space to play *scopa*, drink *benezine*, talk or smoke

"...this was the original school in Castropignano and the prison!": archaeological find; probable origin of universal schoolyard phrae popular in modern usage

Johnny played saxophone: aka Johnny Sax; musician and hero in *Garibaldi's* Court

Navajo cliff dwellings: any home in Castropignano

"No, you don't see that in my country": pertaining to useless or unnecessary things; Italian Measurement Quotient for: "if it didn't exist in my Hometown, you don't need it"

beaded tentacles: common Italian Hometown front door experience; must be brushed off shoulders or head when entering. They come off about twelve feet into the room

"No, non parlo Italiano" (translate: furtive glance, nod and smiles): dialect; the translation in proper or traditional Italian is: "I know, I know, (shrug shoulders here) but he is a nice guy, anyway."

The *mosto* in the mundane: ancient, enchanted practice of squeezing beauty out of the ordinary

The Living Opera: enchanted daily life in the Court of *Garibaldi*

The *Canadese* flyer shot down and befriended: timeless experience of 'marrying into' an entire Italian family

half-hearted translation: sign of fatigue; precursor to matrimonial quarrelling

the privilege of invisibility: exquisite pleasure of just being able to sit down and not interact with anybody; particularly when tired

pours out like water from a fifty-gallon drum: relief and pleasure associated with being in a foreign land and finally being able to communicate in English

sidestep our way down the stairs: safe and proper decent technique when leaving a Castropignano home; see **Navajo cliff dwellings**

gelato: the so-called Italian ice cream that tastes nothing like *Canadese* ice cream and more like popsicles melted and then re frozen; the *lemoni* is nice, you should try it

Act II Scene 2.
Serenade. An Evening at Domenico's

Hi Lo Chikolo: the universal language of play; international icebreaker

the kitchen: *importante* place in the Court of *Garibaldi*; first in the trinity of sacred rooms

Domenico has killed one of his chickens: see **chickens milling about**

pidgin English, blended with Italian nouns and plenty of hand gestures: *Il Vagabondo*, feeling foolish, fluently.

"Moosh-Moosh": see **Rosie**

"pieces of land": rarely side-by-side and always a lengthy distance to walk; source of potential family squabble and compost-moving

Rita Drive: of or pertaining to *Garibaldi's* Court; our quarter of Italian heaven in North York

a paesano: someone who knows where to get rebar and fifty-gallon drums

Ceramica bella: feminine usage; Italian Mr. Clean

Barzula: familiar and popular family friend

little gas stove: is to the kitchen as heart is to the body; good subject for a song by an Italian surf band

magnets of hens pecking roosters: remind me of old Italian men and women in love

"We had nothing": pre-immigration and early post-immigration Italian reference point for stories

... but we were happier than we are today!: boastful phrase, stated with slight contempt aimed at young people today who need so much luxury and technology to have fun; related to an ability to make hard repetitive work socially pleasurable; pertaining to lost Italian laws of the land; see **we had to make our own fun**

re-cre-ati-oni: extreme *Inglese* dialect of the *Court*; nobody speaks this way in real life and I apologize to all of my *paesani*

a lawn chair: frequently seen in or at the front of a garage on clean asphalt; of and pertaining to *"passing time"*

Every square inch seems to have a purpose: Engineering unit of measurement for anything Italian made

"The wine was better back in Italy": frequent claim made by Italian *old guys*; definitely before and apparently after the blight of 1920; interesting source of culinary history and discussion

store-bought wine: silly oxymoron known to the craftsmen of the garage wineries of North York

twisting my arm and flying an *Alitalia* plane across an imaginary ocean with the palm of my hand: prime example of *Inglese Cro-Magnon* dialect see **re-creation-oni**

black olives: canned bitter cousins of green olives which come in jars

"S biscuits": Italian Oreos

making my mouth corners go down like Il Duce: historic gesture used to punctuate a silly point demijohns of red wine: beautiful and uniquely shaped furniture of the *cantina*; glisten like green gold; frequently woven in green, white and red electrical wire affixed to plywood base; *Inglese's* use them to collect pennies

pig: sometimes known by the classic, affectionate pronunciation: *peeg; porco*

Act II Scene 3.
The Cemetery and the Fig Pastoral

They stroke each other's arms and cheeks and beam and nod...: A typical Hometown greeting between an old beautiful woman and a young beautiful woman; pertaining to relatives

pizzeria: '5-Star' hometown restaurant; purveyors of Pizza *Margherita: the green is the basil, the white is the cheese and the red is the sauce*

hard white candy ... wrapped in netting: *bonbonniere* escort; it is still unclear if they are to be eaten or preserved to eternity; tooth-smashers

an up and down chopping gesture with my left hand: dialect-of-meaning; translation: what am I going to do with you?

Piacere: vocabulary builder; easily learned, used and remembered; makes you feel like Rudolph Valentino when you say it; *tu sei romantica*

they look like Maria: clever and curious trick of Italian sunlight on the children which renders *Inglese* gene pool invisible in the Hometown

my character walked through, inspected and left: sensation experienced as outcome of the intense gaze of Italian women into your soul; pertaining but not limited to mother-in-law's and neighbours

when I am pulled down this close to a face: plight of the taller; a sure sign that you are either liked or at least have a face that is interesting to look at

circles of olive oil on salad: thoughtful trance state evoked through silent, repetitive culinary motion; curious practice by Italian elders who never rush this step, even though they have performed it thousands of times; good way to feel like your mother-in-law when grieving

"Come ti chiami?": one of the most important conversational phrases in the Italian lexicon; worth learning; say this and for a split second, they forget you are not Italian

salt cod in rigor mortis: what mass produced *veale* looks like stacked in the freezer section of the kitchen fridge; pry six or so off; fry four or so minutes-a-side in oil; serve with bread and asiago cheese...*mamma mia!*

spicy Molisano sausages preserved in oil: *no cantina* should be without at least three jars

"I taught you everything I know and still you know nothing!": *Inglese* dialect; exaggerated statement of playful frustration at not being understood by one or more Italians

"ehhh, ehhh, ehhh, ehhh": see **eh, eh, eh, eh** or **Choo!**

head cocked in avian inspection: valiant and rarely described Italian head gesture used when trying to understand an *Inglese* attempt to *parle Italiano*

dumb Italian: sneer observed on the face of fast talking, impatient young men in hardware stores; usually wiped off by homicidal stare of young loyal men in the company of *old guys*

the club: scientific phrase meaning center of universe

cereal boxes: ingenious and functional handcraft for preserving *scopa* cards; see **flattened** cornflake box

they showed me how to get on a streetcar: essential urban survival skill taught to Italian men and women in the 1950's

lesson; lezione: pertaining to the speech of love; spiritual matters; of the experience not the *instructione*; a sharing of practice wisdom in the Court of *Garibaldi*

dumb Inglese: frequent and curious experience of having all thoughts run through molasses, thereby immobilizing mouth in large parts of Europe

The sun turns honey gold: distinctive late afternoon play of Italian light off blue sky, white stone and yellow wheat field stubble

Wine and chicken, meat and pasta, orange pop, bread, lasagna and beans, meloni and espresso, liquore: typical Italian culinary orchestra in the *Living Opera*. Encore!

Biagio takes Maria and the kids. Domenico and I follow with the luggage: Italian travel maxim; 1 *Canadese* suitcase = square footage of two Italian automobiles; plan to travel to and from Rome or the train station via caravan

He takes each hair pin turn miraculously: dialect; translation in the proper Italian: "with eyes closed and one hand tied behind his back"

that 'war movie' feel: curious and frequent sensation in Italy, particularly around train stations in small towns

downcast hesitation that leaving brings: sad, aimless fidget of goodbye

Styrofoam cups of espresso: Italian Tim Horton's

fill it to the cap line: Life skill; *cantina* art of siphoning wine without spillage; worth learning quickly

pouring out the heel of the bottle into my glass: universal sign of respect between men

Act III Scene 1.
Canto Primo

Jesu shrine: religious lawn artefact

Black Madonna: women I wish I could make feel better

clean, white concrete: outdoor carpeting of an Italian household

plastic lion in repose/two plastic hens in laying form: standard issue garden furniture

makeshift greenhouse: see **improved on the process**

any tree not a fruit tree, is relegated to the tiny strip of grass owned by the city…: Italian arboreal law of the land

The Father: dramatic third person usage of a frightening figure

red-orange gas station cloths: masculine usage; Italian garage handkerchief

moods cross the Italian face with the speed of clouds moving across a bright blue sky: undefended; honest

solid pair of work shoes: Italian running shoes

healthy outdoor look: perfect tan by mid-May

fluid paunch: seasonal proportion of the Italian male

hiding her face in both hands: romantic gesture of embarrassment

lesser men: the impatient

finish mine in second place: useful observational strategy when meeting new culture for first time; functional definition of obsolete usage: When in Rome etc.

this is the one I was telling you about: of or pertaining to a serious relationship; frightening phrase said by Italian women to their parents; causes The Father to stare and The Mother to worry around the eyes

like a hose on a faucet, trying it out, examining the threads: beautiful thought process of Italian *old guys*

pair of slippers: Italian home welcoming ritual

utility sink near the furnace: primary sink

"downstairs" kitchen table: related to **the club**; center of heaven

eyes are worried in the corners: becoming facial trait of Italian women over, say 55; see above

the plate from the Bahamas: curious Italian trait of prominently displaying gifts from their children of places they themselves have never been

his sister is very important to him: dialect-of-meaning (brother-in-law usage); in the formal Italian: "expect to die if my sister is not happy every day of her life"

the systems of hillside flames: enchanted transformation of soul in *Garibaldi's* Court

You cannot escape your parents: your definition here:

_____

Felice: *importante* word in the operatic libretto; utter bliss

meat sliding off a rib: sauce nuance; time to eat

dry Asiago cheese: I read somewhere that this is the only cheese God serves angels

a silver beauty to a boiling pot of water: How do I say this? When you marry into an Italian family you become both a poet and a *burlone*. It is a gift, I think

Penne rigate: the Italian version of boiled potatoes

Rastrelli: mystical brand of extra virgin olive oil; believed extinct

Act III Scene 2.
Overture to a Side Yard

Ma: endearing contraction of Madre among best friends

dinnermass: typical Italian evening meal

"Non c'e male,": urbane and sophisticated reply to the phrase; how are you doing?

a small man and women: always appear as one angel to me from afar; romantic usage

yellow bags of groceries: plastic equivalent to old-world burlap bags

when I learn to sing the libretto of his Court: the speech of love; the living opera

For Me: phrase used usually after second helping of pasta; full translation: Have some more, or Take some more, for me. Acceptance denotes sign of respect; better to serve self or monitor serving by keeping one hand on mother-in-law's wrist when this phrase is uttered

Cosi sia: amen

There is no rush: of or pertaining to the art of passing time

gleaming berries: I always thought a backyard, twenty-foot cherry tree quivering with bursting red cherries should have been on the Italian flag

silver dollar plant: commonly seen side yard garden plant; excellent to pass time with; so reminiscent of Italian men and women ie., start out green and lush, emerge as beautiful and grey with myriads of black seed children and grandchildren; see **make your own fun**

Mary and I talk and then do not talk: typical Italian speech pattern; romantic usage

painted grey: primary colour of the Italian male; gloss on the basement floor; matte finish on the outside foundation

canned spaghetti: oxymoron; no words for this apparently exist in the Italian lexicon

"Dio! Grazie signore, Grazie, no, per favore, Grazie, no ... Prego, Arrivederci, ciao!": valiant yet unsuccessful attempt by an English person to decline receipt of ten zucchinis

Zucchini Soup School: Zucchini Immersion experience: Lesson One: soup

Ffooooff: common Italian kitchen, backyard barbecue and sauce making sound

Sedano e prezzemolo: see **fagiolini**; there is no point in attempting to learn these words before planting on the long weekend

It has always been there but you have not seen it: as of or pertaining to varieties of basil; olives and the enchanted philosophy of discovery in the Court of *Garibaldi*

"Now, you know": definitive statement acknowledging the acquisition of a *lezione* taught; a permanent understanding

I don't know if I like you and I don't know if I don't like you: preferred and enchanted state of open mindedness; a challenge in the dialect and speech of love

"You never know when you will see me and that way, I will be sure to find some food!": frequent and logical statement made by *Il Vagabondo* in the Court of *Garibaldi*

"No, I am too young for that.": old-world teenage reply to a proposal of marriage

"Ok, Ok, forget about it!": your mind is made up and so is mine

Molise hand dialect: easy to learn and speak fluently

wife's cousin's daughter: classic, Italian descriptor; helpful to have a pen and paper ready if you intend to listen and understand the family connection to the story

a difference of position: i.e. beggar; peasant; well-off farmer; artisan; professional; *caribinieri*; government person

To heck with it.: see **Ok Ok, Forget about it; dead to me** etc.

a feast: or *festa*; place of excellent company; robust food; wonderful music; bird dance

Donato Macoretta: romantic hero of *Garibaldi's* Court

"My parents got a little more than what you got": see **a difference of position**

Saturday night: social Sabbath

"The only thing I could offer her is my love. Other things I haven't got.": masculine usage; see **this is the one I was telling you about**

a good man: someone who believes in God and works hard

Act III Scene 3.
The Garage. Winemaker's Tableau

faint breath of Varsol: garage air freshener

"Eh,": who cares?

homemade work bench: garage sculpture

hybrid tools: the formation of one unique tool to perform a specific job from the leftover parts of two to three different and unrelated tools

homemade screw drivers: see **hybrid tools;** always over fifteen inches long, needed and used once

make peace: what women have to do for their men in the neighbourhood

husbands who do not want to make a problem: men who are too chicken to ask for a tool back

the wine press: mechanical center of the universe, outside

to look at the grapes: Italian code for I am ready to make wine this weekend, the conditions are right; see **"When they are ready you have to go"** and **"we have time to do it"**

the medicine: carcinogenic chemical powder put on the grapes to keep them from ripening en route from California

San Danielle mortadella sandwich with Saputo provolone cheese: the bride and groom of *pranzo*; infinitely better than *Inglese* bologna and process cheese. Trust me

Nutella: curious food resembling hydraulic lubrication loved by children

They take time to make: dialect for "one day I will make them when I am not so tired."

"Bubble Up" Seven Up opener: *cantina* device from the 1960's

***Brio*:** dark haired sister of Mio; takes getting used to; try mixing *Inglese* Dr. Pepper and cola

"Abasta, abasta!": vocabulary builder; correct response to culinary pressure; see **For Me**, above

Meatballs, large ones: slightly smaller than a soccer ball

nice and dark, not too light: a shade of red; preferred colour of *vino*

modification: masculine usage; Italian change of manufacturer's specifications to make something work infinitely better

"You do it once and you learn,": see **Now you know**

"Technology!": *old guy* frustration at how complicated machines are getting

working without a net: the art of eating anything with sauce or oil on it, in a white shirt and not getting any on you; equivalent to balancing on a high wire without a pole

Your wife is going to kill you for working with your good clothes on: common practice of the Italian male

aspetta: vocabulary and self-esteem builder; frequently used in *Garibaldi's* Court; if you are asked to do anything you don't want to do or if somebody is being nervous, say *'aspetta'*

like it was nothing: dialect for to do easily

air lock: of or pertaining to fifty-gallon drums and polyethylene plastic; excellent and well received Christmas present for old guys; see **improve on the process**

"Take your time going, but hurry back,": beautiful Irish goodbye phrase taught to me during a *lezione* with my father

How can I make this easier?: Descartian phrase and perpetual Italian question forged from years of hard, repetitive work; precursor to improving on the process

get the idea in your mind of how a thing should go: this is the secret of how Italian guys figure everything out; of or pertaining to engineering genius

when the job is ready to be done you do it: the reason why old Italian guys a. bend down on the ground to light gas burners; b. climb up on ladders unattended or c. drive in a snowstorm to get something from the hardware store

"I want to taste it,"/ "You can,"/ "It is the only way to learn,": dialogue: "common *Inglese* reaction to all Italian food or drink"/ "common Italian response"/ *"smart alek buffone* response"

Ali Baba's Cave: Italian garage with the door shut during fermentation

Ripete per favore: see Rudolph Valentino words; self-esteem builder

"When the war came,": translation in the proper Italian: "when our life and our land was completely taken over by either the Germans or the allies"

We had nothing to eat: historic reference point; during and just after when the war came

Mussolini: Living History *Lezione*; *Inglese* textbooks portray him as a *buffone*; talk to the old guys about what they actually thought of him

Argentina: Toronto, south; of or pertaining to *paesani*

SS Constitution: Historic reference point demarcating old and new life; ship of a thousand stories; heroic vessel of Garibaldi's Court

PRIMO INTERVALLO

nod like you know it is a good one and ask them to trim the fat: etiquette *lezione*; the correct way to buy sliced prosciutto in an Italian grocery store

veale-by-association: if you buy veals with your mother-in-law they will think you are Italian and later, when you go on your own, you will automatically get good veals, extra sauce and they will serve it to you in an aluminum tray as opposed to ask you if you want the veals on a bun the way cakes do; see **dumb Englishman**

Look like you are ready to yell back if anybody behind the counter says anything: dialect; ignore the signs to use tongs to pick up the buns; demeanor to adopt in an Italian grocery store when ordering cold cuts

veal wars: intense cross-cultural wars and loyalty to stores that sell great veal or veal sandwiches

Gitto di Bondone, Sassoferato, Caravaggio: of or pertaining to art appreciation and pepper making school; if, on the off chance you cannot make it to Firenze or the Louvre, get the Christmas calendar at Commisso's

Briscola: pretty cousin of *Scopa*

sweet table at midnight: curious Italian food worship ceremony practiced towards the end of wedding receptions

Tales of Gusto and Enchantment: spiritual state and philosophy of Life in the midst of my Italians

the winter months: the only time of year when old guys make time to read

Act IV Scene 1.
La via Rita. Song of the Street

St Jane Francis Church: spiritual and romantic center of *Garibaldi's* Court; this alternative definition dedicated to Ft. Claudio Moser, heroic figure of the Court and priest who married *Il Vagabondo* to Maria, Garibaldi's daughter; *molto grazie*

Lamb of God, you take away, the sins of the world, have mer-cy, on me: favoured song of *Il Vagabondo* in the Court;

an extravaganza: of or pertaining to sweet tables and excessive excitement over inanimate things; see **too much of a muchness**

frothy pantomime behind the windshield: universal and cross-cultural usage; road rage

Via Rita is enchanted: a street with a lot of Italians on it during its heyday

wine vinegar: nectar of the gods; *Inglese* white, British malt and store-bought red-mock wine all bow down to it

the salt stings your lips: phenomenon of backyard barbecues in summer; associated with barbecued veal eaten immediately *al fresco*

you must eat six or seven of them: pertaining to figs; etiquette lesson; the correct response when an Italian mother in law offers you the bowl of *frutta* after a meal

Blackthorn and Hope Streets: enchanted places in the Court pre-Il Vagabondo that have completely changed when you drive back there with your *moglie* and kids; bring a handkerchief

JaneSheppard: in the province of North York

they walk so slowly: beautiful gait of old men

wrought iron railing curling up magnificently around perfectly poured cement steps ascending to balconies: typical Italian suburbscape that Caravaggio would have painted if he were alive

red geraniums: regional flower of North York

All small rocks are painted white: curious practice and an abomination in any culture

Italian-pruned: scalped to the point of desolation; always grows back better

"Vagabondo, did your trees die yet?": suburban usage; unbecoming, drive-by, *Inglese* cat call; see **Italian-pruned**

White haired women will shell beans, small hard looking men will braid garlic bulbs: a panel that should have appeared on the Sistine ceiling

'making a life': an old, beautiful, romantic Italian couple putting the garden to bed at dusk

There are times when old men must listen to young men: *Inglese* measurement quotient; when *old guys* stop listening, they become canyons and only interested in hearing their own stories echo back

There are times when young men must listen to old men: a lost art

It is usually the same: preferred state of enchantment in *Garibaldi's* Court

You must even translate love: love has many dialects

all of it for what? For nothing: ancient rhythmic call and response pertaining to those who get nervous

the pills: unimportant medicine forced upon old guys by doctors

"When we need help, we ask for it,": Italian oxymoron; of or pertaining to self sufficiency

He watched me pull out: common Neighbourhood Watch practice on an Italian street in North York or a Hometown

Act IV Scene 2:
Lament: Come Back, Come Back to Rita

young bald men letting themselves go: masculine usage; lament of the middle aged

wives ever so slightly past bloom: feminine usage; see **lament**

little ones piling out of back doors slamming: cross cultural and universal frustration of fathers

wheelbarrow: Italian unicycle

purple pails on their property: sign that household is either Italian; relative of Italians or good friend of Italians

yardbarn: backyard garage

new construction guys: code for hurried substandard work

hammers and screwdrivers: musical instruments of the *Court*

"holiday Catholic": curious disparaging term used to describe the faithful who show up at Church, seasonally

go good together: husband and wife in love

Wonderland: place where Italian Day is celebrated and *Johnny Lombardi*, missed

cherry tree: believed to have grown robustly in the Garden of Eden

I have seen them pronounce a tree dead: arboreal ceremony involving 2 to 3 Italian men, punctuated by shrugs, shaking heads, jackknives and saws

They grow things. It is what they do: Italian e=mc2

At night we will dance: when the lack of light makes it impossible to do any more work

The yard is their living room/The yard is their al fresco kitchen: pertaining to ancient rhythms; it is very rare to find an Italian couple actually inside their home from the long weekend of planting in May to approximately Thanksgiving; or the first frost, whichever comes before

Rita is a lament now: remnant of a street once thriving with Italians

Cars ... tripled up in dirty driveways: a sign that the demographic is changing

the demons on the street: realistic understanding that bad things happen to us all

St. Claire: as in, to go down to St. Claire; the cute *Inglese* translation is 'little Italy'

To get some food you had to work for it: laziness; sloth

yells at me for mysterious reasons: see **nervous**

Act IV Scene 3.
Morte

"Panghe, Panghe": oh, stop worrying or I will give you a little smack for misbehaving"

a thousand smiles wrinkling her eyes: romantic, feminine usage; chorus of little grins around deep, black pools; beautiful to behold

We are all dying now.: what a family goes through when one of them has cancer

baccala: ancient law, loosely translated; "whether you like it or not, we are putting fish in the sauce at Christmas and Easter"; of and pertaining to an acquired taste; see **la tassa**

Italian mass: etiquette *lezione*: like weddings, try to get there just as the previous one is ending; expect to stand

if you don't; if you live close to the church, do not bring
a heavy coat, you will get too hot

chestnuts: Italian Christmas peanuts

panetone e torrone: beautiful culinary cousins that arrive
in December and stay till early January

"I" biscuit: older brother of S biscuit; softer demeanour

insensitive intern: young overworked *doctore's*-in-waiting,
practicing bedside manner

**doors that cowards go through when they have given up
the facts:** entrance to purgatory

**Our eyes share everything. We don't say a word but we
know:** the intimacy of innermost friendship

She left me: ancient usage meaning she has died

'apartments': slang term used to describe compartments in
burial walls

Rizzo's Banquet Hall: one of many places of merriment in
the Court of *Garibaldi*; see **extravaganza**

Act V Scene 1.
Death of a Garden

Memorial candle in a pot of sand: lost heart's evening vigil

"She was my guide, my companion": married couples in
love and in life, eternal

it is at night that he suffers: hardest time of day for the
bereaved

It startles like a slap in the face: walking into an Italian
home when the mother is no longer living

tiny crawlspace: baby *cantina* used to store hundreds of
cleaning products and tools

Every Saturday I had to get up early and help Mamma:
the eternal plight of teenage girls born to second wave
Italian families

That was all we had: dialect meaning we learned to make-do

**You didn't know what life would bring. If you didn't work
hard you would suffer more. Waste nothing. Save
everything. Be prepared in case trouble comes to you:**
what the waves said to the people crossing the ocean
during the 1950's

**Did you drink all the wine or did you pour it down the
sink when you saw it was me?:** common and witty
salutation of *Il Vagabondo* in the Court of *Garibaldi*;
see **"You never know when you will see me and that
way I will be sure to find some food!"**

You arrived too early. There is still some food.: Common and witty repartee in the *Court*

dried red peppers from the garden, slice them up and let them steep in the oil: Italian chili sauce

I butcher the language and turn the libretto into *dolce inglese* sausage: clever food metaphor for the linguistically challenged

I think he wants to take it apart to study it: Italian *old guy* response to modern foreign objects such as micro tape recorders and computers; see **Technology; hybrid tools** etc.

This is not for taking apart: *molto importante* point of clarification; see above

"It is my Solitude. *My* Depression": The Empty Hug of the Spirit of Loss

Metal chairs slide back: the sound of *nonni* getting up and leaving the club to pick up their grandchildren from school

A little pollo zuppa; with soft orange carrots and little pasta stars swimming in it: a beautiful way *nonni* love their grandchildren in the late afternoon before Daddy comes to take them home

The Divine Day Care of North York: how lucky it is to have a *nonna* and *nonno* during the early years of marriage

roasted almonds: Divine Day Care travel snack

Tender old women: widows that didn't become Black Madonna's

The retirement home: Italian Elysian Field if you can't stay at home with your garden; your *cantina* or your garage

an *importante experimento*: dialect; having to do with wine; trying a different grape or grapes instead of carignane, alicante e moscato every year for three decades; or, for example; whether or not wine tastes as good in my home versus yours; begging

steamer trunk: functional treasure chest for the new world

"We don't need that anymore": remarkably rare phrase in the Italian lexicon it means: 'this item no longer has any functional or sentimental value and is not even worthy to send over to the church' see **yard sales all over North York**

yard sales all over North York: the lamentable Bermuda triangle of artefacts from the second wave of Italian immigration

we didn't know what we would find: history *lezione*: the state of mind of the Italian immigrant preparing to leave behind everything familiar circa post-1945

part of their heritage: the preservation of a way of being as opposed to the saving and storage of inanimate objects

The Court of Garibaldi lies in ruin: disinterest that grieving men take in their gardens during periods of grief

The Things They Carried: An Italian Treasury: Title of *Il Vagabondo's* dormant book idea; *professori* of Italian Studies are welcome to call

Torello del Sanio, Oratino, Montagan, Petrella, Sant 'Angelo: Castropignano *scopa* buddies

Act V Scene 2.
March of the Grafted Limbs

It is possible: Ancient Italian *old guy* maxim roughly translated as: anything that is made can be fixed if it breaks

"What tools will you need?/Who could do this back home?": universal thought process of Italian men preparing to fix something

Start to whistle: signal that an Italian man knows how to fix it

time to gather up your tools and bring them back to the work bench: it is a cardinal sin to either misplace a tool or borrow one and not bring it back; see **Violate Rule G**

That ... is how we do it!: triumphant claim of behalf of an entire race when one of them fixes something difficult

You remind me of a young me!: clever repartee by *Il Vagabondo* when someone fixes something; see **That ... is how we do it**

bone: dialect for pit; as in peach pit

The food is good, the work is hard and the company, merry: the pragmatic trinity of daily Italian life

I think you are this way with me because you miss your father: *Il Vagabondo* is speechless ... how do you say it, at a loss for words...

it takes two to grow: the point of both love and life

bingo: if the club is the center of the universe, bingo is the galaxy that contains it

electrical wire: weaving material in various gauges; comes in green, white red and black; sometimes orange for the fine work around glass bowls

Corriere Canadese: Italian Toronto Star/Sun and NY Times in one paper

he makes her sign a little piece of paper that she will pay him back: honour is both a given and an expectation; see **a good man**

She soils the nest of her people: Italian women who answer *Corriere Canadese* newspaper ads and prey on the emotion of desperate widowers; see **dead to me**; may they burn in the putrid hell of their own thoughts along with any relative or friend who knows what they did; ours was named *Pastora*; the only reason why it is useful to know how to use the profanity of a different language; *menge*. Don't get me started.

When she dies, he dies, the house dies: what happens in an Italian family when a mother dies

Act V Scene 3.
A Songbird

It is what I want to do: active usage; resolute state of the Italian mind

My sister is coming down: an important or special meal

the rightful heir to her mother's throne: of or pertaining to royalty; all Italian daughters

Thankfully it is not Sunday: unbecoming, slightly blasphemous thought of those who live on the same street as the church when parking is at a premium

I will get the wine: dialect of meaning translated as: I am looking forward to going to the cantina to start the siphoning process on the bottle of wine; hypocritical; of or pertaining to a false generosity

The distinct aroma of pesce: I never know if I like it, I never know if I don't like it; see *baccala*

I cared little for food: state of young, Anglo Saxons who have not yet met a beautiful Italian women's family

a definitive Mediterranean gesture: slamming the door (they only throw plates in movies)

Ditali Tubetti Gemelli; Stelline Puntalette Quadratini etc.: adopted culinary friends of *Il Vagabondo*

Always make too much: the correct way to cook pasta; trust me on this

Dante: a hero in *Garibaldi's* Court

You look more Italian than she does: a high compliment

Believe me my dears, I can get along by myself: of and pertaining to the character of Italian women

Our generation is different: perennial and cross-cultural claim made by the old in observation and judgement of the young

wise innocenti: nice, old Italian people who know their own mind

loneliness kills my Italians: is the sky blue?

El Dorado: enchanted city of gold

pagliaccio: see **buffone** or **burlone**

Woodibridgi: mythical place, alternately sought after by some, derided by others

is it prophecy, grief or fable that speaks?: confusion inherent to enchantment

SECONDO INTERVALLO

When the pig is big, it is time to kill it: Italian maxim; of or pertaining to practical life

We even collected the blood and made it like a sausage: see *la tassa* or **nothing was wasted**

It is a good house: see **a good man** and debate with an *old guy* whether you can judge a person's character by the outside of their house

flags of convenience to the Italian gardener: election signs

She probably even cleans under here!: feminine usage; spotlessness typical to the inside an Italian home

Act VI Scene 1.
The Life in El Dorado

a bread: masculine and feminine usage; the Italian people do not have a word for loaf-as in 'loaf of bread'; Proper usage: I am going for 'a' bread; Will you go to Molisana's and get 'a" bread; culinary nuance; the only merits of an *Inglese* loaf of bread, which tastes like cardboard after you have Italian bread, is that a. it toasts better and other a. it hold more **lube**, which is *Inglese* dialect for **nutella**; **nutella** may also be loosely translated in the dialect as: *girl-nut*

bruschetta: popular *Inglese* bar and grill appetizer

Saigon Hot Sauce: Vietnamese chili sauce

How are the children?: feminine usage; older Italian women are so used to sacrifice they will often bypass you and get to the beautiful purpose of the life

There is nothing to bring, we have everything: standard reply of the older Italian hostess

the debt to pay: borrowed money used to come to Canada to suffer for the first fifteen or so, years

"you old guys think you know but you don't know": generational lament and frustration of young guys

I don't know how they do it where you are: "your way cannot be more efficient than the way I have learned from the experience to do it'

He is better than an Italian boy: see **he looks more Italian than you do!**

empty Tupperware containers: Etiquette *lezione*: to be on the safe side, if you are not sure if it is a good plastic container or an expendable one, bring them all back for re filling

polenta: Italian mashed potatoes with sauce instead of gravy; avoid store-bought tubes; would you buy a tube of mashed potatoes?

when it is ready, it is ready: "do not be late for dinner"

more moist like: moist

la musica: CD, tape or record

rabbit/hen: Italian farm currency

long wooden stirring spoon: feminine usage; see **hybrid tools**

you do not want to waste the sauce: Italian equivalent of freezing your left-over gravy

reading the cheese is like reading the clouds: see **we made our own fun** or **Hi Lo Chikalo**

They grow it but they do not use it. It all goes to waste now: blasphemous; an abomination

It is not right: to go against the ancient laws of everything I know, my father knew and my grandfather knew before him

Inglese butterfly effect: the cross cultural act of purposely trying to disrupt the ancient rhythmic order that says women do this and men do that; i.e., a daughter helping to make wine in the garage, a father learning to make gnocchi or doing the dishes; a son vacuuming in an ancient household; usually accompanied by protest

Act VI Scene 2.
Venus de Gnocchi

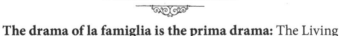

we get old and we get sore: cross cultural and empathic understanding between people

nice and smooth-like: smooth

(I can't believe you take such an interest in these things): the delight expressed by elders when young people enjoy being with them to pass time

pressing and rolling: action required to evoke snake stories or to make *gnocchi*

snake stories: fun to collect; of and pertaining to repetitive stories and acute listening for detail; see **First job**

Can you sing: Over the Hill and Far Away?: Irish dialect meaning your voice is out of tune

That was her job, not his: ancient rhythmic understanding of the way life goes; the living opera; fun to behold and to tease; see *Inglese butterfly effect*

rapini: child repellent

pied piper of gusto: the act of scraping anything off a small cutting board slowly into hot water or sauce when cooking

Welland: Toronto south west

ricotta: I read somewhere that this is what friends of angels serve their children

Highway 400: fastest way to Italian Day Festival at Wonderland if you are late

Act VI:
Finale and Curtain

The drama of la famiglia is the prima drama: The Living Libretto in the Court of *Garibaldi*

The wine is for you and for me: Come, stay a while, be happy

the savory and the sage: secret *Inglese* spices in meatloaf and turkey dressing; favoured foreign food of my Italians.

rubber bands: ancient marking system used to tell the difference between the sauce jars that have the hot peppers in them and the ones that don't

a tragedy: making a large pot of sauce that the children won't eat because the rubber bands broke and you didn't know you were cooking three jars of hot sauce

Your house will smell so good: the enchanted scent of the Italian home

Ciao: the phonetic *Inglese* spelling of the word is *chow*; curious proof, without a shadow of a doubt, that the person has never met an Italian; embarrassing; worse than a *buffone*

(Perfetto. Now, you know)

About the Author

Glenn Carley is a writer and poet who lives in Bolton, ON. Previous books include the creative nonfiction *Polenta at Midnight* (Vehicule Press, 2007); short stories in *Italian Canadians at Table* (Guernica Editions, 2013) and *Good Enough from Here*, an arctic memoir (Rock's Mills Press, 2020). He is a regular contributor (fiction, non fiction, poetry) to *Accenti Magazine* (2018-present). Glenn has four books coming out in the 2021 calendar year: the libretto *Il Vagabondo: An Urban Opera* (Guernica Editions); *Jimmy Crack Corn, A Novel in C Minor* (Rock's Mills Press), along with two children's books, coauthored with and illustrated by his son Nick Carley: *The Long Story of Mount Pester* and its sequel, *The Long Story of Mount Pootzah.* (Rock's Mills Press).

This book is made of paper from well-managed FSC® - certified forests, recycled materials, and other controlled sources.